# De-Hegemonizing Language Standards

## Learning from (Post)Colonial Englishes about 'English'

Arjuna Parakrama
*University of Colombo, Sri Lanka*

First published in Great Britain 1995 by
**MACMILLAN PRESS LTD**
Houndmills, Basingstoke, Hampshire RG21 6XS
and London
Companies and representatives
throughout the world

This book is published in Macmillan's *Language, Discourse, Society* series
Editors: Stephen Heath, Colin MacCabe and Denise Riley

A catalogue record for this book is available
from the British Library.

ISBN 0–333–61634–0 hardcover
ISBN 0–333–61635–9 paperback

First published in the United States of America 1995 by
**ST. MARTIN'S PRESS, INC.,**
Scholarly and Reference Division,
175 Fifth Avenue,
New York, N.Y. 10010

ISBN 0–312–12316–7

Library of Congress Cataloging-in-Publication Data
Parakrama, Arjuna.
De-hegemonizing language standards : learning from (post)colonial
Englishes about "English" / Arjuna Parakrama.
p.   cm.
Includes bibliographical references and index.
ISBN 0–312–12316–7
1. English language—Variation—Commonwealth countries.
2. English language—Provincialisms—Commonwealth countries.
3. English language—Standardization.   4. English language—Sri
Lanka.   I. Title.
PE2751.P37   1995
427'.95493—dc20                                                94–25478
                                                                CIP

10   9   8   7   6   5   4   3   2   1
04   03   02   01   00   99   98   97   96   95

Printed and bound in Great Britain by
Ipswich Book Co Ltd, Ipswich, Suffolk

# Contents

# Preface

This book is the culmination of my doctoral study at the University of Pittsburgh, USA. I have changed only the most obvious of errors and corrected only what seemed to me to be the most glaring omissions. I have expanded some explanations, removed and changed some names from the conversations cited in Chapter 3, and tightened the argument where I felt it was most urgently needed. I have tried, however, to preserve the tone and style of my dissertation because to alter this would be to go against the spirit of this work.

I meant the text then to be unconventional in that it did not conform to the dominant paradigm of detached academic writing. I had wanted to maintain the tension between the hortatory, activist component of my work and its abstract theoretical underpinning, stylistically as well as in content. Footnotes are sometimes more important than the so-called main text, and the book does not insist on a sequential reading. I strategically repeat my key arguments and constantly go back and forth from chapter to chapter in order to reinforce the commonality of the insights I have to offer, whose very 'banality' sometimes works against their importance.

I have no wish to pre-empt your response to this text as unpolished, disorganized and repetitive – this discomfort, this strain is fundamental – but merely to call into question the bedrock primacy of these standardized discursive concepts or norms of good writing. It is when these fairly arbitrary rules have become 'natural' and self-evident that they are the most insidious. In such a situation, variations are allowed only in certain 'special' cases such as 'creative writing' where they are ghettoized.

I had wanted to write the whole of this book in form(s) of non-standard English, but it became too difficult because I am very much a product of these standards I wish to problematize. This task to change the way we have looked at language, in concrete as opposed to abstract terms, is hard – *really* hard because it has much less to do with individual ability than structural and discursive hegemony.

The basic claim for the classed,[1] 'raced', gendered, regioned

---

1.  The fact that 'villain' originally meant 'peasant' and 'blackguard' derived from 'kitchen worker' only goes to show just who is winning the war of words – power is ultimately the ability to make meaning stick.

nature of the standard language is hardly contested now, yet little is done to work against this, except in the insistence on linguistic 'table manners' in order to subvert the most blatant sexism in, say, standard (or, for that matter, not-so-standard) English. Examples of scholarly work in 'dialect' exist both in the US and Britain, but as isolated experiments that seek, quite rightly, to legitimize certain group-interests, rather than as part of a project to broaden the standard itself. Across the spectrum of disciplinary and ideological views, therefore, there exists a shared and 'self-evident' premise that the standard is clearer, more amenable and, to put it in a nutshell, *better* than the other variants/dialects/forms. If, in fact, the standard is all these things, and, in a sense, it is *now*, given the history of its evolution, this has as little to do with the inherent superiority of the standard, as has the fact that more men are good chess-players than women to do with superior intelligence or ability. In any case, none of these arguments can be used against a systematic effort towards broadening the acceptable range of this standard.

I offer instead my most theoretical work to date, written in a mixture of marginalized varieties of English, alongside its standard (both in terms of language and style) 'translation', which I consider to be a fair synopsis of the work undertaken in this book. To me, the *Concrete* far surpasses the *Abstract* in rigour as well as impact, but I want you to be the judge of the difference.

The difficulty of writing 'theoretically' in the non-standard is, then, structural and not accidental. We must continuously chip away at this monopoly by, paradoxically, adding stuff to it. The hardest part for us, within these dominant paradigms, is, of course, the *unlearning* of our privilege in/through language. In the three or so years that I have been discussing these ideas with academics, teachers, intellectuals and anyone interested, the most persistent anxiety has centred around this issue of (the loss of) authority/control, though it is invariably couched in worries about 'What will be taught in the classroom, then?' *or* 'Who will decide what is right and wrong?'

The question of which rules apply and where, of what is unacceptable and why, becomes fraught in the new framework I am advocating here. In fact, the most therapeutic moments in the discussion of my work have been precisely the debate and disagreement over what I chose as 'infelicitous' or 'mistaken' use. In each case, what was seen was the very tentative, even weak grounds on which any particular usage could be rejected.[2] This dramatically reiterated the fact that once the standard, *qua standard*, was negotiable, all rules of exclusion became provisional and contestable, which is exactly how it should be! Moreover, then, the rules themselves become the site of this contestation.

For those readers who are non-Lankans, for those who have no special interest in the Indian subcontinent, is the material of Chapters 3 and 4 too specific, too esoteric? I offer no apology because the implications and ramifications of the Lankan context must resonate for you, or else the text has greater flaws than merely the emphasis in these two chapters. In addition, the mapping of non-standard language onto 'non-standard' discourse, articulated through an analysis of the 1848 rebellion in Ceylon on the lines of the subalternist project, is crucial to the understanding of the implications of this work in the hierarchized topology of everyday life.

*Colombo*                                    ARJUNA PARAKRAMA

---

2.    See, for instance, Chapter 4, pp. 125ff.

# Acknowledgements

Professor Colin MacCabe, my dissertation adviser, taught me a great deal and inspired me to work harder than I have ever done before. Professors Paul Bové, Dennis Brutus and James Knapp helped me with particular aspects of this work and were always very supportive, as did Professor Alan Durant. Professor Gayatri Spivak has influenced my thinking so much. Professor Thiru Kandiah, whose own work served as the inspiration and impetus for mine, was most generous with constructive comments and criticisms. I am also most grateful for his Foreword to this book. My friends and colleagues, both in the USA and in Sri Lanka, helped me in a thousand ways, cheerful in the face of my outrageous demands.

I wish to thank all those who made this work possible.

# Introduction

## CONCRETE

I done shown Standard spoken English as standing up only for them smug-arse social élites. And it ain't really no different for no written English neither. The tired ways in which the standardized languages steady fucked over the users of other forms had became clear when we went and studied them (post)colonial Englishes. Them 'other' Englishes came and made it impossible to buy into sacred cows like native speaker authority because there from the getgo there are only *habichole* users, not natives!

I ask why is it that, say, 'She say I is not good people' and 'She telling I no good fello, no!' are murder to the 'educated' except in the ghetto of 'creative' contexts, whereas something like 'In the conversations that have transpired during our acquaintance, she has intimated to me personally that she cannot bring herself to consider myself to be admirably suitable with respect to my individual character' is only deemed 'wordy', but clearly shows a 'command' of the language? The hegemony of hep standard languages and cool registers which hide where they are coming from, by a shitload of 'arbitrary' rules and 'other-people-in-power-require-'isms is read for points by these non-standard varieties like and unlike the ones I be mixing and jamming here.[3]

---

3.  Two observations. This is a mish-mash because the brother wants to show-off essentialist notions of dialect use which ghettoize non-standard forms. Black English is not spoken only by blacks, nor do all blacks speak it, no? This means also that questions of 'authenticity' and 'appropriateness' (semi-literates can only talk in 'vulgarisms') must also be questioned like a mutherfucker. This, of course, does not let whatever dialect or *tuppahi* mish-mash language off the hook if it is racist, regionalist and so on and so forth. Second, why is the 'appropriate' liberal response to this *achcharu*, a snicker-giggle? What does this cover-up? At what point in these matters does proving a point become also interventionist practice, not tokenism?

If hegemony be maintained through putting up and policing standards, and if a kind of 'passive revolution'[4] manages opposition by allowing for a piss-trickle of the previously non-standard into the standard, then you's resisting when you's refusing the self-evidence of the rules and the proper. Mistakes and bad taste, whether deliberate or not, whether in organized groups or not (as counter-hegemony), is always subversive, though sometimes 'wastefully' so, because they cannot be absorbed into the standard as easily. These non-standard stuff is therefore 'natural' resistance and a sensitive index of non-mainstream against-hegemony. Persistent mistakes and bad taste fuck the system up because they cannot be patronized if you dont accept the explaination, so they fail your ass at the university and say you need remediation like its the pox.

The lastma final word, then, is to go like crazy for the broadest standard and to be psyched up to steady talk in it, teach your head off in it, write like mad in it, despite of its sometime 'oddness' to our ears, refusing of the uncomfortable laughter, inspite the difficulty, paying no mind to some non-standard users and their liberal advocates having an attitude bout it. The ideal, then, is for what is standard now to become contaminated with what is non-standard now, and arse backwards, so much so that everyone will have to know more about what everyone else speaks/writes, and so that not knowing, say, 'black english' will be as much a disqualification as not knowing 'general american'. There should even be room for a certain amount of self-inconsistency as well. Complete intelligibility is a cheap hoax anyway, so it's necessary, yar, to bring this to the up front level, nehi? Alas, putative private languages are the only ones

---

This operation can then be termed 'strategic de-essentialization' to parody or upside-downify Spivak's phrase. It attacks notions of (originary) purity even in the oppressed linguistic situation, and confronts the issue of mediated representation through language form. To trash Wittgenstein for a worthy cause, if language be a form of life, then the form of language is telling us nothing epistemologically new about the form of this form of life. What is up for grabs are habits and practices, contextually creative vocabularies and so on, but not systems/possibilities/limits of knowing, because, after all, standard and non-standard forms of language are so differentiated for political reasons, not philosophical ones.

4. *Contra* Gramsci, not merely restricted to relatively weak hegemony, but also strong, pre-empting effective counter-hegemony.

that are out, at least until someone refutes Wittgenstein[5] or until they go public.

All this wont be in place for a long time, and mebbe never, but anything else isn't worth this pul try. As teachers we don't often let blatant sexism and racism get by from our students just because their views are shared by many in power all over the world. Why the hell do we excuse away language values and non-language values hidden within language values, then? All things considered, and *ceteris paribus*, it is my expert and dispassionate opinion, therefore, that, in punishing 'error' so brutally yet so selectively and in laying the blame elsewhere, or in saying in the appropriately subdued tone, 'what else can we do?', the language teacher is pimping with a vengeance for the system while masturbating his/her conscience with this 'empowerment' crap.

## ABSTRACT

Champions of the so-called Other [or (post)colonial] Englishes have operated on the basis of the special status of these varieties, thereby justifying the formulation of different criteria for their analysis. A careful examination of the processes of standardization as they affect these 'Others' (particularly 'South Asian English') strips the camouflage from standardization which can be seen as the hegemony of the 'educated' élites, hence the unquestioned paradigm of the 'educated standard'. These standards are kept in place in 'first world' contexts by a technology of reproduction which dissimulates this hegemony through the self-represented neutrality of prestige and precedent whose selectivity is a function of the politics of publication. In these 'other' situations, the openly conflictual nature of the language context makes such strategies impossible. The non-standard is one of the most accessible means of 'natural' resistance, and, therefore, one of the most sensitive indices of de-hegemonization.

---

5. This refers of course to the celebrated Private Language Argument, but there is a critique of 'ordinary language' itself embedded here which confuddles the hell out of the 'ordinary' as always-already hegemonic through the collective (mis)use of words such as 'attitude' and 'read' in this piece.

Treating these Englishes as equivalent in every way to their 'parent' forms leads to the re-evaluation of cherished linguistic paradigms such as 'native speaker authority', since hitherto self-evident categories such as this are fraught in the (post)colonial contexts.

Taking the discriminatory nature of the standard seriously and also accepting the necessity of standards, however attenuated, this thesis argues for the active broadening of the standard to include the greatest variety possible; it also holds that the 'acceptable' bounds of general linguistic tolerance will expand with the systematic and sanctioned exposure to such variety.

A case study of de-hegemonization at work exemplifies this theory of resistance in/through language as it focuses on the Sri Lankan context both in colonial times and today, where the 'English' language is shown to exist in non-standard form, at once theorizable, resistant and innovative. The analysis of written and spoken discourse, supplemented by a historical account of attitudes to English (culminating in a current attitudinal linguistic survey), serves as a prolegomenon to the work that lies ahead for language planners and teachers who wish to widen, strategically, the acceptable range of variation within the standard. This would force (post)-colonial hybridity-as-conflict in the periphery upon the ('western') centre, which will in turn pre-empt 'business as usual' there.

# Foreword

## Centering the Periphery of English: Towards Participatory Communities of Discourse

THIRU KANDIAH

*Department of English Language and Literature*
*National University of Singapore*

Linguistics appears at a quick glance to be one contemporary academic discipline that has managed to insulate itself considerably from the currents of thought generated by the post-colonial and post-modern projects that have come to assume such significance in the contemporary world. Avoidance of the conditions that this thinking addresses and of the concerns that these conditions differently raise is, of course, impossible, for these are pervasive conditions in our times, and the study of virtually anything will inevitably bring up topics and issues that are intimately part of them. (Almost?) everything that sociolinguistics, for instance, have looked at belong very definitely within one or the other of these two conditions of our existence.

The problem is that in linguistic studies they are not seen in the way that either post-colonialism or post-modernism sees them. The rigorously structural, positivistic, empirical perspectives and methodologies that are brought to bear on the phenomena examined yield descriptions that, as far as they go, are indeed often very good. But they show reluctance to take on board what can be argued to be the crucial task, namely that of critically analysing and interpreting the dynamic interrelations between language, individual action, social structure and culture, against a framework of general assumptions about humankind, society and nature, and with clear recognition of the ontological, epistemological, ideological and other such dimensions of the task. The goal of such an exercise would, ultimately, be to search out through linguistic study a way towards a world in which all human beings can be happy. The result of this reluctance is that the descriptions that are produced tend too often to lack the kind of explanatory adequacy that alone can validate them, issuing in fact as comparatively static legitimations of the prevalent social structures and relationships, the ontological, epistemological and other assumptions they are based on and the power and dominance patterns and the hegemonic appropriations that are all too often built into them (see Marshall, 1986; Kandiah, 1986, 1991a; 1994b; see, too, Skutnabb-Kangas, 1989, for some very pertinent remarks on the role of researchers in such legitimation).

Not that post-colonialism and post-modernism are identical projects. Post-modernism cannot, for instance, be expected in many of its versions to show as much enthusiasm as post-colonialism for preoccupations of the kind just mentioned, particularly in the way in which they have been stated here. For, in a sense it does, after all, mark a kind of tired, disillusioned end, arrived at through the dissociated sensibility (Eliot's currently unfashionable term!) and the positivistic abridgement of reason (Habermas, 1963, 1987) that in post-Enlightenment times the excessive individualisation and materialisation promoted within the kind of social structurings dominantly associated with Western modernism misbegot.

Like post-modernism, post-colonialism, too, marks an end, the end of empire; but it is not just that. It marks also for millions of people spread out across the globe a hopeful beginning, the possibility after centuries of degrading dispossession and subservience of lifting themselves out of the backwardness they had been condemned to during the colonial visitation, and of rediscovering, reconstituting and realizing themselves again in the terms they best understand. These people are faced with the very urgent task of making a life for themselves that they never had. This makes it imperative for them to engage immediately with problems such as the recovery and reconstitution of individual identity, legitimation, and also material deprivation and poverty (more specifically, rice and curry problems of alimentation, sarong and banian problems of attire and so on, without addressing which the other problems can hardly be meaningfully taken on). They cannot afford, therefore, to indulge with the same relish as the comparatively affluent elite world of Western post-modern scholarship a luxurious sense of alienation and negation, without striving as hard as they can to put these things, which in any event they know only too well, behind them. The narratives of their own immediate realities do not make it a possibility for them not to take very seriously the known existential, epistemological and other priorities and claims of the complex modern reality that they suddenly find themselves acknowledged to be a part of. These narratives demand instead that they engage closely with all these priorities and claims and make a strenuous effort to refashion or replace them with viable, more adequate and stable alternatives, drawing wherever necessary on resources of their own that post-modernism does not have direct access to, namely the long-neglected indigenous cultural and intellectual traditions that they are heirs to. None of this can they validly dismiss on the grounds that it will trap them within transcendental totalizing metanarratives that have nothing to contribute to their understanding of themselves and their condition and to the practical improvement of their situation.

For them to do so will be to miss their historical moment of emancipation. Instead of remaining with the emasculating indeterminacy and anxiety of a great deal of post-modernism, therefore, they need to try to seek out the kind of unabridged reason that will allow them to draw on the full learning potential in their contemporary condition as well as on their own inherited cultural capital for the purpose of critically examining and recognizing the deformations of life in their post-colonial and post-modern realities. This it is that will equip them to work towards a praxis of social change which will enable them to rediscover and legitimate themselves, improve their material conditions and evolve, among themselves as well as together with those spread out across the globe, into communities which are marked by true social solidarity, mutual participation and conviviality and within which they therefore know themselves meaningfully to belong.

Clearly, the affirmative, integrative and, too, implicitly non-relativistic, even normative nature of these tasks of post-colonial recovery and reconstruction will not recommend them too strongly to many forms of post-modernism, making the two enterprises look qualitatively very different. Yet, under the light shed on its own problems by each of the two efforts – the post-colonial and the post-modern – it is possible to see that for all their great differences, these two sets of problems are very much of a kind. This is as it should be, for they are both alike a consequence of the kind of society that has come to assume precedence in our times, with its capitalist organization of the economy, the dominance it assigns to the industrial mode of production and to the associated notion of unlimited growth, its assumption of the superiority of technology and its not-too-perfectly-concealed neo-colonialist global outlook. The insights generated by each of these enterprises can, therefore, be expected to extend beyond its own boundaries and contribute to an understanding of the problems that preoccupy the other – problems that in either case are among the most pressing problems of our times.

If all of this is of immediate salience to linguistic study, it is because, as will become clearer as we proceed, right at the centre of what is going on is language and the communication and discourse it facilitates. In fact, language, communication and discourse, seen in this or related ways, have increasingly engaged a whole wide range of thinkers: Bakhtin, Gramsci, Foucault and the critical theorists, critical linguists, social constructivists, philosophers, genre theorists, writing specialists, and so on. For Habermas, among these thinkers, for instance, 'the two fundamental conditions of our cultural existence' are 'language, or more precisely ... the form of socialization and individuation determined by communication in ordinary language', and an interest in them 'extends to the maintenance of intersubjectivity of mutual understanding as well as to the creation of communication without domination'. What is particularly to be attended to is that when this interest is pursued, it allows us 'to disclose the fundamental interests of mankind as such, engaged in the process of self-constitution' (1968, p. 113). For linguistics (the object of study of which is human language) to cut itself off from immediate engagement with such concerns and to remain asocial and ideology-blind is to miss an opportunity to renew and assert important sources of its validity.

All of which will explain why when I now say that I consider it a privilege to have been invited to contribute this Foreword to Arjuna Parakrama's book, I am not just making a routine gesture of polite reciprocation. Parakrama's theorization of the post-colonial Englishes (or New Varieties of English [NVE], or New Englishes, as they have also been called) and the interrelationship, or rather the socially-politically-ideologically loaded encounter, between them and the standard language, does more than simply put on a rigorous, principled basis a field of study which has hitherto tended to remain content with, largely, a set of often disparate, essentialist observations and claims and inadequately explanatory descriptions.

Driven as it is by the post-colonial imperative and carrying, for that reason, considerably beyond the parameters within which such linguistic investigation generally takes place, this theorization allows Parakrama to open important insights into NVEs and their encounter with the standard language, under the light of some of the crucial concerns of our times, as these have been described above. It does so through a problematization of the objects of study and their complex dimensions which reveals and brings to crisis the structures of hegemony that are built into them within their historically determined situation, and which in this way discloses dimensions of them that, though comparatively disregarded hitherto, are central to their understanding.

The value of this accomplishment extends well beyond just the study and understanding of NVEs. For, in increasing our understanding of NVEs, it also enables better understanding of important dimensions of English itself as such, and, further, of human languages in general as well. By Parakrama's account, the theoretical insights he arrives at on the basis of his investigation of the 'subaltern' usage that the NVEs represent allow us to learn about the 'parent' language itself. This they do by indicating that it is this 'other' usage, not the standard usage of the 'parent' form(s), that represents 'the most general cases'. The increase in our understanding of 'English' that results from this is, then, something which goes along with a better understanding of 'the way language works in its most general form(s)'. Both the subaltern usage Parakrama looks at and the response to it have their existence within 'a social text of far wider spread than its immediate colonial weave', so that what his study of English and its colonial context and history does in fact is to 'make visible' a far more general issue about 'language production in all societies'.

The problematic they help define, therefore, shows up in all kinds of other situations, including many which have hitherto not been seen in quite these terms, and this facilitates valuable new insights into a wide range of language-related issues. Consequently, to the extent that what Parakrama says is heard, it can be expected that it will challenge scholars to take another, very different look at what is going on in a whole range of familiar areas of linguistic investigation, not only in post-colonial contexts but across the board. This will enable them to see issues and dimensions of issues which both post-colonialism and post-modernism are very interested in but which linguistics (even in the more societally-oriented forms that can be expected to be attentive to such matters) has tended not to look at in this light. Among the areas of linguistic investigation which can as a result be expected to come out looking quite different would be not just NVEs (and also the literatures associated with them), but also, more outreachingly, the very notion of standardization and its conceptualization, variation in language in general, code switching/mixing, language teaching and language education, language planning, and so on.

Given the overt dehegemonizing stance the book adopts, there is one claim made above (and explicitly stated in the second part of the title of the book) that calls for special comment: namely that this study of subaltern NVE usage will lead to a better understanding of the 'parent' language itself. The reason is that in practical terms this claim startlingly reverses an assumption that has, through the long centuries of the colonial ascendancy, acquired the status of a given. This is that the directionality of the flow of ideas and insight in studying the issues and problems of our times must necessarily be from centre to periphery, as these territorial notions have been determined by colonial history. The exuberant readiness of large numbers of scholars from the ex-colonial countries simply to apply intact and confirm these ideas and the accompanying methodologies in their work has only strengthened the assumption. In two recent papers (Kandiah, 1993 and 1995), I have suggested that it is time for this perspective to be changed, that it needs to be recognized that the conditions that prevail at the periphery often allow more satisfying insights into general theoretical problems (my attention as a student of language has, of course, been on linguistic problems) and give more useful pointers towards their solution than those at the dominant academic centres which are regarded in some sense as 'home' to both the problems and the thinking, so that some significant reversal of the direction of the flow of ideas, guaranteeing true mutuality within the scholarly quest, would be highly beneficial all round.[1]

Parakrama's independent demonstration of the way in which subaltern NVE usage can teach us about 'English' itself is the most substantial and convincing demonstration of the validity of this kind of claim that I have seen. For, if it does not allow itself to be seen as a provocative endeavour at a sort of coup, an irreverent attempt to, as it were, beard the (British, but also American, etc.) lion in its own den, this must be because the approach to scholarship that is under challenge is not in fact valid. For if it were, it might, because of the kind of territoriality and claims to proprietorship it incorporates, justify a claim that English ought to be allowed to look after its 'own' affairs without seditious interference from 'outsiders' on the periphery.

There is, however, one large question that insists on raising itself: how, in these post-colonial times, can it be that English, the language which more than any other is associated with the colonial disruption and whose salience the task of post-colonial restoration can, therefore, be expected to reduce, calls as much attention to itself as it does in post-colonial scholarship and tolerates the assumption that solutions may be sought through its study to important post-colonial problems? The fact, after all, is that there are very many more people in the world who do not use English than use it. This has always been the case, but post-colonialism seems to assign it actual consequentiality. For, with decolonization huge numbers of these non-English-using people have acquired the kind of visibility that will not allow them any longer to be disregarded as they had been during the long period of the colonial visitation. Liberating, democratizing and nationalizing movements have drawn them irrevocably out of the obscure backwaters and margins to which they had been consigned during that period to active and essential participation in the construction of the communities that they belong within and of the lives they lead therein. Through the emergence and development in their countries of whole ranges of activities extending from the momentous and the profound to the ordinary and the mundane (most dramatically attested perhaps by the spectacular post-colonial outburst of creativity in the arts), non-Western cultures and peoples and the ways of thinking, seeing and doing that they find meaningful have begun to reclaim for themselves just recognition and also eminence. Inevitably going together with all this, of course, has been the ever-increasing rise in significance of a host of non-Western languages across the world.

The paradox is that, in the face of all these facts, post-colonialism still needs very much to take the language seriously, and for reasons that go immeasurably beyond the familiar mechanistic and instrumental matters of numbers, utilitarian functions and so on, in terms of which the discussion of the importance of the language is popularly framed. The point is that the realities of the world that the ex-colonial countries occupy decree that the task of repossession and reconstruction that they are determinedly engaged on can only be pursued *within* the global order created for our times by the very history that dispossessed and disempowered them in the first place. The effective pursuit of their goals leaves them no viable option but to seek to become meaningful participants within the modern global community that that history forged, largely, so the conditions of their modern order determine, through modernization and growth. This in turn makes it essential for them to cultivate the new bodies of knowledge and the new practices and activities through which history constituted that order, namely, science, technology, industry, commerce, communications, transportation, travel, diplomacy, and so on.

This is what makes English so important for these countries. For, the same history that created the modern order also assigned to English, even as it was doing so, a privileged position as the *de facto* first language of that order. English, therefore, became the most prominent and dominant language of the globe, or, as Quirk, Greenbaum, Leech and Svartvik (1972, p. 2) would have it, 'the most important language in the world', and all the evidence points on an objective scrutiny towards further enhancement of its standing in the foreseeable future.

This importance, stemming from the crucial functions the language performs within the modern global order, makes it impossible for ex-colonial countries not to keep it very much within their range of preoccupations. Looking at these functions from the point of view of Halliday's classification (1975, pp. 3, 87; 1985, p. 7), there are two functions of English within the modern order that it would be particularly useful to pay attention to: namely, its 'pragmatic function' ('language as action', as 'a resource for doing with') and its 'mathetic function' ('language as reflection', as 'a resource for thinking with', which serves in 'the construction of reality').

As regards the former, English is very evidently the primary language in which many of these countries carry out the activities which will enable them to participate in the global community, as part of their efforts to reduce the material, technological, economic and other disparities that, the formal end of empire notwithstanding, still maintain them in unequal positions within it.

It is when we consider English in its mathetic function, however, that the full implications of the post-colonial role of English become transparent. In this function, the language serves to construct the modern reality. As Wittgenstein (1953) and Foucault (1972) among several scholars have differently made us aware, linguistic signs cannot, as de Saussure assumed, be taken simply as signifiers of a pre-existing essentialist reality about which they passively transmit messages/ideas; rather they need to be recognized as entering into the constitution of linguistic patterns and discursive practices which systematically construct reality for their users, and the meanings associated with that reality. That is to say, these patterns and practices, and the forms and conventions associated with them, bring into being whatever sense the users of a language will have of themselves and their natural and social world, and establish the way in which they see all of this. In that sense, the language that they define can be considered to reflect what might be called its users' model of reality.

Given this, it will not be difficult to see why it is not too paradoxical that English continues to call the attention of the ex-colonial countries to itself. The history already referred to ordained that England would play a powerful leading role in the development of all of those matters that define the modern global order, namely, industry, trade, commerce, science, technology and so on, and also, through empire, in the spread and establishment of these things across the globe. This guaranteed that its language, particularly in the standard prose form favoured by the middle and professional class who were at the helm of these developments and also by academia, who undertook to serve the interests of this class, would enter centrally into the construction of the model of reality that drives the modern order. In addition, it ensured that, of all the languages which entered into the process, this would be the one which would provide for the ex-colonial countries the most immediate access to this model. A control of its linguistic patterns and discursive practices would enable them to take hold of the model of reality which these patterns and practices construct and which preeminently defines the modern global order within which they need to seek out their destinies. This would allow them to become meaningful communicating participants within the modern global community of thought and action – which, if Lemke's claim (1992, p. x) that 'communication is always the creation of community' is correct, they would also, therefore, be able to play a real role in making.

Prabhu (1989) draws out an aspect of the way in which all of this would contribute to the task of reconstruction these countries are engaged on. What constitutes knowledge in our times and determines our understanding of our modern world includes the ideas of famous thinkers such as Galileo, Newton, Einstein, Darwin and others, together with notions of rational enquiry, individuality and individual rights, freedom, democracy, equality, the possibility of progress and so on, and a host of other such things. These go to make up the knowledge base of all contemporary human endeavour, the current 'knowledge paradigm', of which English is the effective first language. In its mathetic function, English would allow the ex-colonial world to access this knowledge paradigm. In doing so, it would contribute considerably more towards the task of reconstruction than it would in its pragmatic function. For, while in its pragmatic function, English would allow such important things to take place as the transfer of technology and so on, it would still keep the world divided 'between knowledge generators and knowledge receivers', with 'the future course of the knowledge paradigm being shaped in one part of the world while the other part continues to depend on its future products'. English in its mathetic function would change that, by allowing 'a widening circle of thinking minds across the world' to participate on an 'unprecedented' basis of parity in 'the knowledge-generating process'.

Unfortunately, the actual workings of language and discourse within the realities of the modern order do not permit us to luxuriate too long in the excitement this prospect generates. The paradox contains within itself a further paradox. For, even if a control of the linguistic patterns and discursive practices of the relevant form of English could contribute to the task of post-colonial reconstruction in the manner indicated, making the language an important object of interest to ex-colonial countries, the fact nevertheless remains that these patterns and practices are not neutral or innocent because they carry ideological loadings that can militate against the best interests of these countries.

The versions of reality they construct cannot be taken as Reality, with a capital 'R'. As Mészáros (1986, p. xiii) puts it, 'the fundamental structural characteristics of a determinate social order assert themselves on the relevant scale' during the construction. In the particular historically constituted social context within which it takes place, these patterns and practices create and maintain particular structures of knowledge and particular social relations, which assert particular ontological and epistemological claims, especially those that serve the interests and the ideology of the dominant group who occupy the positions of power and authority within that context. In doing so, they 'circumscribe the alternative modes of conceptualization of all the major practical issues' (Mészáros, 1986: p. xiii), effecting closures on the way Reality may be seen and determining what issues may be considered to be valid and acceptable, even which questions may legitimately be asked, what kinds of social relationships may be recognized as normal, what kind of social behaviour and action are permissible, and so on. Through conformity with these patterns and practices (which, of course, is exactly what the notion 'standard language' is designed to ensure), therefore, individuals and groups allow themselves to be consensually constituted as subjects who occupy a space within which 'the universal reign of the normative' (Daudi 1983) prevails. Those who do not assent in this way are, then, constituted as the 'other' and excluded, and their voices thus silenced (Dalby, 1988). The outcome is the establishment and consolidation through the linguistic patterns and discursive practices of the hegemony of the ideology of the dominant group.

In the case of English, what is considered to be normative was determined by versions of reality constructed over the centuries by the emerging middle class to serve them in their task of building the radically different social, economic and political order which came to be the modern order and which they came to dominate, through the pursuit of their consuming interests, namely industry, trade, commerce, science, empire and so on. It was in response to these exertions that the modern English prose medium that is at the centre of our discussion emerged, to be fixed and standardized, largely in the eighteenth century, on the basis of implicit as well as explicit norms such as intellectual capacity, urbanization, prestige, rootedness, community acceptance, flexible stability and so on (Garvin and Mathiot, 1970), and also, beyond the 'purely' linguistic, order, reason, unity, consensus, integration, truth and so on. Doubtless, these norms and the positives associated with them have always claimed for themselves 'the self-evident reasonableness of ... "moderation", "objectivity" and "objective neutrality" ' (Mészáros, 1986, p. x). Given what has been stated above, however, they may be seen to be but reifications of the values and the ideological concerns of the dominant group, which, through their normalizing claims, serve to legitimate and extend their hegemonic position and purposes.

All of this raises the prospect that the kind of community which the ex-colonial countries might become a part of through their acquisition of control over the currently favoured English discourse could well be what Anderson (1983) calls an 'imagined community', that is, a community which 'achieve(s) ... solidarity on an essentially imagined basis'. That this is much more than just an unfounded misgiving is demonstrated by the literature on the discourse of development, which shows how this discourse has 'made possible the advance of social control over the Third World' and the effectuation and maintenance of 'domination over it' (Escobar, 1984, pp. 390, 377).

This raises a huge contradiction for the ex-colonial countries. On the one hand, they desperately need to get hold of this medium which offers them the best chance of taking into their hands the resources which alone within their modern realities will enable them to carry out their task of reconstruction. On the other, for them to enter the discourse and to be socialized into the community which produced it would be for them to run the danger of complying with the task of reproducing the structures of knowledge and power relations built into it. The cost of such co-option would be the acceptance of the hegemony of the dominant group within the modern order and the subversion of their own endeavours.

In the heady days of nationalist liberation and independence, the resolution of the contradiction appeared somewhat simpler than many nations appear to see it to be today. All that needed to be done was to throw the offending language out. But even then there was some acknowledgement, be it of a modest kind, of the complexity of the issue – which is why, for instance, it was the governing party which was responsible for the 1956 act (which withdrew official status from English in Sri Lanka) that also appointed the first two Committees of Inquiry into the teaching of English in the island, the first in fact immediately after the passing of the act. The situation is somewhat different today. The 'failure' of India to implement the clause in its Independence constitution relating to the eventual replacement of English, the restoration of English to official status in Sri Lanka in 1988, the increasing recent interest in the language in Malaysia, China, Cambodia, and so on, all partly signal some recognition of some of its positive potential as described earlier. This is a recognition that has been made possible by the confidence generated in these countries by the knowledge that the de-colonizing changes which have been made in them are irrevocable and irreversible.

This has not prevented latter-day resurrections of some the earlier arguments, clothed now in more sophisticated language, drawn at times even from the post-modernist discourse – see, for instance, Tripathi (1992). Tripathi's elegant exposé of 'the establishment position on the current spread of English' lays bare important and too-often unrecognized dimensions of the matter that demand corrective attention. But, his reluctance to acknowledge positive potential in English condemns him to a conclusion which it is very difficult to come to terms with: 'I do not know wherein lies the greater tragedy, the more terrible destiny: in the refusal to compromise, leading, if not to immediate extermination, then to slow lingering death in iso-lation, or in the uncertain chance, even the positive certainty, of a richly endowed corner in a large harem'. The rhetoric here is, of course, deliberately tendentious, intended to suggest that none of the human agents involved in the situation have any real choice.

But, even if this were a true description of the situation and these were in fact the choices available, it is interesting to note that while the cost of the first choice would have to be borne by the unfortu-nate mass of people who have no English, the benefits of the second would be reaped by an elitist bilingual middle class secure in their control of it. Indeed, this elite have never shown too much com-punction in publicly recommending the first choice to their people in the form of a nationalist rejection of the language, while making the second choice, often surreptitiously, for themselves, without any sense that there is anything 'tragic' or 'terrible' about any of it. The practical result of this course is that they are able to ensure for them-selves both a place in the international harem which by these means they make a reality, as well as a position of dominance and power within the less-endowed abodes they share with their own people (see Kandiah, 1984, for an examination of how this strategy works).

From the point of view of the underpersons, this leaves them with one of two prospects: either they wait for the arrival of Utopia, when all these problems of theirs will be solved, or, and this is the solace Tripathi offers to them, they seek comfort in the assurance of the workings of a blind and indifferent history which will sweep both the harem of the elite as well as their own painful deprivations (all 'petty considerations' as Tripathi would have us believe) into oblivion. Their own perceptions of the situation, generated by the more immediate sense that they are likely to have of their own reali-ties than their elite spokesmen, seem, however, to be substantially different from this, as poignantly evidenced by Annamalai's foot-note to his paper on English in India: 'Even slum dwellers prefer to send their children to English medium schools.' (1994, p. 274). The realities of the situation give this statement a tragic complexion. But at least it represents an effort by these people to assert their human right to wrest from even a hopeless situation some choice, beyond mere 'compromise', for themselves *now*, instead of succumbing in effect to the kind of defeatism that only a comparatively well-provided elite can afford.

One of the things which recommends Parakrama's book very strongly is precisely that in it he resists such seductive temptations and the comfortably facile 'solutions' they bring. Instead, he accepts the far more difficult task of engaging responsibly with what is clearly an impossibly complex situation, and he searches out responses to it which can make a difference that matters to the lives of the human subjects who are immersed in it. Recognizing clearly the hegemonic dimensions of English that are at the crux of the paradox confronting ex-colonial countries, he problematizes the situation in a manner that significantly enhances its study by carrying it further than it has been in any of the work done till now. Particularly valuable in this respect is Parakrama's rigorous theorization of NVEs and their encounter with the standard. This provides for the field of study something which it has not given sufficient attention to so far but which any such field cannot do without, namely a principled basis, by reference to which everything which belongs within the field may be properly and adequately identified, understood, explained, evaluated and validated.

The kind of benefit this procures for the field is illustrated throughout the book by the way it forces insightful re-examination of positions adopted by a range of scholars, including myself, based on new ways of seeing them which open out new possibilities of dialogue about the objects of study. A fuller appreciation of this point will, perhaps, be provided by a consideration of the interaction between the approach he develops in his book and the position I argue for in my recent work (Kandiah, 1993, 1994a) for instance.

In these papers, I adopt the position that the way that the ex-colonial countries may resolve their paradox is for them to enter as fully as possible into the dominant discourse and take control of it, but with a conscientiously cultivated Freireian kind of 'critical consciousness', which will lead them to see how its patterns and conventions maintain the knowledge structures and social practices of the dominant group, by re-opening 'the closed structures into which (these patterns and conventions) have ossified' (Silverman and Torode 1980, p. 6). This will enable them to avoid co-option into it and its knowledge structures and social practices by ' "interrupting" it [Silverman and Torode 1980], interrogating its formulations of reality, intervening in its modes of understanding, resisting its normalizing tendencies, challenging its hegemonic designs and, eventually, transforming its patterns and conventions in such a way as to allow their own meanings to be expressed and their own voices to be heard' (Kandiah, 1993).

This act of linguistic praxis will fundamentally alter the linguistic medium to make it adequate to the new kinds of message that these new users find it meaningful to express, even while allowing it to remain 'the same'. And, the argument continues, it is something which the NVEs have already, by the natural process of their dynamic socio-historical development, carried out, so that their users may now move into the discourse with the confidence that they are equipped to stand up to its negative workings – even, when necessary, to turn it against itself.

Parakrama's independently developed conceptualization provides for this position the kind of theorization that it needs to put it on a principled basis. Extending the Gramscian notion of language as a site of struggle, and arguing that the non-standard is 'one of the most accessible means of "natural" resistance', he characterizes the NVEs as an 'interventionist project' within which their users 'confront the hegemonic meanings and norms of standard dialects through alternative meanings and anti-norms for the "same" practice'. On this basis, he calls for an 'active broadening of standards to include the greatest variety possible'.

It is clear how this will help define for my position, as it has been described above, a principled, theoretical basis. While doing so, it also makes it more possible to identify and better understand aspects of that position that may not be fully transparent without it, thus facilitating more productive engagement with them.

Among such matters are several that have considerable significance for the field of study as a whole. One of the most important of these arises out of my observation that custodianship of the NVEs (which provide for their users the counter-hegemonic linguistic weapon the ex-colonial countries need) remains in the hands of local elites who are not averse to using them as means of imposing *their* hegemony on their own people in their local contexts. This further paradox within an already highly paradoxical situation raises a problem the solution to which it 'is by no means easy to see' (Kandiah, 1994a, p. 160). Parakrama's theorization of a 'broader standard' which accommodates 'so-called uneducated speech' makes it easier to see where a principled solution may usefully be sought.

In doing so, it also throws the focus sharply on a set of very complex issues that demand far more mindful attention than it has received up to now. This involves the issues of proficiency and competence. At an earlier stage of language study there was only one view on these issues, namely that they were virtually the only real

issues that NVEs, as simply irregular collections of deviations from
the expected norms, raised. In spite of several decades of systematic
study of these varieties, that view has by no means been left behind.
Davies (1989), for instance, having led us on a highly diversionary
excursion through the issue of the claim of NVEs to native status,
suddenly informs us at the end that this issue 'disappears as unsolv-
able and in its place remains the old and tired but very necessary
question of proficiency'.

It might not, perhaps, be unfair to suggest that the persistence of
this view even at the present time is something that has been made
possible by the failure of the liberal scholarship that rehabilitated
NVEs to take seriously enough the issues of proficiency and competence, which simply cannot be avoided in the countries in which these
varieties are used. This scholarship tends to treat any form whatsoever that, purporting to be English, issues from the mouths or pens of
natives of the countries in which NVEs are spoken as a valid datum
for the characterization of these varieties. This obliges it to come out
with such constructs as the cline of bilingualism or the cline of proficiency to account for what is actually incompetent or non-proficient
usage which, in fact, has no role in their characterization, using the
norms of standard (British or American) English for the purpose (see
Kandiah, 1987, for a discussion of this matter). The resulting reinforcement of such standard norms, coming from within this scholarship, makes positions like Davies' entirely possible.

Parakrama's problematization of NVE usage, precisely by insist-
ing on the necessity for standards and then going on to make a case
for these standards to be defined as broadly as possible, does not
allow such positions to be sustained. At the same time, it raises a
whole new problematic, involving now the precise characterization
of the new broadened standard and, most particularly, of the criteria
on the basis of which forms and practices are to be assigned or
denied a place within this standard. Parakrama recognizes the challenge, and in his third and fourth chapters explicitly addresses the
new issues it raises.

But the positions he develops raise, for me, some rather worrying
questions. It is not just that his criteria do not at times entirely convince, though that is in fact so. For instance, even a native speaker of
Lankan English like myself cannot always see clearly the basis on
which the various examples of usage that he considers are distinguished as admissible or not. Similarly, the tendency to use a version of intelligibility, namely, the ability to get a message across, as a

criterion for acceptance raises some discomfort, for two people with hardly any knowledge of a language might be able to get their messages across to each other in it in some very minimal kind of way, but that would hardly constitute competent use of that language.

But, these are the lesser problems which but reflect the real big one. A great deal of the 'uneducated' usage (Parakrama's term) that would make its way into the redefined standard on the basis of such criteria has the potential, it appears, not to advance but to seriously weaken the dehegemonization battle that drives the entire project. To appreciate this, we need to remind ourselves of some of the matters we looked at earlier. Community is created through communication, in a discourse which uses linguistic patterns and discursive conventions whose nature and manner of use are agreed on or authorized by those who go to make up the community. Indeed, it is by virtue of such agreement or shared authorization that these people emerge as a community. What induces such agreement or sharing is that it is just these patterns and conventions that construct for them the model of reality that makes sense to them, the structures of knowledge and so on that maintain it, the precise kinds of meaning that they need to convey, and so on. Not to know and control these patterns and conventions is to remain outside of the commmunity they define, to be characterized as an 'other' who has neither the entitlement nor the ability to participate actively in it. (See, for instance, Lemke's discussion, 1992, of how such patterns and conventions define membership in one important community of discourse, that of science.)

To return with all this in mind to the problem at hand: the historically determined realities of the modern order have placed ex-colonial countries, as well as large numbers of their people, within global or local communities as the case may be which are dominated by powerful groups. These groups exercise their domination through a discourse which marginalizes these countries and people, precisely on the basis of the fact that the latter do not control its patterns and conventions in the manner authorized by them. At the same time, there is no way in which these countries and people can make for themselves the kind of equal and liberated life they are now in search of, except within the realities of the world which they occupy but which at present they have no control over by virtue of the marginal status that they have been assigned.

This defines their course of action for them, which is to rid themselves of their marginal status and make themselves effective participating members within their community, whose voices are heard and whose meanings are respected. The linguistic praxis which such an act of self-empowerment will entail will require them to enter the discourse which defines the community and take control of its authorized patterns and conventions for the purpose of engaging purposefully with the knowledge structures and so on that they define for the powerful, all the while transforming them to enable them to express, in ways that cannot be set aside on the basis of what constitutes authorized usage, their own meanings, understandings and so on.

One problem from this point of view with the 'uneducated' usage to which Parakrama would assign this task of empowerment is that it can and will easily be set aside as the unauthorized usage of the 'other'. This, as Pattison (1982, p. 154) reminds us, is in fact what happened to the Chartists when they took on the nineteenth-century British Establishment. The failure of the 'monster petition' of 1848 which eventually brought their agitation to an end was due, Pattison suggests, to the fact that 'they did not participate in the literacy of power', and that they did not control 'the authorized uses of language' which would have obliged those they petitioned to listen to their voice.

Perhaps more important, however, is the fact that a great deal of this usage does not possess the kind of linguistic and discoursal resourcefulness and versatility that will allow it to engage effectively with the authorized knowledge structures, meanings and so on. It is not just that the resources that it does have are adapted to alternative meanings that, though they matter to these marginalized users, are irrelevant to the discourse of the powerful. The point is that a fair amount of this usage represents what appears to me to be a genuine lack of proficiency, a true inadequate learning of it. It does not, therefore, reflect the kind of choice that competent users of the language in such ex-colonial contexts exercise when using it, drawing purposively in the process from a range of alternatives that they have available to them in making their different kinds of meanings. Rather, it seems to represent genuine difficulties of the kind that learners have in using the language in a rule governed way and that get in the way of making it effectively serve their purposes. As such, rather than functioning as an effective means of resisting the discourse and subverting it, it will only serve to disadvantage them. The West Bank and South Africa of yesteryear dramatically demonstrate how great the cost of battles fought with grossly unequal weapons can be in the real world. In the linguistic world, the only way to avoid paying a similar cost is for the participants to enter the discourse of power and take control of the weapons it offers them, for the purpose both of surviving within it and of resisting, and eventually transforming it to make it effectively serve their own purposes.

The best illustration of the point I am trying to make is provided by Parakrama himself, in his 'Concrete' (see p. x), a virtuoso performance, if anything. But, that *is* the problem, it is a virtuoso performance, be it a very significant one. Parakrama himself informs me that he offers the Concrete 'as perhaps the most theoretical work I have done to date, and certainly the most difficult to write'.

The difficulty is entirely understandable. No one actually speaks or writes like that, so that the Concrete is, in fact, a self-conscious, purposive construction out of forms and expressions drawn from widely different communities of discourse with widely different views of reality and structures of knowledge, within which they function naturally to communicate meanings and perceptions that they are immediately adapted to. What it does, therefore, is to 'manufacture' a new medium out of existing ones to carry a new message made up of essentially different kinds of meanings and perceptions.

This itself need be no problem, and that in any event is not my point. My point, rather, is that to the extent that the Concrete works in the way that Parakrama wants it to and that it certainly does – it does so because its writer has assured access not only to the marginalized forms of the language but also to the forms authorized for the purpose of making the kind of meaning that the Abstract and the rest of the book so effectively make by means precisely of these authorized forms. Indeed, close examination of the way the Concrete works will, I think it is not unfair or distorting to claim, reveal that the burden of its thought and argument is carried largely by the authorized forms, and that what the other forms do is, as it were, to weave an intricate pattern around it which invests it with a kind of experiential immediacy that belongs in a rather different world from the 'natural' world of that thought. Without the latter kind of forms, we would still be left with the thought; without the former kind, we would have not even the experience.

And, yet, the Concrete works, and precisely from the theoretical point of view that Parakrama highlights in his communication to me cited above. Not that we can know with any certainty that the kind of de-hegemonized discourse he is making a case for will emerge looking anything like the Concrete. That discourse is something the nature of which can only be determined by real, live interaction among real, live people in real, live situations. If the Concrete works, it works because it gives body to a possibility that the book as a whole awakens us to an awareness of. This is a possibility that current modes of thinking about the matter too often block out of our vision, even in the face of the persistent evidence we get in its support every time we watch the international media or run into the large numbers of 'international people' who are now found wandering all over our increasingly interacting world, and respond with openness to the rich variety of accents, forms and meanings that come across to us with such persuasiveness and power. But, it is a possibility that it is crucial for us to be aware of, for it will allow us, in our-not-too-perfect time and place, to see our way towards the emergence of truly participatory communities of discourse, and through them to a world in which, if I might be permitted to come back to my earlier humanist modification of the words of the Buddha, all human beings may indeed be happy.

For awakening us to the reality of that possibility, Parakrama deserves our gratitude.


## NOTE

1.  This is not just an ineffectual, kite-flying gesture of post-colonial defiance. For, it does appear that the colonial experience, negative though its impact undoubtedly was in too many ways, also bestowed on the former colonies an unintended advantage from the point of view of making adequate responses to some of the important problems of our culturally highly complex and variegated modern world. Precisely owing to what were at that time the intrusions of colonialism, these places acquired a kind of complex, multi-faceted richness that makes them today, in some very important respects, better endowed laboratories for discerning inquiry into some of the intellectual problems of our heterogeneous modern world. More particularly, out of the centuries of dialectical interaction between their indigenous cultures and what came in from outside, there emerged an interesting symbiotic nature and outlook, together with language codes (including NVEs) and other symbolic systems that naturally evolved to handle this nature and outlook and the experience they generated. This allows the users of these codes, if my rhetoric might be permitted to draw on the Lankan situation I am familiar with, to access from deep within themselves Shakespeare *and* Sarachchandra, Tolkaappiyar *and* Chom-

sky, Western technology *and* inherited craft skills, and so on, with a far more experienced immediacy than is possible to the users of the codes associated with the more considerably monotype Standard Average European culture (to use the Whorfian descriptor) which is home to the dominant academic centres (see Kandiah 1979/81, 1989, 1991b). In the increasingly heterogenizing modern world that the different peoples and cultures are presently in the process of constructing, this would in principle equip them to make more perceptive and meaningful responses to the actual *needs* of this world than others who do not have this advantage.

# REFERENCES

Anderson, Benedict (1983), *Imagined Communities: Reflections on the Origin and Spread of Nationalism* (London: Verso).

Annamalai, E. (1994), 'English in India: Unplanned Development', in Kandiah, Thiru and John Kwan-Terry (eds), *English and Language Planning: A Southeast Asian Contribution* (Singapore: Times Academic Press) pp. 261–77.

Dalby, Simon (1988), 'Geopolitical Discourse: The Soviet Union as Other', *Alternatives* **13**, pp. 415–42.

Daudi, Philippe (1983), 'The Discourse of Power and the Power of Discourse', *Alternatives* **9**, pp. 317–25.

Davies, Alan (1989), 'Are Non-native Speakers just not Native Speakers', paper presented at the Conference on English in South Asia, Islamabad.

Escobar, Arturo (1984), 'Discourse and Power: Michel Foucault and the Relevance of his Work to the Third World', *Alternatives*, **10**, pp. 377–400.

Foucault, Michel (1972), *The Archaeology of Knowledge* (London: Tavistock Publications).

Garvin, Paul and Madeleine Mathiot (1970), 'The Urbanization of the Guarani Language: A Problem in Language and Culture', in Fishman, Joshua A. (ed.), *Readings in the Sociology of Language* (The Hague: Mouton) pp. 365–74.

Habermas, Jürgen (1963), 'Dogmatism, Reason and Decision: On Theory and Practice in a Scientific Civilization', in Seidman, Steven (ed.) (1989), *Jürgen Habermas on Society and Politics: A Reader* (Boston, Mass.: Beacon Press) 29–46.

Habermas, Jürgen (1968), *Toward a Rational Society: Student Protest, Science and Politics*, trans. Jeremy J. Shapiro (London: Heinemann).

Habermas, Jürgen (1987), 'The Tasks of a Critical Theory of Society', in Habermas, Jürgen, *The Theory of Communicative Action*, vol. 2: *Lifeworld and System: A Critique of Functionalist Reason*, trans. Thomas McCarthy, (Boston: Beacon Press); reprinted in Seidman, Steven (ed.) (1989), *Jürgen Habermas on Society and Politics: A Reader* (Boston, Mass.: Beacon Press) pp. 77–103.

Halliday, M. A. K. (1975), *Learning How to Mean: Explorations in the Development of Language* (London: Edward Arnold).

Halliday, M.A.K. (1985), *Spoken and Written Language* (Victoria: Deakin University Press).

Kandiah, Thiru (1979/81), 'Disinherited Englishes: The Case of Lankan English: Part 1', *Navasilu*, **3** (1979), pp. 75–89; 'Part 2', *Navasilu*, **4** (1981), pp. 92–113.

Kandiah, Thiru (1984), ' "Kaduva": Power and the English Language Weapon in Sri Lanka', in Halpé, Ashley and Percy Colin Thomé (eds), *Honouring E. F. C. Ludowyk: Felicitation Essays* (Colombo: Tisara Prakasakayo) pp. 117–54 .

Kandiah, Thiru (1986), Comment on Marshall, David M., *The Question of an Official Language: Language Rights and The English Language Amendment, in International Journal of the Socology of Language*, **60**, pp. 183–9.

Kandiah, Thiru (1987), 'New Varieties of English: The Creation of the Paradigm and its Radicalization', Sections I–III.2.ii.3, *Navasilu*, **9**, pp. 31–41.

Kandiah, Thiru (1989), 'Adolescent Nationalism and the Perpetuation of the Twentieth-Century Conflict Syndrome', *Commentary*, **7.4**, pp. 26–32.

Kandiah, Thiru (1991a), 'Extenuatory Sociolinguistics: Diverting Attention from Issues to Symptoms in Cross-Cultural Communication Studies', *Multilingua*, **10.4**, pp. 345–79.

Kandiah, Thiru (1991b), 'Perceiving the "Other" within One's Own Unique Self', in Thumboo, Edwin (ed.), *Perceiving Other Worlds* (Singapore: Times Academic Press) pp. 283–96.

Kandiah, Thiru (1993), 'Whose Meanings? Probing the Dialectics of English as an International Language', paper presented at the Fourth International Pragmatics Conference, Kobe, July 1993.

Kandiah, Thiru (1994a), 'New Varieties of English: The Creation of the Paradigm and its Radicalization, Sections V.2–V', *Navasilu*, **11 and 12**, pp. 153–163.

Kandiah, Thiru (1994b), 'English and Southeast Asian Language Planning Practice: Extracting Regional Patterns and Theoretical Principles', in Kandiah, Thiru and John Kwan-Terry (eds), *English and Language Planning: A Southeast Asian Contribution* (Singapore: Times Academic Press) pp. 281–305.

Kandiah, Thiru (1994c), 'Exploiting the Theory of Universals in Adult Second Language Teaching', *International Review of Applied Linguistics*, xxxii/2, pp. 111–39.

Kandiah, Thiru (1995), 'Syntactic "Deletion" in English: Learning from a New Variety of English about ...', in Baumgardner, Robert J. (ed.), *South Asian English: Structure, Use and Users* (Urbana and Chicago: University of Illinois Press).

Lemke, Jay L. (1992), *Talking Science: Language, Learning, and Values* (Norwood, NJ: Ablex).

Marshall, David M. (1986), 'Rebuttal Essay', *International Journal of the Sociology of Language*, **60**, pp. 201–11.

Mészáros, István (1986) *Philosophy, Ideology and Social Science: Essays in Negation and Affirmation* (Brighton: Wheatsheaf Books).

Pattison, Robert (1982) *On Literacy: The Politics of the Word from Homer to the Age of Rock* (Oxford: Oxford University Press).

Prabhu, N.S. (1989) 'The Mathetic Function of English', paper presented at the International Conference on English in South Asia, Islamabad.

Quirk, Randolph, Sidney Greenbaum, Geoffrey Leech and Jan Svartvik (1972), *A Grammar of Contemporary English* (London: Longman).

Silverman, David and Brian Torode (1980), *The Material Word: Some Theories of Language and its Limits* (London: Routledge and Kegan Paul).

Skutnabb-Kangas, Tove (1989), 'Legitimating or Delegitimating New Forms of Racism – The Role of Researchers', plenary paper, Fourth International Conference on Minority Languages: Comparative Research and Development of Theories, 20–24 June, Ljouwert/Leeuwarden, The Netherlands.

Tripathi, P.D. (1992), 'English: "The Chosen Tongue"', *English Today*, **8.4**, pp. 3–11, reprinted in *Navasilu*, **11 and 12** (1994) pp. 169–73.

Wittgenstein, L. (1953), *Philosophical Investigations* (Oxford: Basil Blackwell).

# 1

# The Politics of Standardization and the 'Special' Problematic of (Post)Coloniality

## INTRODUCTION

I must risk two generalizations about language attitudes that taken together describe the environment of consensus which I wish to question in this book. First, just about everyone has an opinion about the issues surrounding standardization, and, second, this 'common sense' (and I should add, 'conservative') view is hardly different from the thinking on the subject by the most radical intellectuals and experts. On the one hand, the question of language standards is not considered by the non-specialist to be a complex one best left to the disciplinary expert, and, on the other hand, many specialists who hold theoretically sophisticated positions on other related issues are either silent on this one, or sound just like the 'know-nothingists' they denigrate elsewhere.

Remarkably, none of the claims made in favour of language standards and standardization as a valid and necessary process which cannot be broadened indefinitely, are supported with arguments from first principles or even with the empirical evidence of hindsight. At best, language as the site of struggle[6] becomes a pious credo that has been emptied of theoretical bite as well as political agenda. In pedagogic terms this translates to the notion that standard language is unfair to marginal groups and minorities but that it is the least of all evils. Other dialects or forms of the language in question will, the argument goes,

---

6. As improvements on Volosinov's classic formulation in *Marxism and the Philosophy of Language*, which states that 'Sign becomes an arena of the class struggle' (1986, p. 23)

discriminate even more against these peripheral elements within the community. In mainstream linguistics even this piety about language-as-the-site-of-struggle is dissimulated by a privileging of the investigator as transparent (both 'neutral' and 'detached'), and the positing of the act of investigation as merely a meticulous recording of what takes place, which leaves everything as it was before the investigation. Even in the best sociolinguistic work I have encountered, the political and social status quo is valorized because data are collected and analysed on the basis of 'choices' opted for by subjects *within the current context*, which is hardly a transcendental *a priori*. Subjects are never given the option of proposing other 'choices' in the best of all possible worlds or at any rate a better one than exists for them at present. For example, in the discussion and description of the so-called social norms and rules that govern language usage as well as of pejorative and complimentary attitudes to selected utterances, inadequate attention is paid to the fact that these language-values may be 'Hobson's choices' of a kind. In not recognizing that the over-arching social text is also a variable that the investigation cannot consider outside its scope, sociolinguistics too becomes an apology for the 'way things are' and the 'way things will gradually become', as if the linguist and his/her investigation is not an influence on this process.[7]

---

7.  See, for instance, John J. Gumperz, *Discourse Strategies*, pp. 60–5. This is an excellent book, and Gumperz's work remains among the most innovative and challenging in the field. I discuss the detail of his argument on conversational code switching in Chapter 4, but here I wish to merely point to the ubiquity of the kind of social fatalism that inflects even the most pathbreaking sociolinguistic work.

    Gumperz discusses here the negative attitude that many bilinguals have towards their own conversational code switching which varies from evidence of a lack of education and bad manners to improper control of the two grammars. The most positive comment was that it was a 'legitimate style of *informal* talk' [my emphasis]. It would seem important here to try to understand the role that hegemony plays in the reinforcing of such attitudes and in the resisting of others. Gumperz's position which can only allow language attitudes a subordinate and derivative role is clearly visible in the following formulation:

    'When political ideology changes, attitudes to code switching may change also' [63].

    My position is that these are not necessarily *different* phenomena, much less temporally divergent ones. If it is the case that the change in language attitude is only *observable* to an *outside* investigator *after* overt political change, all this establishes is that the attitudinal changes have received sufficient *legitimacy* to become safely expressible. See also p. 188 in this text.

Within the discipline of linguistics, self-styled descriptivists affirm that no single language or dialect is inherently superior to any other. Acknowledged prescriptivism is quite rare among influential linguists, and today the descriptivists present the most useful theories on language for the study of so-called non-standard forms of discourse. However, descriptivism, despite its avowed intentions, tends to valorize certain dialects (and indeed languages) by focusing excessive attention upon them. This unequal emphasis is not so much the fault of individual descriptivists as a problematic of description itself, which can never be a neutral activity. In other words, description is always a weak form of prescription. The 'situating of the investigator' – a self-conscious attempt to try to understand how a particular 'I' in a particular place at a particular socio-historical juncture determines the outcome of the enquiry – must, therefore, always be an ongoing part of the process of description, rather than a generalized gesture that is made at the outset and then forgotten.

In linguistics, however, much of the most exciting recent work in post-structuralism has gone unnoticed.[8] There are many reasons for this, of which I suggest two as most important: the conceptual framework of linguistics as a *science* which still remains in place even within the subdisciplines of sociolinguistics and applied linguistics; and the historical complicities between linguistics and colonialism (both 'internal' and 'external') which still pervade its 'neutral' systems of classification and nomenclature.[9]

It appears that linguists, both descriptive and prescriptive (and including shades in between), do not even require token disclaimers to rationalize their exclusive concentration on prestige (and standard) forms of language. On the margins, however, theoretically important work deals with non-standard forms, particularly those

---

8. There are, of course, some important exceptions, but somehow these remain on the periphery of the discipline, and these scholars often operate from other disciplinary niches such as anthropology, literary theory or philosophy.

9. Nowhere is this more apparent than in the teaching of English as a foreign language. In this burgeoning field, Eurocentric 'half-truths' such as Robert B. Kaplan's description of the circularity of Chinese and the meanderings of Indian languages (as opposed to the directness of English) take on the transparency of objective fact, and are presented in a spirit of liberal relativism. See, for instance his *The Anatomy of Rhetoric: Prolegomena to a Functional Theory of Rhetoric* ... (1972).

that are restricted to distinct geographic locations. The over-arching tendency in these cases is still consonant with the central preoccupation with standard language since these other varieties are presented as exceptions and special instances, albeit those that have individual validity. As a result of their special status as languages, these 'other' forms are not allowed to influence our perception of the theoretical construct of standardization.

The point to be emphasized is that these marginal forms of language foreground attitudinal presuppositions that cannot be accounted for in the paradigm. In this chapter an attempt will be made to show how the very notion of a standard comes undone when a group of these other varieties, specifically of the postcolonial kind, are considered to be fullyfledged languages in their own right and not specialized, exceptional forms, however legitimate. The theoretical insights obtained from the study of these forms can then be used to re-examine their so-called parent forms.

The argument will be made through a consideration of English, where I shall show that these other Englishes are not merely special cases, but, rather, that they are the best examples we have of the general case of language as such, before standardization has regularized, smoothed out and displaced the struggles that are constitutive of the communicative processes. What can be seen in these examples, paradoxically, is both an *acceleration* (telescoping 500 years into 150 or so), and a *slowing down* of change brought about by the military-administrative imposition of a foreign language combined with the self-consciousness of the negotiations, conflicts and so on that result from this imposition as it confronts/collaborates with developed native languages. This complex set of phenomena would clearly have taken place in any context of language imposition, but not so self-reflexively (by calling attention to itself, by being visibly 'fought out'), nor at such close remove where it can be studied in so much depth.

The standard language (or dialect) *appears* to be viable in the case of British English, for instance, and it does have some claim to widespread acceptance, but the doubts and qualifications that, however, do not seem to quite nullify the usefulness of the concept, become impossible to ignore in the other context. We are thus nudged into the consideration that perhaps our judgement in the first instance is too 'interested'.

The case of South Asian English will be examined in some detail thereafter, in order to show that the assumptions that appear to have some validity (even as theoretical fictions) in Britain are less acceptable here. The burden of this analysis will be to show how the establishment of a Standard South Asian English (or Indian English or Lankan English) *excludes* too much of what is spoken on a widespread basis.

It will be shown that the reference to an 'educated' standard is particularly problematic because many of the examples of the distinguishing features of this variety of English have been taken from 'uneducated' speakers or as 'unusual' cases, though perhaps not consciously. The Lankan English component of this standard will be analysed in order to establish the basis for theorizing a South Asian Standard. This argument, which calls for a broadening of the standard to incorporate aspects of 'uneducated' speech as well as for a recognition of its radical potential within the post-colonial context, must be distinguished from the position of Prator (and others), who dismiss these varieties of English because they do not have clear-cut standards in place.

My analysis sets out to establish that the evidence from the subcontinent, if taken seriously, leads to a radical re-evaluation of the concept of the standard itself and to a situating of its unexamined privileging of the 'native speaker' as arbiter of this standard. This becomes visible because the mechanisms for inaugurating and maintaining a standard are not yet in place, and therefore the struggle for hegemony is more clearly seen. The standard functions to anaesthetize this conflict. It is precisely when the standard is stripped of its reasonableness that its operation is most clearly visible.

The role of the 'native speaker' in establishing and nourishing the standard is problematized since this category is ambiguous and fraught in the post-colonial context. Easy generalizations and convenient over-simplifications become less tenable, and the very category of native speaker competence has to be revaluated once it is stripped of its mystique.[10] The language contact situation is at its most sophisticated and complex, thus providing for important insights into borrowing, mixing, code-switching, translation and so on that linguists must generally theorize (at least in the context of English) using unreliable historical data and conjecture.

---

10. You may wish to read pp. 17ff, 39ff, 87ff and 182ff where this argument is fleshed out in the light of insights obtained from these (post)colonial Englishes.

Thus, if it is true that language is the site of the heterogeneous struggles of class, race, gender, age and region, and if it is the case that standardization dissimulates these struggles, then the so-called other Englishes (as evidenced here by 'South Asian English' and Lankan English) provide better examples of this aspect of language at work.

## STANDARDIZATION

A typical formulation of the distinction between the standard and non-standard forms of the 'same' language is: the standard dialect is the prestige form of a language which has been accepted through time by the linguistic community.[11] David Crystal, the pre-eminent linguist, writes.

[A Standard is] a term used in sociolinguistics to refer to a prestige variety of language used within a speech community. 'Standard languages/dialects/varieties' cut across regional differences, providing a unified means of communication, and thus an institutionalised norm which can be used in the mass media, in teaching the language to foreigners, and so on. Linguistic forms or dialects which do not conform to this norm are then referred to as sub-standard or (with a less pejorative prefix) non-standard – though neither term is intended to suggest that other dialect forms 'lack standards' in any linguistic sense.[12]

We shall have occasion to refer later to this gesture of disclaiming responsibility for the explicit hierarchy of values that these terms exhibit.[13] At this point, however, it is important to note the apparent

---

11. 'Standard English is the customary use of a community when it is recognized and accepted as the customary use of the community. Beyond this ... is the larger field of good English, any English that justifies itself by accomplishing its end, by hitting the mark' (George P. Krapp, 1985). Emphasis must be made upon the ease with which the problems with this formulation are dismissed or disarmingly acknowledged.
12. David Crystal (1985) p. 286.
13. See, for instance, the discussion of Daniel Jones that follows, and the analysis of Braj Kachru's work on South Asian English at the end of this chapter.

ubiquity and naturalness of the Standard, as it seemingly cuts across differences.

The concept of a Standard is fundamental to the study and teaching of language, and for this reason perhaps the notorious difficulty of defining the Standard in any satisfactory way, has not been perceived as a problem with *this* concept, so much as a problem with particular descriptions, or as one inherent to linguistic description itself.

> The dominant or prestige dialect is often called the *standard dialect*. *Standard American English* (SAE) is a dialect of English that many Americans almost speak; divergences from the 'norm' are labeled 'Philadelphia dialect,' 'Chicago dialect,' 'Black English,' and so on. ...
>
> SAE is an idealization. Nobody speaks this dialect, and if somebody did, we wouldn't know it because SAE is not defined precisely. Several years ago there actually was an entire conference devoted to one subject: a precise definition of SAE. This convocation of scholars did not succeed in satisfying everyone as to what SAE should be. The best hint we can give you is to listen to national broadcasters.[14]

This 'typical' introductory text goes on to describe the process by which certain dialects become favoured, a 'development' justified in the most naturalistic terms that dissimulate the struggle that takes place in and on language among differing interest groups. It is precisely these struggles that are covered over in the move to make standard forms the 'most natural', and in the analogous attempt to efface conflict in the metaphorics of 'inevitability.'

> But how does one dialect become so prestigious? Once a dialect gets a head start, it often builds up momentum. The more 'important' it gets, the more it is used; the more it is used, the more important it becomes. Such a dialect may be spoken in the political or cultural center of a country and may spread into other regions. The dominance in France of Parisian dialect, and in England (to a lesser extent) of the London dialect, is attributable to this cause.[15]

---

14.  V. Fromkin and R. Rodman (1983) pp. 257–58.
15.  Ibid., p. 257.

The operative verbs are all in the passive voice. The 'active' use of standard language as a means of power for the élite is thus covered over. I am not, of course, suggesting here that there is a self-consciousness on the part of the users to this end, but rather that the conceptualization of language-users as passive and powerless is misleading, especially as concerns the 'innovative' users of the so-called prestige dialect.

The example of Standard (British) English shows that the identification of a standard dialect with the speech of a particular region (that is, the political or cultural centre) is misleading since this dialect is determined more by education and class than by locality *per se.*[16]

Professor Tony Crowley in his book *Standard English and the Politics of Language* (1989) has presented an invaluable analysis of the history of the concept of Standard English in Britain, and I shall have recourse to his research in this section, which seeks to place the current debate on the post-colonial Englishes within the larger framework.

Crucial to Crowley's argument is the distinction that he makes between the written (or literary) standard and Standard English as a spoken norm.

> There appeared ... from within the 'history of the language' and the texts it enabled a concept of a standard literary language *and* a standard spoken language. The standard literary language was traced as an historical phenomenon by the linguistic historians as it emerged into its role as the national, uniform, written language. The standard spoken language, however, was not the same type of phenomenon.

It is this difference in the standard spoken form that provides the basis for Crowley's critique of standardization in the context of 'British' English. Whereas it makes some sense to refer to a standard literary form of the language which is kept in place by various technological and infrastructural mechanisms, such a position is untenable with regard to the so-called spoken standard since it is neither uniformly accepted nor practiced by the majority.

---

16.    See the discussion of Joseph in Chapter 2, where he goes to the other extreme by denying any sense of geographic location to the standard.

Although some linguists did see it as a possible uniform mode of speech, others (the majority) saw it as a form with a particular value deriving from the social status of those who used it: the literate and educated. This in turn created new ways of evaluating various forms of spoken discourse as it gave certain values to specific usage and devalued other usage.

This conflation of the two different senses of the concept results, for Crowley, in a confusion that is hardly accidental. It must be noted here that the situation that Crowley identifies is not one of diglossia, since these are not two 'very different varieties of a language [that] co-occur in a speech community, each with a distinct range of social function [where] both varieties are standardized to some degree, are felt to be alternatives by native speakers, and usually have special names'.[17]

Within the ambiguous phrase 'standard English' the two concepts are often indistinguishable: sometimes it refers to the common language of writing and sometimes to the valued spoken form. And its significance in some senses stems precisely from this ambiguity since in particular debates it could lend proscription (the banishment of certain forms of discourse) the more acceptable face of prescription (guidance in use) and thus be the more effective. (Crowley, 1989 pp 162-3)

Crowley undertakes to delineate the 'continuities and ruptures of the use of the term' Standard English (ibid., p. 164). In this he examines the influential theories of Daniel Jones who 'undertook much of the work that was to facilitate the early-twentieth-century consolidation of the sense of the term "standard English" as a standard to be met by all speakers' (p. 165). Crowley then derives from Jones's corpus

a precise definition ... of the 'standard' that was to serve as the model for non-native and native speakers: it was essentially the careful conversational style of men educated at the English public schools in the South of England. That is, it was the formal, monitored style of the men of a particular class. (p. 171)

---

17. David Crystal, pp. 93ff. Usually, diglossia corresponds broadly to different levels of formality within a community, according to Crystal.

The standard, in this view, is

> proposed on the grounds of recognition: internally it is that form
> by which those whose home is elsewhere than southern England
> and whose 'dialect differs' from the 'standard', can make them-
> selves 'more generally understood'. Externally it is the 'generally
> recognised form of speech'.[18] Significantly, in both cases, the
> model for the 'standard of speech' is the 'common literary lan-
> guage' since the 'standard speech' is allegedly to function like the
> literary language in that it is to be nationally uniform, not belong-
> ing to any particular region or class. Its basis is alleged to be
> national intelligibility.   (p. 172)

This notion of intelligibility, which is the crux of current non-
prescriptivist arguments for the perpetuation of the standard, is,
however, vitiated by a new element since, for Rippman, the
'standard' now must be 'not merely intelligible' but 'pleasing to the
greatest number of educated speakers of English', and not only
'unobjectionable pronunciation' but 'good voice production'.

For Crowley such a position creates two main problems:

> The major contradiction in the argument is that the 'standard' in
> this case is clearly not the form uniformly intelligible but the form
> counted as 'pleasing', 'unobjectionable' and 'good'. In fact, how-
> ever, another contradiction takes place earlier and is based on a
> false comparison between the 'common literary language' and the
> 'standard speech'. The 'common literary language' had a clearly
> delineated history as a uniform linguistic practice since, as was
> argued earlier, it had been and was still the form recognised by
> anyone who wanted to write in English. It was not the preserve of
> any particular region or class and there were no rivals to its use.
> With the spoken language, however, the situation was different,
> since the 'standard speech' was not used by all who wanted to
> speak English, as it had not been and was not a uniform linguistic
> practice. It was, as its definition declared, *precisely* the preserve of
> those of a certain gender, class and region: the men educated at
> the private, fee-paying schools in the South of England. The
> exclusiveness of this definition could not have been clearer and

---

18.   Crowley is quoting Rippman, the editor of Jones's *English Pronouncing
      Dictionary* (1917).

given that it was a narrowly defined and privileged 'standard' that could be used to evaluate other forms, it could not become a uniform linguistic practice. (p. 173)

He holds that the literary standard is universally acknowledged and adhered to, and confines his objections only to the arbitrariness of the spoken variety. His criticisms of the spoken standard are, moreover, cogent and well researched. It seems to me, however, that these same objections, this same problematic, obtains with reference to the literary form. The difference lies in the inaccessibility of the non-standard written language since the politics of publication ensure the exclusive and ubiquitous exposure of the normative standard whose very exclusivity is thereby masked. The literary standard appears, therefore, as the most natural since its competitors are systematically denied public visibility except precisely as 'mistakes' and 'deviations' that often provoke humour or sympathy.

As a result, the applicability of the very arguments that Crowley adduces for the class, gender and regional 'interest' of the spoken standard are denied in the case of the literary standard since through successful 'naturalization' they have 'disappeared' from our view.

'Description' provides the alibi here, as elsewhere, in linguistics. Jones in his introduction argues that 'the book is a record of *facts*, not of theories or personal preferences. No attempt is made to decide how people *ought* to pronounce' (p. vii). He describes himself as not 'a reformer of pronunciation or a judge who decides what pronunciations are 'good' and what are 'bad', but as an objective, scientific observer'. Jones makes, moreover, the characteristic disclaimer which, I shall argue, is symptomatic of the dilemma of descriptivism. He writes that he believes in neither the 'desirability or the feasibility of constructing a "standard"', and that he does not consider the pronunciation of the public-school speakers as 'intrinsically superior to any other'. In this context, it is important to note that this position is identical with that of Trudgill, Stubbs and others.[19]

Crowley's analysis of this position taken by Jones is instructive since it remains in place as a general critique of the prescriptive consequences of descriptivism as well as the inadequacy (even, in a

---

19. Cf. Crowley (1989) p. 261.

sense, irrelevance) of motivation as a criterion of evaluation in these matters.[20]

> However, in spite of such self-justification, it is clear that Jones was instrumental in the theoretical and practical construction of a particular form of speech as the 'standard' to be met. In spite of any conscious intentions that he may have had, his work was placed within a context that could only have led in one direction.

In the detailed analysis that follows, Crowley shows us how Jones's claims of impartiality can have no bearing on the outcome of his work, which can only result in valorizing the standard. Here, however, it is important to see that Crowley's argument remains valid even if one were to substitute 'the literary standard' in place of the spoken.

> In rendering the description of the 'facts' of public school pronunciation and in calling this the 'standard of pronunciation' Jones's texts fitted easily into a structure whereby the discourse of that class was counted as the 'standard' for evaluating the discourse of other classes. His intent may have been otherwise, but the effect of Jones's work was both prescriptive and proscriptive. It assigned a particular form of pronunciation as 'correct', 'educated', 'standard usage' and it banished other forms as 'cockneyisms', 'undesirable pronunciations', 'dialectal peculiarities', 'indistinct' and 'artificial'.

What we can deduce then is an analogous process by which the literary standard became 'universalized'. This gradual change was further facilitated, no doubt, by the fact that the written language is less democratic in its dominant form as published text due to the costs and the politics of publication. In fact, therefore, there is much less access to non-standard forms of language in published material, so 'models' of this writing are unavailable for would-be practitioners. Unlike the spoken varieties, non-standard writing, even when systematically and consistently divergent from the 'norm' as when

---

20. See also Chapter 4 in which motivations (of peasants in the Lankan Rebellion of 1848) are deliberately not accorded the importance traditionally attached to them.

it reproduces non-standard speech, has little legitimacy except in restricted and specialized 'creative' contexts.[21] Thus, those who

---

21.  Here is an example of a 'Basic Writing' student at the University of Pittsburgh (in autumn 1989) who failed the course, but whose essay showed a superb command of the language. In fact, the evaluator who was 'reluctantly' forced to fail him took a copy of his essay, saying that it was 'poetry'! I cite a portion of the paper in question below:

> A project is a building made out of brick and is shaped like a giant shoe box. One building can hold twelve families. There are two to four bedrooms in each apartment. The walls between each apartment are very thin so you can hear everything that your neighbor is saying or doing at all hours or the night. I might add that there were no fire escapes on these buildings so if you lived on the top floor and there was a fire I guess you would die from the flames or just jump to your death it was your choice. Two buildings face each other separated by a courtyard. The court, as we called it, was around fifty yards long and twenty yards wide. Some courts would be filled with flowers andother types of yard arrangements. My court was horrible. The cement and ashfalt that covered the grounds was so old that it had huge cracks everywhere and was crumbling. There were areas closer to the building thaat were reserved for gardens but that dirt was harder than the old cement. At the main entrance into the court there was a slight hill and then it would level off. Whenever it would rain a huge brownish puddle would form. The puddle was so large that people had to go around it in order to get into there buildings. Because of the puddle being so large we nick named it lake Allequippa. It was so bad I didn't want to bring my friends over.

The essay had not been proof-read carefully. In addition, there were the 'Black English' 'mistakes' such as

> I was about eight ... when she first brang his Rasta Man Vibrations album home.

OR

> The Quiet Storm was the perfect thing when I needed to *relax me* before I went to sleep.

There were also attempts at phonetic spelling such as 'endore' and 'ashfalt'. Yet, the spirit of the writing, the attention to descriptive detail and the avoidance of sentimentality deserve recognition. It has been noted by instructors at Pitt that often the minority student will 'learn' the rules of standard usage *and* standard subject-matter (that is, crudely put, 'white' issues) at the expense of his/her identity, by producing 'safe' and uninteresting papers.

write 'ungrammatically' (as they speak, for instance) are less likely to defend their *writing* in the face of 'correction' by teachers, peers, superiors and even strangers, whereas dialect (so-called non-standard) *speakers* receive a little more tolerance. A reason for this growing acceptance of *certain* dialectal variants is partly the result of descriptive sociolinguistic work in the field, which has in turn led to a self-consciousness among users to whom the dialect in question provides both a means of identification and a medium of protest against hegemony. This disciplinary legitimization through its construction as an object worthy of study has not, however, taken place within written English, even though many of the same considerations apply as in the case of the spoken varieties.

As we make the move from the discourse of standardization and Standard English to certain non-standard (post)colonial forms of the language, it is imperative that we reiterate the historical complicities between the imperialist project and the rise of English studies. Crowley identifies the widely held belief among influential philologists, linguists and statesmen in the middle of the nineteenth century (the beginnings of high colonialism) such as Archbishop Trent, Max Müller and De Quincey that 'the English language and nation had one thing in common: their greatness. The more the English nation extended the boundaries of its empire, the more the English language was praised as a superior language and subjected to extensive study' (p. 71). The radical shift from relative obscurity and disdain (only women and the working class studied English, which was the 'poor man's classics') to disciplinary status is intimately, if complexly, woven into the very fabric of the colonial enterprise. Unfortunately, the extent and detail of this connection has hardly been determined, and is beyond the scope of this study.[22] In the absence of a careful analysis of the implications and

---

22.  Notable is the doctoral dissertation of Gauri Viswanathan, which explores the construction of the discipline of English within the displaced arena of India (since published in revised form as *Masks of Conquest: Literary Study and British Rule in India*; 1989). Yet, the definitive work on English studies, *The Social Mission of English Criticism* (Chris Baldick, 1983), makes only one reference, albeit a strong one, to the role of the colonies within this disciplinary narrative. Crowley too, in an otherwise fine analysis, appears to gloss over the colonialist imperative by identifying it as one influence among many of equal importance. Also worth reading is Venkat Rao's 'Self Formations: Speculations on the Question of Postcoloniality'.

repercussions of such a disciplinarization, however, we must rely on MacCabe's description of the broad text of colonialism as it seeks to provide a continuist version of the English national identity through a self-conscious homogenization and unification of heterogeneous elements.

> The cultural monolith that was institutionalised in the study of English literature is now broken open as a contradictory set of cultural and historical moments.... English as a subject was created not only on the basis of a unified cultural tradition but, as importantly, on an almost total subordination of speech to writing.... ['Broken English']

And it is this 'almost total subjugation of speech to writing' that is operative within much of the debate on standardization. Yet, it is a complex phenomenon in that though speech is normed by writing, speech remains at the same time the 'shibboleth' as well as the possibility of protest.[23]

> We have Old Testament authority ... for the social and deadly significance of speech but we hardly need recourse to any authority to prove what we all experience every day – a differential and contradictory sorting of approved forms of speech. And this is as true of the written language as it is of the spoken – only someone insensitive to the imbrication of power and language would confuse, as equivalent, sentences written in popular textbooks and those chalked fleetingly on convenient walls. If we are concerned with how a language reproduces itself, then these questions become pressing. ... In fact American and British English have not grown further apart. The shared technologies of communication from print to the more recent forms of speech reproduction in film, television and gramophone records have made for greater interchange and intercommunicability between the two dialects.[24]

MacCabe's conclusion marks an important moment in the standardization of language. Notwithstanding all the distinctions and reservations outlined so far, it does make sense to speak about a

---

23. See below for the articulation of this problematic in terms of South Asian English.
24. Colin MacCabe (1990) p. 3.

standard in the 'British' context. This standard needs to be broadened, it needs to be continually revised, and even then it is not to be entirely trusted, but whether we like it or not, it remains more or less in place. The standard is in effect, and is based, however loosely, on shared assumptions and on a network of mechanisms such as the school system, a common historical narrative, and, perhaps most importantly, the conservative consequences of printing and communication technology which literally fixes the language.

At least, this is what *seems* to be the case. As we examine each of these assumptions, we find that they derive their cohesion from systematic exclusion or selectivity in the manner outlined by Crowley and others. Yet what makes them appear tenable is the complex history of the construction of language nationalism in England, which has become in a Foucaultian sense a signifier-turned-referent, or, crudely put, a bedrock premise that requires no further justification within the discourses it inhabits. Yet even these parameters that obtain in the British context do not work in the same way in other language situations, and particularly those that involve the colonial imposition of English.

## THE STATUS OF THE 'OTHER' ENGLISHES

At the outset it is necessary to distinguish my position from that of opponents of the 'other' Englishes such as Clifford Prator whose prescriptivism has been powerfully critiqued in an exemplary text by Braj Kachru. I can do no better than re-read this essay, in which he refutes 'a colonialist' argument against the acceptance of the 'non-native' Englishes into the linguistic canon, both as an acknowledgement of my indebtedness to Kachru and as a measure of our divergence.

In addition to his critique of Clifford Prator's 'The British Heresy in TESL',[25] I shall also discuss other influential linguists such as Halliday and LePage who are 'more tolerant' than Prator, as well as Kachru's own attempt at suggesting alternative methodologies for dealing with the 'non-native' Englishes. I aim, in this manner, to show that even the most liberal and sympathetic of linguists – of

---

25.   In Joshua A. Fishman, Charles A. Ferguson and Jyotindra Das Gupta (1968) pp. 459–76.

whom Kachru is an outstanding example – cannot do justice to
these Other Englishes as long as they remain within the over-
arching structures that these Englishes bring to crisis. To take these
new/other Englishes seriously would require a fundamental
revaluation of linguistic paradigms, and not merely a slight accommodation or adjustment.

Kachru sets out to discuss the 'linguistic feud, primarily one of
language attitudes, between the native speakers of various varieties
of English (and some non-native speakers, too) and the speakers of
the non-native varieties of English, such as Filipino English, West
African English, Indian English, etc.,' and begins by 'clearing away
a few attitudinal cobwebs ... about non-native varieties of English.'
He notes, however, that he is not 'out to destroy an imaginary linguistic straw man,' and that Clifford Prator is a 'distinguished and
active scholar in the area of the Teaching of English as a Foreign
Language' (Kachru, 1986, p. 100).

Prator represents the quintessentially purist position in Anglo-US
linguistics which usually looks up to a simplified French model. The
main objection to legitimizing alternate varieties is that it sets these
up as equivalent to Standard English. Therefore, for Prator,

in a nutshell, the heretical tenet I feel I must take exception to is
the idea that it is best, in a country where English is not spoken
natively but is widely used as the medium of instruction, to set up
the local variety of English as the ultimate model to be imitated
by those learning the language.    (Prator, 1968, p. 459)[26]

In Prator's initial formulation quoted above, Kachru does not take
exception to the implied categorization of, say, India as 'a country
where English is not spoken natively.' I do not really know what it
means to speak English 'natively', but given Kachru's acceptance of

---

26.  Both Prator and Kachru adopt this register of religious terminology:
     Kachru responding to Prator's invocation of 'heresies', 'dogmas', and
     'doctrines', enumerates the 'seven attitudinal sins' committed by Pra-
     tor. English has magical properties – the title of Kachru's most recent
     book is *The Alchemy of English* – and its acquisition leads to a 'linguistic
     reincarnation': the religious metaphor is symptomatic. It is not the case
     that *any* language is able to transform its users, but rather that English
     is *the* language that is able to do this. The 'alchemy' of English is its
     ability to effect a transmutation of the base metals into gold, its myste-
     rious transmuting of something common into something special.

this classification (native/non-native), surely he needs to differ? At any rate, Indian English is theoretically important precisely because it renders such unexamined categories such as the native/non-native dichotomy suspect.[27]

Kachru faults Prator for 'the sin of ethnocentrism' by pointing to his 'intellectually and empirically unjustified view concerning the homogeneity and speech uniformity of American society'. Prator makes the strange claim that 'social classes are difficult to distinguish in the United States, and social dialects show relatively little systemic variation' (p. 471). Kachru notes that in this case Prator has not been affected by the vast empirical evidence to the contrary which he cites, and concludes, 'that it is this view which makes him (Prator) adopt an unrealistic attitude to homogeneity and linguistic conformity in non-native varieties of English' (p. 102).

This extrapolation is cryptic, however, since it is precisely Prator's contention that there is little if any homogeneity in the so-called non-native varieties of English. It must be that the unjustifiable homogenization in the 'American' case stems from the same cause as the equally unjustifiable heterogenization of Indian English. Even though this cause has been identified for us by Kachru as 'ethnocentrism' we are unclear as to how it works.

It is in his questioning of the systemicness of these other varieties of English that Prator raises the most fundamental, if misguided, objection to their legitimacy. Referring to his obvious *bête noire*, Indian English, Prator writes:

> the rub is that very few speakers limit their aberrancies to the widely shared features: each individual typically adds in his *(sic)* own speech a large and idiosyncratic collection of features reflecting his particular native language, educational background, and personal temperament.    (p. 464)

The point, however, is that standard speakers do more or less the same. Prator admits as much when he agrees that the 'mother-tongue varieties of English also lack complete consistency, and

---

27.  It seems quite clear that the moment one accepts such categorizations and 'theoretical fictions' such as the native/non-native binary, one has already begged the question of the subordination/inferiority of the 'lesser' term in the hierarchy. At best, thereafter, one is reduced to rehabilitating the subordinate term until it achieves some respectability.

idiolects vary with circumstances'. Kachru shows that Prator's concern that the definition of Indian English as 'the English spoken by educated Indians' has no specific meaning, is unfounded since the same sorts of 'impressionistic' and 'scientifically meaningless' [Prator] concepts obtain in the British context as well. Kachru's example is from Randolph Quirk's *Survey of English Usage*, in which he presents the goal of the survey in terms of the analogous concept of 'educated English':

> The *Survey* is concerned with 'educated' English: that is, no account is taken of dialect or sub-standard usage. But it is necessarily acknowledged that these terms are relative and that the varieties of English so labelled are by no means entirely contained within hard and fast boundaries. It is an important feature of a language's 'style reservoir' that there should be a periphery of relatively dubious usage which the timid avoid, the defiant embrace, and the provocative exploit; we may compare our mild fun with 'he didn't ought to have ate it' or 'who-done-it.' ... A working definition like 'Educated English is English that is recognized as such by educated native English speakers' is not as valueless as its circularity would suggest. (Quirk, 1968, p. 79)

Having pointed to the 'arbitrariness' of linguistic normativity, Kachru does not wish to show that even this arbitrariness, which rests, broadly speaking, on a class–race–gender–region–based consensus, is disrupted by the 'non-native' varieties of English even whose 'educated' form must challenge the definition. The definition becomes 'bad' not because of its circularity so much as because the significer-turned-referent 'native speaker' is suddenly shorn of its reference. The 'educated native Indian English speaker' becomes far less easy to homogenize, and indeed to identify at all. Even if they can be located, the social, political, economic 'situation' of such speakers renders the privileging of their 'nativity' all but impossible. In fact, elsewhere Kachru identifies this group as 'the Indian English speech community', using the term 'native' to describe the privileged site of Standard English discourse (RP).

Prator quotes Halliday, McIntosh and Strevens from *The Linguistic Sciences and Language Teaching* (1964) – their book forms the basis on which Prator identifies the 'heresy' that he critiques in the article – approvingly in the following extract:

It is possible to suggest two basic criteria to determine whether a variety of English is acceptable for use as an educational model. First, it must be a variety actually used by a reasonably large body of the population, in particular *by a proportion of those whose level of education makes them in other respects desirable models*. This means that we would exclude forms of English which have been invented or imported and bear no relation to *the professional and educational standards* of the country. Second, it must be mutually intelligible with other varieties English used by *similar professional and educational groups in other countries*. ... It follows from this that the extent of deviation from Standard English grammar and lexis must be small. It also follows, as far as phonology is concerned, that while the actual quality of vowels and consonants may vary a great deal between one accent and another, the number of contrasts, the number of phonological units, and the number of systems being operated must also remain fairly close to those of other *'educated accents'*, since otherwise speakers of one would have great difficulty in understanding speakers of others.

The disagreement derives in part from the fact that while Halliday and colleagues 'believe that suitable variations of English, meeting their two criteria, actually do exist in the countries in question and that there will thus be no need to "invent" one,' Prator feels that this is not the case (p. 462). Halliday and others agree, according to Prator, that 'if a local variety of English gains acceptance as the instructional model in a given country, the chances that the language will continue to play a significant role in the life of that country will thereby be considerably increased'. The urgency of the situation is best captured by Le Page, who is quoted by Prator as saying that

'unless an *"educated standard* variety of English" can be identified or created "in those countries where English is not the native language of an indigenous *white* population", the only alternatives may be some form of Pidgin as an indigenous lingua franca which may flourish or English spoken simply as a foreign language by fewer and fewer of the population'. (p. 463)

In these quotations the emphases have been mine. I have tried to show by this means where I feel these linguists agree even though there is a tendency to make much of their divergences. Prator,

Halliday and Kachru surely have their differences, but they share strong feelings on the necessity of 'an educated standard'. In fact Prator's thesis amounts to a critique of the lowering of standards in the name of TESL.

This universal support for an educated standard, which has remained unquestioned in the discipline, displaces issues of class, race and gender in language. It is due to this insensitivity to the social dynamic as struggle against hegemony that linguists can defend post-colonial Englishes on the grounds of neutrality, in the following manner:

> It seems to be in general true that, if the people of these countries identified the English language with colonial rule and lack of independence, this was very largely through the social and educational accent-markers of the professional and governmental Englishmen they were accustomed to meeting; English without these markers, and a fortiori English with local markers, is quite neutral and can the more readily become a tool for communication, to be used or discarded according to practical considerations. (Halliday *et al.*, 1964, p. 294)

The fact that in a restricted and radically circumscribed space such a contention is not untrue, does not detract from the fact that an obsession with this narrow stratum provides a distortion of the broader linguistic context.

In fact, this thematic of the neutrality of English is recurrent in the writings by linguists studying the 'new' Englishes. Examples of this neutrality generally cited concern code-mixing of a 'trivial' kind and involve, for instance, the use of non-caste-marked alternatives to lexical items in the speaker's 'first' language (see Kachru, 1986. pp. 9ff).[28] Having identified the preferred contexts of lexicalization as 'kinship, taboo items, science and technology, or in discussing sex organs and death', Kachru agrees with Moag's description of the 'social neutrality' of English in the case of Fiji as applicable 'in almost all the countries where English is used as a non-native language.' In the Fijian context, Tongans and Fijians,

---

28. The situation is, of course, more complex than this. Please see below where a detailed analysis of code-mixing in Sri Lanka identifies the various 'motivations' at work. I am grateful to Professor Siromi Fernando for helping me see this phenomenon in a less simplistic manner.

find English the only safe medium in which to address those of
higher status. English not only hides their inability in the specialized vernacular registers, but also allows them to meet traditional
superiors on a more or less equal footing.   (Moag, 1982, p. 276)

Not only is this factually incorrect in the case of Fiji, but it is quite
absurd when one generalizes the phenomenon to cover 'almost all
the countries where English is used as a non-native language'. Even
when English is, in fact, the 'only safe medium' to address those of
'higher status', it is so not because English is 'socially neutral', but,
on the contrary, because it is virtually inseparable from that very
'higher status' that it marks. If English hides anyone's (in)ability 'in
the specialized vernacular registers', it is that of the traditional
superior – generally a post-colonial – who has had class-based
access to 'western' education.

These pleas for the neutrality of English in the post-colonial contexts are as ubiquitous and as insistent as they are unsubstantiated
and unexplained. It is as if the neutrality of English is a metonym
for the neutrality of linguistics itself, so that there is more at stake in
this displaced valorization. Kachru even seeks the authority of history to legitimize English in India when he accuses Prator of 'failing
to see the role of English as identical to that of Sanskrit in earlier
Indian history, or that of Indian Persian in the North of India during
the Muslim period' (p. 107). Thus, it would seem that the neutrality
of the colonial language[29] is dependent on the neutrality of colonialism itself, and that this in turn obtains the neutrality–objectivity–
scientificity of the derivative discourses of colonialism.

To return to our reading of Kachru's reading of Prator, however,
the second 'sin' that Prator is accused of committing is the 'wrong
perception of the language attitudes on the two sides of the Atlantic'
(p. 103). Prator makes the argument that the British linguists' position is typified 'by the deep-seated distrust of the African who pre-
sumes to speak English too well' (p. 471), whereas the 'mistrust of
the French and Americans seems rather to be directed toward the
outsider who does not speak French or English well' (ibid.). Prator's
'explanation' is that 'the American's greater experience with large
numbers of immigrants, whose presence in his [sic] country he has

---

29.  I am only using a shorthand here since I hope to show in Chapters 3
      and 4 that 'English' is more than this in the context of Sri Lanka/
      Ceylon.

felt as an economic threat and a social problem, undoubtedly helps to explain his greater antipathy toward foreign accents. In France the tourist and the expatriate may have contributed to a similar attitude' (ibid.).

Kachru is, of course, right in saying that 'the sociological asides supposed to provide bases for the two types of language attitudes, *unfortunately*, are not only counter-intuitive, but without any empirical basis' (p. 103). My emphasis on 'unfortunately' seeks to locate the reason for Kachru's sympathy with Prator's untenable position. Why is it that what Kachru finds most objectionable in this formulation is Prator's attempt to 'structure the language attitudes of the speakers of English on the two sides of the Atlantic in a neat dichotomy'? It seems that Kachru is raising the one, undoubtedly valid, criticism which leaves the underlying language attitudes themselves intact. The real issue concerns the different prescriptive attitudes to language normativity which are a function of sociohistorical processes, the analysis of which will shed light on struggles for dominance through ideological production within 'linguistic' and 'national' communities. There are certainly sufficient differences in the two caricature positions outlined by Prator, even if one were to discount their neat dichotomy, to merit a more serious response by Kachru, if, in fact, he did disagree with their substance. Instead, he seems to be disappointed that they are empirically unsupportable.

The seventh sin is that of Prator's 'exhibiting language colonialism'. Kachru writes,

An enthusiastic defender of the non-native varieties of English will not be too wrong if he [*sic*] detects traces of linguistic and cultural colonialism in Prator's arguments. If this attitude does not manifest itself in the imposition of a particular language, it shows in an unrealistic prescription with reference to a model.  (p. 106)

There are so many qualifications here that attenuate and anaesthetize what must be an obvious conclusion. The defender must be 'enthusiastic' and therefore a little emotional perhaps, and yet he[30]

---

30. The sexism is not limited to the 'stylistic variation' (Rorty) of choice of personal pronouns, of course, but is implicated in the over-arching humanism of these texts which tend to universalize the state of *MAN* by smoothing over and devaluing the moments of difference and crisis.

will not be right but only 'not too wrong' in the 'detection of traces' of linguistic and cultural colonialism!

It is symptomatic of this discourse that both sides exaggerate the differences and minimize the commonalities that they share. What better way to do this than by accusing each other, albeit diminutively, of being 'colonialist'? In this manner, colonialism becomes merely an insult to be bandied about, and does not require any further analysis or unpacking. The strike is clearly pre-emptive in the case of Prator, who begins his essay with the assertion that 'the doctrine of establishing local models for TESL thus appears to be a natural outgrowth of the much deplored colonial mentality' (p. 460). It *appears thus* according to him because 'such proposals seem to arise spontaneously and inevitably in every formerly colonial area where English has been the principle medium of instruction long enough for the people to begin to feel somewhat possessive about the language'. He cites India, Pakistan, Ceylon,[31] Ghana and Nigeria as countries where such notions are 'particularly prevalent'. For Prator, the fact that 'it (the plea for legitimizing localized forms of English) does not seem to flourish in countries that have little or no recent history as colonies' is proof of its complicity with the colonial mentality. The existence of distinct local forms of English obviously derives from the extent and duration of the colonial experience itself, but from this causal connection, Prator extrapolates that the demand for the recognition of these forms must be fundamentally colonialist. The fact that Kachru does not respond to this patent *non sequitur* masquerading as critique is telling.

Kachru's alternative to Prator's 'attitudinal sins' involves the acceptance of

---

31.  The following figures of students attending 'vernacular' as opposed to English schools even at independence debunks the popular upperclass myth that 'in the old days everyone studied in English, and it is only now that standards have declined'. I have culled these statistics from such diverse sources as de Souza,'Tests and Targets' (1977), *Census of Population & Housing 1981* (Sri Lanka) and the Special Committee on Education Report (Ceylon Sessional Paper XXIV of 1943).

|                        | 1931    | 1940    | 1948    | 1981      |
|------------------------|---------|---------|---------|-----------|
| English schools (fees) | 84,000  | 92,049  | 180,000 | NA        |
| Bilingual              | NA      | 15,917  | NA      | –         |
| 'Vernacular' (free)    | 476,000 | 650,910 | 720,000 | 2,831,960 |

two premises concerning Indian English as we should about any other Third World variety of English. First, that the users of Indian English form a distinct speech community who use a variety of English which is by and large formally distinct because it performs functions which are different from the other varieties of English. Second, that Indian English functions in the Indian socio-cultural context in order to perform those roles which are relevant and appropriate to the social, educational and administrative network of India'.   (p. 111)

Here we have the typical move distancing the 'third world' Englishes, and making them special *vis-à-vis* standard/native English, or, by implication, English as such. It seems to me, however, that the two premises, supposedly peculiar to these Englishes, are valid for all types of English in use. There may be variations in degree, but these variations are present even within the 'same' type of English.

Referring to the so-called deviations in Indian English, Kachru finds that they result from a 'process of acculturation which has rightly made the non-native varieties of English culture-bound' (p. 112), as if this phenomenon were again peculiarly appropriate or symptomatic only of the 'non-native' Englishes.

Kachru takes issue with Prator in terms of the so-called functional differences of Indian English, and he never really questions the primacy/desirability of the standard for transnational communication. For interaction with 'first language' users of English, Kachru suggests the model of *educated* Indian English.

A little effort on the part of the native speakers to understand Indians is as important as a little effort on the part of Indians to make themselves understood by those who use English as their first language. The result will be a desirable variety of English with the distinctiveness of Kissingerian English, intelligible, acceptable and at the same time enjoyable. Let us not make over twenty-three million Indian English speakers sound like WASPS lost in the tropical terrain of India, nor should they sound, as Quirk notes, like the RP speakers sound to the Americans, 'clipped, cold and rather effeminate'.   (Quirk, 1972 p. 22)

The context of centre–periphery relations within the international division of labour is thus obliterated by the polite exchanges of genteel society, where all that is required is 'a little effort' exerted mutually. The smoothing out of struggle within and without language is replicated in the homogenizing of the varieties of English on the basis of 'upper-class' forms. Kachru is thus able to theorize on the nature of a monolithic Indian English, and Quirk can report on 'American' perceptions without the slightest embarrassment that it is not merely male chauvinist but also white racist in that it excludes the perceptions of blacks and hispanics entirely. The image of WASPS 'lost in the tropical terrain of India' can be read as recuperating the primal colonial scene, as can, in a different argument, the interested use of Kissinger as the 'intelligible, acceptable and ... enjoyable' model.

The example of the other Englishes is sufficient to show Kachru that 'the universality of pedagogical models is suspect' (Kachru, 1986, p. 123), and he is also aware that 'in pedagogical literature the term "model" entails a prescriptivism with reference to a specific variety of a language or a dialect' (ibid., p. 117). However, he wishes to retain this prescriptivism, attenuating its harshness by suggesting two different models instead of one. For Indian English as a means of communication among Indians, he advocates the use of parameters such as Firth's *Context of Situation* in the formulation of a new model. He emphasizes the need to recognize the nature of individual *speech events*, the *cline of intelligibility* and the differing nature of the *roles and types of linguistic interaction*. The implied model of language as such is still communicative in the narrow sense, however.[32]

Kachru writes that 'those who recommended a local model of English for the non-normative varieties (of English) are not out to get even with the past colonizers by nativizing the language of the Raj, or to demonstrate a nationalistic pride, or exhibit a linguistic perversity without realizing its ultimate consequences' (p. 120). He accepts the validity of the normative varieties of English, only wishing to garner some respectability to the non-normative varieties as well. In so far as he does, therefore, make a special case for TESL or Indian English, he is reinforcing the linguistic hierarchy. When he restricts the validity of Indian English to situations of context in which Indians communicate with each other, he is,

---

32. Cf. Chapter 2, particularly n. 66, for a discussion/critique of narrowly communicative models of language.

willy nilly, reproducing the old colonialist categories of a Hugo Schuchardt.[33]

Kachru makes apologies for going too far. He is worried about being perceived as a linguistic anarchist, perhaps. He is at pains to show that he is not undermining the basis of all the linguistic work that has gone on so far. To do this he has to avoid contention with the 'nativity' of English as metonym of the First Language.

> It is generally thought that the goal for excellence in language teaching and learning is acquiring a 'native-like' command, and, as a consequence, *acceptance* by a native speaker. This argument seems to be valid for a majority of language-learning situations. One would, however, be reluctant to accept it as a crucial criterion for TESL. (p. 118)

The double-bind is that, having accepted the model as appropriate in most situations, Kachru is doomed to devalue those contexts that are inappropriate to the model, even if only in terms of linguistic patronization.[34]

---

33. See, for example, Schuhardt's pioneering work on pidgins and creoles, but it is important to note that scholars do not seem to have progressed much in the past century or so. For instance, here is an indication from a recent work on South Asian languages, which, for all its self-avowed innocence, does not convince:

   > We have also elected to include a discussion of some of the literature on varieties of South Asian English. A word of explanation is clearly in order. We obviously do not wish to imply that all, or even many, varieties of South Asian English are essentially pidgins or creoles. Rather we would claim that some of the same linguistic processes that have occurred in the genesis of pidgins and creoles have also occurred in the formation of some varieties of South Asian English. But clearly there are differences. The decision to include a discussion of South Asian English in this chapter is, then, a reflection of our inability to find any natural and appropriate place to locate a discussion of the matter in the pages of this work. (1983, p. 194)

34. The argument can been made that Kachru and others are not theoretically sophisticated from a post-structuralist standpoint, but that this critique leaves the major thrust of their work unaffected. I do not agree, of course, and submit the following section on South Asian English as an 'empirical' proof of these 'theoretical' problems.

This contradiction that Kachru unwittingly inhabits is best described in a recent essay by the Sri Lankan linguist Thiru Kandiah, which I discuss in detail in Chapter 5 of this book:

> Measured by the norms of standard OVEs (Old(er) Varieties of English), as the cline (of bilingualism) requires them to be, many of the forms of these NVEs (New Varieties of English) would most certainly be 'aberrant' or, as Kachru calls them 'deviant' (1965; 1983, 186), so that the varieties would necessarily remain but 'partially learned' languages (Richards: 1977, 172). Which, in fact, is why, for Kachru, even the intelligibility of the NVE forms to OVE users would not imply 'that the user's command of English equals that of' such OVE users (1983, 129); and why, again, even the educated or standard variety of IE (Indian English) can guarantee its users a place only somewhere 'around the central point' along the scale (Kachru: 1983, 26, 71. Verma: 1982 expresses essentially the same position, though rather differently) (See, too, Kandiah: 1980/81, 1981). The best users of IE have, then, gone only about half way towards acquiring control of *the* language.    (1987, pp. 36–7).

What remains to be argued, however, is precisely who these 'best users' of IE (or, in this case, Lankan English) are, and it is in this respect that we shall diverge from Kandiah by suggesting, only partly in mischief, that the 'best users' may also be the 'worst'!

## SOUTH ASIAN ENGLISH, INDIAN ENGLISH AND LANKAN ENGLISH

In Kachru's discussion of South Asian English,[35] he appears to conflate both the written and spoken varieties, and this remains generally true for subsequent writing on the subject, thereby re-enacting the situation outlined by Crowley and alluded to by MacCabe in

---

35.  I shall refer to two pioneering essays by Kachru on South Asian English: 'English in South Asia: An Overview' in *The Indianization of English* (1983) and 'A Nativized Variety: The South Asian Case' in *The Alchemy of English* (1986). These draw on thirty years of research in the field, and remain the definitive work on the subject.

terms of the Euro-American model.[36] Specifically, this problematic operates within the linguistics of the other Englishes by conflating speech and writing into one form which is then unravelled on an *ad hoc* basis. Sri Lankan English, for instance, has been mainly

---

36. The situation is described powerfully by Kandiah in his analysis of 'New Varieties of English':

> The significance of the proposal (to compile NVE dictionaries) is that it would help resolve a curious ambiguity that users of NVEs tend to show towards their own usage. As already mentioned, these users do control rule-governed systems that they freely operate in their everyday usage. However, when they are in any doubt, for instance, (as to) the pronunciation of a word, they do not turn to an examina-tion of their own usage, but, instead, go directly to the authority of a dictionary of Standard British or American English. This does not, in actual fact, mean that they have forsaken their own norms; for, after they have procured the phonological information sought for, they would proceed, in their usage, to 'reinterpret' it in terms of their own inbuilt phonological system, realizing the form involved in terms of their own phonemic and phonetic counters. ...
>
> More careful reflection shows, however, that there is no real ambi-guity in the attitudes of these users. Since their own usage has never been codified or standardized by the usual means, they have no published authority to go to but the current ones, which happen to be based on Standard British or American usage. ... Since as Kachru points out, 'the compilation of dictionaries (for NVEs) is a crucial first step towards their standardization' (1983, 166), his proposal, if acted on, will help to rectify the situation that is responsible for this apparent contradiction, and also go some way towards dispelling the schizoid attitudes that the users of NVEs often have towards their own usage. (1987, p. 34)

The argument that I wish to emphasize here is that the mechanisms of standardization that are in place in, say, Britain do not obtain in the case of these 'other' or 'New Varieties of English' thereby problematiz-ing standardization itself in ways that are difficult to see today in the 'West'. On the one hand, there is a need for institutional mechanisms such as dictionaries and grammars which would legitimize and repro-duce the standardized versions of these NVEs. On the other hand, however, since these dictionaries and grammars are not in place, it is possible to broaden the self-conscious standard in a manner that would be impossible if there were mechanisms to police the NVEs. Here we have a situation, then, where the standard itself can be fought over without the élites having recourse to an authority established locally. The only authorities that can be invoked are those that the élites themselves can be shown not to conform to, thereby undercutting the force of their claims.

characterized as a spoken variety in the linguistic literature, though written elements, and particularly creative writing, have been analysed for distinctive features as well.[37]

In this regard, Kachru's diagnosis of the peculiar mix of literariness and formality of South Asian varieties (or dialects)[38] of English is especially relevant.

> The third factor which contributes to the 'South-Asianness' of South Asian English is the fact that English is taught through the written medium in South Asia. The curriculum does not make any special provision for spoken English. It is therefore natural that many features of 'South-Asianness' in pronunciation is based on spelling. ... Spoken models are exclusively Indian, and the written models are provided by the classics of English – mostly of the eighteenth and nineteenth centuries – which Indian graduate students relish.  (p. 38)

The diglossic situation as concerns Sri Lankan English has been noted by some scholars, but has never been examined systematically.[39] For instance, Kandiah discusses the tensions between the systems of Standard English and Lankan English for Lankan users of the language (pp. 78ff), but the contention that Lankan English closely approximates Standard English in its written form seems to me to beg the question. In less formal contexts such as personal

---

37.  See, for instance, Kandiah, 'Lankan English Schizoglossia' (1981a) p. 64, though the preoccupation with spoken forms is quite pervasive, and requires little further evidence.

38.  Manfred Gorlach, editor of *English World-Wide* in a footnote to Kandiah's essay writes in 1981:

> in fact, a great proportion of the non-BrE (or non-international English) (*sic*) features encountered in Sri Lanka is shared by other varieties of SAsE. No exhaustive scholarly investigation of the distribution of these features has been undertaken so far, so that claims about LknE vs. IndE vs. SAsE remain more or less impressionistic.  (p. 64)

39.  It seems to me, for instance, that though there appears to be diglossia in the case of Lankan English, it is hardly as pronounced or as important as in either Sinhala or Tamil. In comparison, it is almost a distortion to refer to the Lankan English situation as diglossic, particularly since elements such as 'slang' and intimacies form the bulk of the difference in the respective varieties.

correspondence within the educated variety, and certainly ubiqui-
tously in the other varieties, there are distinctly Sri Lankan elements, which, however, become less acceptable to habitual users as
the level of formality increases. In this sense, the situation is a mirror
of the spoken form, but since informal written contexts are relatively less common, it appears different. The more important point
concerns the identification of the contemporary non-standard written elements which break with the earlier ornateness and over-for-
mality of Lankan English prose. These non-standard elements are
certainly the result of 'first language interference' or transfer, but
that fact does not seem to me to be sufficient reason to dismiss them,
particularly since they are systemic and predictable, and, moreover,
since the language conflict situation they reproduce cannot be
wished away. In my own writing in this book, I have made no
attempt to 'correct' the numerous archaisms ('albeit', for instance),
though the academic content and tone has resulted in fewer Lankan
expressions than, say, US ones, where I did my graduate work!

In this respect, it is crucial to my argument that much of the distinctiveness attributed to South Asian English is derived from syntactic
and idiomatic examples that would not be acceptable to educated
speakers of, say, Lankan English whose usage is defined as the distinctive variety in question. A detailed examination of the grammatical characteristics of South Asian English as identified by Kachru
follows. Here, I shall interpose data from the Sri Lankan linguistic
context in support of my contention that these 'deviations' are not of
the so-called educated standard or prestige dialect, but, rather, from
non-standard speech which is looked down upon by habitual
English-users who are said to establish the norms of Lankan English.

The identification of grammatical characteristics of South Asian
English inevitably leads to complexities. The attitude toward grammatical deviations is not identical to the attitude toward deviations
in pronunciation. Since there has not been any serious attempt at
codification of such grammatical characteristics, it is naturally difficult to distinguish a deviation from what may be considered a mistake. In grammar, therefore, the idealized norm continues to be a
native prescriptive model. Perhaps the largest number of users of
Fowler's *Modern English Usage* are in South Asia. ...

It has impressionistically been claimed that there is a tendency
in South Asian English to use complex sentences which result in
large-scale embeddings. ...

The transfer (or 'interference') from the first languages also results in deviant constructions in, for example, interrogative sentences and the formation of tag questions. There is a tendency to form interrogative constructions without changing the position of the subject and auxiliary items: *what you would like to read?* or *when you would like to come?* ... Transfer thus results in South Asian English constructions such as *you are going tomorrow, isn't it?* and *he isn't going there, isn't it?*[40]

Kandiah identifies these forms of tag-questions with hypercorrection in Lankan usage, but is careful to note that the 'sentences are clearly ungrammatical'.[41] For Kandiah, *'Upali returned the book, isn't it?'* is the kind of sentence produced by many people who have come to stigmatize and reject their own distinctive tag-element, 'no?'[42] However, even the sentence, *'Upali returned the book, no?'* would not be considered acceptable by educated speakers of Lankan English, and would certainly not be written by them except in specialized creative contexts. Antoinette Fernando makes the point that, in general, the examples of hypercorrection offered by Kandiah are 'more characteristic of the speech of speakers of a fossilized interlanguage than that of the average educated speaker of Sri Lankan English' (p. 32).

Hypercorrection itself when taken as a symptom of linguistic insecurity provides insights into the pressures that obtain in the larger linguistic environment. Kandiah is, therefore, quite right to focus on this phenomenon inspite of the fact that its manifestations are not, by his own definition, examples of acceptable Lankan English. If, however, it were possible to imagine the unthinkable by incorporating these constructions into the standard; this new standard would provide a much better reflection of the way language works in such a post-colonial context, indeed in any context. In this sense, it is possible to read, against the grain of mainstream linguistics, as it were, 'hypercorrection' and other exorbitant and persistent 'mistakes' as attempts to de-hegemonize the once-colonial-and-now-class-based English language. Here, as elsewhere in this section, these arguments and suggestions will be fleshed out in terms of concrete examples from the current Sri Lankan language-in-crisis situation in Chapters 3 and 4 of this book.

---

40.  Kachru (1986, pp. 39–40).
41.  Thiru Kandiah (1981a, p. 71).
42.  More about this in the last chapter, pp. 186ff, when I discuss hypercorrection and motivation in Lankan English usage.

Other differences in South Asian English are the result of the extension in selection restrictions in syntax and semantics as, for example, in the use of stative predicates. These are English verbs which are ungrammatical when used in the progressive form (*is having, seeing, knowing*). Therefore the following constructions, transferred from the first language of the South Asian English bilinguals, are unacceptable to a native speaker of English:

> *Mohan is having two houses.*
> *Ram was knowing that he would come.*
> *I am understanding English better now.*   (Kachru, 1986, p. 40)

The fact is that such sentences would be unacceptable to the majority of habitual English speakers in Sri Lanka too, though they are very widely used by others.

> The use of articles in a South Asian English ... has (been) aptly classified ... as 'missing,' 'intrusive,' 'wrong,' 'usurping,' and 'dispossessed.'
> Reduplication of items belonging to various word classes is a common feature of South Asian English and is used for emphasis and to indicate continuation of a process.... Consider, for example, Lankan English *to go crying crying, small small pieces,* and *who and who came to the party?*   (ibid., pp. 40–41)

Again, the examples used are from the repertoire of those 'low' on the cline of bilingualism. Even then, these examples taken from Passe (1948) are not widely used, though examples of reduplication as in *'hot hot hoppers'* are used in certain informal contexts by those higher on the scale.[43]

---

43   The discussion in Antoinette Fernando's unpublished dissertation (1986) is important in its attempt to explain why some such expressions are acceptable while others are not.

> The culture conditioned conception of certain things goes some way in explaining why an expression such as hot hot hoppers is more acceptable than *she went jumping jumping. Jumping, jumping* is merely a translation from the Sinhala *pane pane giya:* used to describe the movement of skipping along. Though this is an apt description of the movement it is not culture specific in that this movement is the same whoever does it and under whatever circumstances it is done. *Hot hot hoppers* on the other hand is the expression of something that is typically culture conditioned. While *pane pane giya:* and *skipped along* conjures the same mental image *hot hoppers* and *unu a:ppe* conjure two different images. Sri Lankanisms then are not the result of translating from one language to another but from one culture to another: it is the result not of language transfer as such but of culture transfer.   (p. 33)

Kandiah who, more than anyone else, is responsible for legitimizing Lankan English writes:

> Although at the morphological level LnkE does not appear to differ from StE, at the syntactic level there are many phenomena that are distinctively Lankan. Among these are focalization, illustrated by 2., topicalization, illustrated by 3., and the non-specification of certain redundant features that may be recovered by means of Gricean-type conversational rules involving contextual and other aspects of the speech act, illustrated by 4. ...

> 2.  Before five o'clock, Nimal woke up.
> 3.  Kasy, I expect him to make an exciting contribution to Tamil studies.
> 4.  If Rani asks Mahes to help her, sure to oblige (= 'he is sure to oblige her'). (1981a, p. 64)

As Fernando points out, however, both (3) and (4) 'cannot be said to be characteristic of *all* "habitual" users of Sri Lankan English or even of *most*' (1986, p. 28). Even (2), though it may be acceptable, is certainly not the usual or preferred formulation.[44]

The situation as regards Lankan English (and, for that matter Indian English) is further complicated by the fact that *all* the writing to date has been based on random examples and personal experience. Nothing like a large-scale sociolinguistic survey or a systematic empirical study has been undertaken. As a result, the findings of linguists remain more impressionistic than necessary, and even the acceptability of the few cited examples are contested. There is, however, broad agreement as to the phonological features that mark Lankan English (or Ceylon English). The distinctive features of Sri Lankan speech affect not merely vowel and consonant sounds but, perhaps more importantly, stress, rhythm and intonation. Siromi Fernando analyses the dynamic of Lankan English phonology as it adapts to social and attitudinal transformations in the 1980s, pre-

---

44.  In any case, it appears that, in general, insufficient emphasis is placed on context in the viability of examples from speech. The immediate context of a speech act as well as its broader environment provide the crucial determinants of acceptability of an utterance. It seems, therefore, theoretically at least, simplistic to provide absolute (negative) judgements on the linguistic credibility of isolated sentences.

senting a convincing case for a more complex model that is more tolerant of hitherto unacceptable patterns:

> Changes in the phonology of SLE ((Sri) Lankan English) today mirror the following patterns of change in the variety as a whole. SLE today is an uncertain system at many points. A large number of variant forms are acceptable at several of these points, and these variations are sometimes unsystematic, even within the speech of a single speaker. Children who acquire SLE as an established variety, are confronted with this uncertain system, and are often bi-dialectal in these indeterminate areas.[45]

Chitra Fernando, writing in 1976, identifies three 'main patterns of bilingualism' involving English in Sri Lanka, and using a variation of Kachru's *cline of bilingualism*, she describes the first group as having 'a highly Anglicized life style and speak(ing) a virtually uniform variety of English whatever its racial [sic] origin, i.e. Sinhala, Tamil or Malay'.[46] She characterizes these bilinguals as

> typically members of the legal, medical and educational professions, civil servants, commercial executives etc., at the top and middle of the social scale; at the lower end are clerks, nurses, stenographers etc., who would shade off into Group Two depending on their pronunciation and the degree to which they use English in domestic or social intercourse. ...
>
> Group Two bilinguals, generally of peasant, lower-middle or working-class origin, would regard English very much as a foreign language unlike the bilinguals of Group One, especially the older ones to whom it has become an adopted mother tongue. Differences of racial origin [sic] would show up quite clearly in this group....
>
> Phonology is important because it is the salient criterion that distinguishes bilinguals of Group One from bilinguals of Group Two. Members of Group Two are not significantly different from Group One in grammar and lexis....

---

45. Siromi Fernando (1985) p. 56.
46. Chitra Fernando (1976) p. 354. See also p. 102ff where Fernando's work is taken up again in relation to non-standard Lankan English usage.

Group Three consists of bilinguals whose fluency in English is small but who are typically of the same social background as those of Group Two i.e. either peasant, lower-middle or working class or of such origins.... They are essentially receiver bilinguals who learn English because it is compulsory to do so in all Sri Lanka [*sic*] schools.... Poor teaching, weak motivation, little or no exposure to the language outside the classroom result in Group Three bilinguals having very little receptive or productive skill in English. Their position on the Bilingual cline is towards its zero end.... The majority of bilinguals in present-day Sri Lanka would be of the receiver type....

What is most striking about their (Group Three) grammar in English is the extent of its deviation from Standard English as a result of the influence of the mother tongue.... All groups of Sri Lankan bilinguals show areas of departure from Standard British English, but whereas the departures of Groups One and Two are slight, those of Group Three are radical and numerous.

It is also clear that those at the top of Group One tend to use English in their homes and in everyday activities: it is the language they think and dream in, for instance. Sri Lankan English has been defined in terms of these 'native-like' 'habitual' users to whom it serves as an effective 'L1' or 'first language.'[47] Kandiah considers this number to be 'not inconsiderable' (p. 63); if one were to risk an estimate on the basis of the Census for 1981,[48] which defines literacy in a language as the ability 'to read and write with understanding a short statement on everyday life' in that language, I would argue that around 0.7 per cent of the total population over 10 years of age is literate only in English. Thus, the number of those to whom English is an effective 'first language' would be between 0.7 per cent and 12 per cent (the percentage of literates in English, 10 years and older, according to the Census, though this figure seems unacceptably high) or between

---

47. See Kandiah (1964, p. 64), S. Fernando (1986, p. 1) A. Fernando (1986, p. 30) C. Fernando (1976, p. 349).
48. As contained in the *Census of Population and Housing 1981: General Report*.

75,000 and 1,210,000.[49] The actual number is clearly closer to the lower end of the scale, perhaps somewhere around 150,000 or 1.5 per cent. Though this figure is small, the influence and power wielded by the English-speaking élite remains considerable.[50] It is to this group, then, that linguists appear to have gone 'naturally' in their characterization of Lankan English.

A small fraction of the English-using population (in South Asia) claims that English is their first language, but this fraction is so small that for the purpose of the present discussion it can be ignored. Most of the English users are at least bilinguals, and in a majority of cases it is even difficult to say which is their dominant language. However, all such users of English have a language repertoire in

---

49. The estimate of effectively monolingual English speakers was made on the basis of the differences between the percentages for total literacy by ethnic group and literacy in the 'mother tongue' for that group. For instance, 89.3 per cent of Sinhalese over 10 are literate, and of them 89.0 per cent are literate in Sinhala. It is reasonable to deduce, therefore, that the balance of 0.3 per cent must be literate only in English (and not in Tamil), based on an empirical understanding of the language context in Sri Lanka.

    My estimate is somewhat higher than the 'definitive' version provided by Coates in 1961 – 0.17 per cent of the *total* population – but must not be taken to account for an increase in the ratio since the methods of computation differ, and since there is no other external evidence to support this claim.

50. S. Fernando writes that though educationally and in terms of status this group has 'an edge over' the others,

    the liberalism of his [*sic*] anglicised cultural background, and the ideological and moral framework he has inherited, ironically enough from this very westernisation, often gives him a sense of guilt and embarrassment about this slight edge, and triggers off in him an attempt to identify with the other group.  (1985, p. 6)

    This change in linguistic environment, though not surely as widespread as Fernando implies ('he himself belongs to an endangered species'), must be taken into consideration in any contemporary account of English in Sri Lanka. For instance, Fernando's thesis on recent changes in Sri Lankan English phonology are explained in terms of the growing insecurity of SLE speakers.

which English dominates in some functions and one or more South Asian language in others. 'South-Asianness' within this group, then, is typified by features of transference.   (Kachru, 1986, pp. 37ff)

Thus, Lankan English has been defined in terms of its acquisition as an L1 by speakers who 'pick up' the language 'in action' at home and in school (S. Fernando quoting Kandiah. p. 2). It is also identified in terms of its function, again as used habitually as an effective first language, and as an educated variety. Even S. Fernando who considers that 'in terms of the 1985 situation, to label SLE (Sri Lankan English) an "effective first language" (Kandiah, 1979) seems too hasty' (3), argues paradoxically that the variety of English used by L2 speakers would only more or less equate to the system of SLE (p. 4). This inability to distinguish between those who use English as an L1 and an L2 marks an important difficulty with C. Fernando's three groups of Sri Lankan bilinguals. As articulated by S. Fernando, 'Group One subsumes both L1 and L2 users of SLE, while Group Two comprises only those who use English as an L2 or foreign language, but who use a variety that is neither Std.E. nor SLE' (4). In terms of the current situation that obtains, then, for S. Fernando

Socially, the speaker of SLE today is (generally) privileged, affluent, upper or middle-class, with a tradition of formal westernised education behind him [sic], usually educated in urban schools, many of them private; also with a tradition of anglicised cultural patterns, in employment generally in the professions, learned occupations and upper rungs of the government or commercial hierarchy. Although still privileged, he is less assured today of those privileges than earlier.

In terms of language acquisition, he still acquires English at home. This is reinforced at school only in a few urban private schools where English continues as the official medium of extra-curricular activities. At home, English is still acquired for speech by the age of five at the latest, and what is acquired is the established variety, SLE. Socially, the younger generation, but also all speakers of SLE, are more mobile and interactive today. They interact more than earlier with those to whom SLE is not an L1, both in Sinhala (and Tamil) and a variety of English that is neither Std.E. nor SLE. In the case of interaction in English, he is exposed to the non-Std.E., non-SLE variety mainly in listening, but in some cases he may use this variety as well.   (1985, pp. 5–6)

In the case of Standard (British) English, the question as to which variety is to be considered normative was, as we have seen, not without controversy. However, in this case, the 'native speaker' of each variety or dialect was not really the issue, but rather the legitimacy of one variety over another. There always remained a prototype native speaker, however mythologized, whose arbitration and judgement was sought whenever a particular controversy over usage got out of hand. One of the firmest linguistic rules of acceptability to this date has remained the acquiescence of native speakers. In the case of South Asian English, or more specifically Lankan English, however, no such sacrosanct arbiter obtains. Linguists use every other formulation but 'native speaker' to describe the legitimate users of this dialect. They are termed 'native-like' or 'habitual' or 'first language' (L1) users of Lankan English, but their judgement (as to what is and is not acceptable) clearly does not have as much conviction as in the British case. As de Souza and Goonetilleke have emphasized, Lankan English does not pervade every aspect of the lives of any of its users.[51] This problem of identifying appropriate users of Lankan

---

51.  Doric de Souza's classic formulation of the problematic of the habitual speaker of English in Sri Lanka is relevant even today if one remains within received notions of what can legitimately constitute the domain of (educated) Lankan English:

> In India and Sri Lanka, English never became the language of all the people, but served only a small minority. Further, for this very reason, the language cannot serve all purposes, even for those who know it. English did not penetrate into the kitchen and bedroom even in the best regulated families. English was never adapted to deal with the local religions, kinship systems, meals, topography, fauna and flora. There are some people in Ceylon (*sic*) who claim to know only English. If so, most of the plants, animals, fruits, vegetables, spices and I also suspect their actual kinship relations must remain nameless, for there are no English words for them. This fact is of great importance to our targets in teaching English.   (1977, pp. 38–9).

> Though it is not possible to agree with the notion that a language must be free of borrowings or mixing in order to reflect adequately the experience of its native-like users, it is necessary to understand the context within which Professor de Souza here intervenes. In this sense, he can be taken to be refuting precisely the claim, made by many more at that time than today, that (Standard British) English was their native (and only) language, by showing that this was an absurdity. If English was, in fact, the only language they knew, then this English could only be an English inflected with Sinhala and/or Tamil lexis and structures, or, in other words, a Lankanized English.

English is inflected in the problem of identifying the appropriate variety of Lankan English to be valorized. This has been 'resolved' so far by finding the closest approximation to a native speaker available and by legitimizing his/her speech. It must be noted that this approximation has not been uniformly accepted, nor is it based on numerical superiority, nor even on proximity to Standard English *per se*. I am suggesting here that since the native speaker as a self-evident category has been irrevocably problematized in this context, it may be possible to bring to crisis concomitant notions of the standard as well.

My view is that it is precisely this 'non-Std.E., non-SLE variety' that should become the object of study and of legitimation. In fact, the labelling of this variety 'non-SLE' is arbitrary and sometimes self-contradictory since the oft-quoted examples of Lankan English outside phonology belong to this category. A. Fernando makes this important point when she writes, 'While the phonological features of these two groups of bilinguals (Two and Three) are not regarded as being characteristic of Sri Lankan English, some of the syntactic, lexical and idiomatic features of their speech seem to be incorporated in the descriptions of Sri Lankan English' (1986, p. 30). Kandiah's defence of the examples used by him is that they were actual utterances by habitual speakers of Lankan English. Yet, the use of an expression is not the same as the acceptance of its legitimacy. We all say things that we would not consider to be acceptable, even though in the flow of the conversation we may not immediately correct ourselves.

The most insistent objection to such an agenda would be that the variety in question is merely 'a fossilized interlanguage' (A. Fernando, 1986, p. 32) or that it comprises 'some incomprehensible and even, at times, apparently unsystematizable items' (extrapolating from Kandiah, 1981b, p. 63). Notwithstanding the hegemonic linguistic attitudes that such views exemplify, this remains an empirical question that is systematically addressed in Chapters 3 and 4 which outline many of the ways in which speakers/writers who have been traditionally marginalized as producing 'non-educated' or 'sub-standard' and 'unacceptable' or 'ungrammatical' linguistic elements, do in fact engage in productive, creative and systematizable discourse which constitutes a crucial component in the de-hegemonization of English in post-colonial Sri Lanka.

# 2

# Towards a Broader Standard: The 'Non-Standard' as 'Natural' Resistance

## INTRODUCTION

This section will present the *linguistic* perspective(s)[52] on standardization and the function of standard languages. Chapter 1 was primarily concerned with arguments against the standard from outside the discipline of linguistics. Here, I shall consider, in a sense, what standard languages *do* in real situations where they function as standards in the face of strong theoretical 'proofs' against their viability and fairness.

Chapter 1 argues the following:

1. Standard languages, despite all disclaimers to the contrary, discriminate against minorities, marginal groups, women, the underclass and so on, albeit in different ways, in the subtle manner that our 'enlightened' times call for, since overt élitism is no longer tenable. The 'neutrality' of Standard Language/Appropriate Discourse has thus become a useful way of dissimulating hegemony.

---

52. There is, however, too much made of this distinction within the discipline which cannot account for the fact that, in the final analysis, scholarly *bona fides* are not reflected at the same time in general attitudes to language. Thus, notions of 'non-standard' usage may not carry negative valuation within the *linguistic* use of linguists, but within their language practices as well as outside the discipline these value judgements are firmly in place. At best, we can posit a deferred change in general attitudes to language as a result of disciplinary intervention, but even in this case the question of standardization remains one in which linguistics has been influenced, willy-nilly, by popular attitudes rather than the reverse.

41

2. The theoretical validity of critiquing the standard, though uncontestable, is vitiated by the fact that standards do, *in fact*, exist and have to be dealt with at the level of linguistic reality. Given the fact of the operation of a standard in language communities, therefore, linguists (and others) should work towards broadening the standard to include so-called uneducated usage (in speech *and* writing) in order to reduce language discrimination. The crucial issue that arises here concerns the limits placed upon a standard if it is to function as one: how broad can a standard become before it effectively ceases to be a standard? Are there such limits to diversity and acceptability of alternatives beyond which linguistic anarchy will usurp the standard? Will this anarchy in turn militate against the underclass even more than the arbitrary standard does, since the Standard, however skewed, presents a tangible and attainable paradigm?

3. It was argued that this broader standard could be theorized from a careful examination of marginalized forms of language which had historically been devalued or, at best, excused away as special cases: the (post)colonial dialects. When these 'varieties' (or dialects, or languages) were considered seriously as languages in their own right, many of the paradigms of linguistics which were based on the study of standard languages would be rendered suspect, and would therefore have to be re-evaluated even in the cases where they were hitherto held to be descriptively accurate.

Here, these arguments will be complemented by the following theoretical discussion:

A. An examination of the boundary conditions placed upon the standard which enables its function as such: here the available literature is unequivocal in its concurrence that the standard implies a limit to breadth. The following, taken from Joseph is fairly typical,[53] and yet no theoretical arguments, nor empirical evidence in support of this position is forthcoming:

---

53. I refer to analogous assumptions in the work of Haugen (1966), Garvin and Mathiot (1968), Kratochvil (1968), Das Gupta and Gumperz (1968), but nowhere have I come across specific limits/limitations argued for, either on a theoretical or empirical basis.

Every standard language, by virtue of continuous change and conscious elaboration, contains a minimum level of variation. Every standard language, by virtue of inherent stability and conscious control, imposes a maximum limit on variation.

Linguists sometimes speak of a language's 'degree' of standardization or of control, based on the relative amount of variation it admits. (1987, p. 127)

B. In this chapter, it will be seen that one of the paradigms that becomes untenable in its present form is the concept of standardization itself, which cannot even account for the incipient standardization of the post-colonial Englishes much less theorize their future as standard languages. In this regard, I shall try to bring together what little work there is on standard varieties of post-colonial English (specifically those identified as Indian, Sri Lankan and South Asian) with the most interesting recent work on standardization in order to suggest that these 'other' Englishes may provide new directions in this area, refuting, incidentally, Joseph's 'monogenetic' approach.[54]

C. The theoretical basis for valorizing marginal or non-standard forms of language will be outlined here, using Derrida's critique of Austin as a springboard for conceptualizing the importance of accounting for marginality, rather than, as is customary, simply explaining it away as exceptional. I shall also attempt an outline of a theory of discourse which will lay the ground for the empirical studies that comprise Chapters 3 and 4. In this context, I shall point to a hybrid use of Wittgenstein, Volosinov and Marx by (mis)reading their respective projects onto another arena. Emphasis will be placed here on an alternate understanding of protest and resistance through a witting and/or unwitting refusal to submit not merely to the 'form' of normative discourse but also to the acceptable boundaries of 'content'.

---

54. This may be too ambitious here, though it does seem important to point to the ways in which these Englishes as standard dialects, or at least on the way to standardization, create new paradigms.

## STANDARDIZATION AND STANDARD LANGUAGES

It is regrettably true that theoretically important work on standard-ization and standard languages is scarce. There remain no more than a handful of recent books in English,[55] and these too deal with case studies of language planning situations rather than with the theoretical questions posed by standardization, resulting even in confused articulation of the characteristics and functions of the stand-ard. The thinking in the area is well summed up by James Milroy in the following:

> In modern linguistics, the phenomenon of language standardiza-tion has not been a central interest, and it is noticeable that lin-guistic scholars have often been content with *ad hoc* and incomplete definitions of 'standard language'. Usually the stand-ard language is said to be merely a dialect or variety on a par with other varieties, and the difference between standard and non-standard loosely characterized in several different ways. Some-times a standard language is defined (in passing and without fur-ther elaboration) as the 'variety' that is most widely comprehended; at other times, it is said to be the variety that has the highest social prestige, and at yet other times the variety that is official and used by government. …
>
> Modern nation states normally have a standard language in addition to other varieties, and this standard is popularly thought to be THE language, the dialects being corrupt deviations from it. Standardization, therefore, is influential in the way we evaluate our own usage and that of others, and it has many other socio-political consequences. Strong feelings can be aroused. … [S]tandardization has a bearing on the relationship between speech and writing, and as training in literacy is a major aim of educational systems, the characteristics and consequences of standardization need to be understood by educators and other professionals who deal with language.   (Foreword to Joseph, 1987. pp. vii–viii)

In order to substantiate these issues, as well as to situate them within their linguistic sphere of influence I shall in the following

---

55. Notable is recent work in German and Italian which I am unable to examine in depth, but that I have access to in terms of synopses and evaluations provided by Joseph and others.

pages present an analysis of John Joseph's book, *Eloquence and Power: The Rise of Language Standards and Standard Languages* which has been identified as 'the fullest account of language standardization that we have'.[56] In the first instance, Joseph points to the ubiquity of standard languages and the hierarchization of dialects within the popular idiom, albeit dissimulated as 'sensitivity to language quality'.

> Just as there exists no human speech community without variation, there exists no speech community, literate or otherwise, whose members are not consciously sensitive to language quality in one form or another .... [However], while language standards occur universally, and vary in shape according to the structure of the individual language, the same is not true of standard languages. They are not universal, but represent a specifically Western concept that has been spread by cultural tradition. This tradition, the process whereby standard languages come into being, we may call standardization.   (ibid., pp. 4, 7)

Joseph makes the radical distinction between the existence of language standards and standard languages, which, for him, is essentially a process of 'modernization' (for him synonymous with 'Westernization'). He defends this position against the charge of Eurocentrism by arguing that the system of classification is all that is at stake here, but one is not clear how he will deal with the reality of standard languages that remain radically outside these paradigms.

> To call all languages Standard *x* which display some of the constituent features of standardization forces one, for reasons of clarity, to posit a continuum of the sort discussed above and to arrange these languages along it. This continuum clearly constitutes a hierarchy. The criteria used in determining this hierarchy depend entirely on the concept and definition of standard language which has arisen within Western civilization. The Western and Westernized standard

---

56. James Milroy, in his introduction quoted above. I shall also have recourse to the Milroys' book *Authority in Language: Investigating Language Prescription and Standardization* (1985) in this chapter. These two works appear to stand out in an otherwise neglected field, at least among linguists writing in English.

languages will always end up further along the continuum than will non-Western(ized) languages. That is already culturocentrism. Moreover, the continuum model implies historical progress: languages toward the right end of the continuum are more highly developed than those back toward the left. That is really culturocentrism, a vestige of the time when scholars took for granted that the attributes of Western languages were superior, and that their absence indicated primitiveness.

It is culturocentric to believe that the constituent features of one's own civilization are intrinsically so good that all cultures, left in isolation, would eventually arrive at them. It is not culturocentric to admit that the societies to which one's civilization has been attached have achieved massive political and cultural domination that has led to imposition of features of this civilization throughout much of the world, any more than it is to accept the evidence that alphabetic writing has been developed only once in history, and that its subsequent appearance in various parts of the world are accounted for by transmission rather than spontaneous generation. ( pp. 21–2)

Joseph appears here to be conflating two aspects of the standard: in the specific sense that he outlines, perhaps standardization is typically western, but there is no doubt that standard languages predate western 'influence' in other parts of the world. Standard languages exist outside of western influence, and standardization has taken place, therefore, by other means than stipulated by Joseph.[57] The scrupulous disclaimer of the western bias of standard-

---

57. This requires a much more detailed argument (the subject of another book, perhaps) which must be supplemented with empirical evidence from Sanskrit, Tamil, even Sinhala. According to Joseph, classical languages were once standard ones which have lost their native communities of speakers (173), in which category he includes, after Kloss, Arabic, Sanskrit, Classical Sinhala and Classical Chinese. This recognition of the prior standardization of these languages appears to contradict Joseph's thesis about standardization itself.

A starting point for such work could be Hubert Devonish's *Language and Rebellion: Creole Language Politics in the Caribbean* (1986), which claims that 'Diglossia was the norm in pre-capitalists states such as Ancient Egypt and China. The rise of industrial capitalism and the development of the modern nation-state which usually accompanies this development, however, favours the destruction of traditional diglossias' (p. 21).

ization becomes then a way of privileging one particular way of theorizing this phenomenon by identifying it with the phenomenon itself. In order to remain consistent on this score, Joseph must maintain that

> If language standardization names a specific, culturally transmitted tradition of processes effectuated upon language, and if we recognize ... that civilizations can grow in the absence of this tradition, then we no longer have to assume that the constitutive processes of standardization are naturally superior to any alternative, and that all languages would accede to them independently over time. We can maintain that they form one pattern of development among many possible effective ones. As with the alphabet, other methods would have been possible; perhaps the greater efficiency of cultural adaptation as opposed to reinvention accounts in part for the spread of both the alphabetic and the standard-language principles. (p. 54)

And yet, how does this account for the historically prior development of standardized forms of Sanskrit and Chinese, for instance, where the influences of the Greek–Roman model is tenuous to say the least?[58] The alternative to standardization is not indicated even in the sketchiest form, moreover, and it is one that seems impossible even to conceptualize here, *unless perhaps it is the model that derives from broadening the standard to the point at which the widest possible acceptance of variation is the norm, which is our agenda with the NVEs.*

This none the less functions as a standard, however broad its tolerance, and is, therefore, not a difference of kind. As the Milroys write in the Coda to their book, 'For a standard language remains as necessary as ever in a complex, large scale society such as ours, and needs to be available as a resource to all English speakers' (1985, p. 175). There is no controversy or disagreement here, only in what precisely constitutes or should constitute this standard in order to maximize its benefit to all concerned.

---

58. Historical linguistic work on these languages too is needed to establish this argument. Is Joseph talking of self-conscious standardization, with the concept itself literally 'in place', or of the processes that are involved? In either case, his position seems untenable, but the 'proof' is beyond the scope of this study.

[B]ecause of the cultural functions in which they are employed, standard languages are acquired largely, even primarily through INSTRUCTION, CORRECTION, IMITATION, ASSIMILATION, ACCULTURATION – precisely the ways in which one's native language is not acquired.   (p. 19)

For Joseph, then, the distinguishing feature of standard languages is the fact that they are learned, non-natively, by all users. Again, there is no doubt that in theory he is right: the standard contains some components that are not found in any of the source dialects, and these have to be learned afresh by prospective speakers. Yet this position distorts the radical inequality of such learning, since the standard approximates élite dialects, or at the very least accommodates such variants within the range of acceptability, whereas it explicitly devalues other divergences often associated with the underclass.

It seems to be almost universal that within linguistics there is no sense of hegemony at all. Language-as-the site-of-struggle, which has become a commonplace in critical theory and cultural studies over the past fifteen years, appears heretical within the discipline of linguistics. Linguists are thus able to identify language change with the acceptance of the community at large, and present standardization as the culmination of this community acceptance over time.

Even when Joseph acknowledges the role of power and social hierarchy in language standardization, it is done in terms of homogeneous communities rather than élites within these groups.

The rise of one community's dialect as synecdochic within a linguistically fragmented region is both a manifestation of that community's power and a base for expanding it. A few users of the standard language accede to positions of authority which permit them to direct the future course of standardization. Individuals learn standard languages in order to increase their personal standing. And 'eloquence' in the use of language almost universally functions as a mantle of power. ... It is in the interest of the powerful and prestigious to develop means of keeping their language difficult of attainment.   (1987, p. 43)

And yet, as a result of this blind spot, he is able to generalize that 'in no society does learning the standard language actually provide entry into the "leisure class"' (p. 44) where it should be acknowledged that knowledge of the standard is clearly a necessary though not sufficient condition for upward class mobility. This 'imposition' of the standard is thereafter presented merely in terms of a choice of imitation of a 'prestige' dialect by those of 'lower status' who wish to emulate the élite. Joseph provides 'prestige' with a dynamic of its own which, since it is abstracted from any recognizable materiality, gives it the mystical character of a fetish:

> Political and cultural imperialism are two quite independent forces. If the culture of the conquered possesses higher prestige than does that of the conquerors, it is likely to prevail in spite of the conquerors' superior forces. Indeed, a superposition situation regularly develops after such a conquest, with the language of the conquered serving as a model for standardization of the language of the conquerors. (p. 45)

> In the case of a discrepancy between political-military power and linguistic-cultural prestige, history shows that the latter is likely to prevail over the former in directing the course of development of the language. Political and military might, after all, must be transferred and rechanneled into cultural prestige before they can exert a linguistic influence. (p. 49)

The fact that prestige is hardly a given in the sense of *a priori* knowledge and, therefore, requires 'interested' evaluation by widely different groups is dissimulated here. It seems to me that in the few cases that the language of the conquered remains super-posed over the language of the conqueror,[59] the reasons for this have more to do with the specific aspects of the *elaboration* of the former to environmental conditions (in the broadest sense, including area-specific employment, climate, religion, kinship patterns and so on) than 'prestige' itself. In fact, this notion of 'prestige' is most prob-lematic for me since it hangs out for these linguists precisely where

---

59. I am following Joseph's terminology, which defines superposition as the coexistence of two or more languages of significantly different pres-tige within a single-speech community (p. 48), and is identified as a precondition for standardization. The superposed 'high' system is des-ignated by H and the more widely used 'low' system, which is under-going the standardization, by L.

struggle and the possibility of subversion are covered over. Thus, in the process of standardization, Joseph feels that

> 'L speakers who betray their culture (whether or not their motives are really mercenary enough to merit this judgement) are usually perceived as doing so only in hindsight, when the status of L culture has improved. Prior to this *their community* respects and even envies them. Ultimately, they may deserve a sort of backhanded martyrdom: the prestige they earn for themselves, and which threatens to cut them off from their *home L community* reflects in a positive way upon that *community as a whole* (whether the *L community* desires this or not)'.   (pp. 52ff, my emphasis throughout)

What may be appropriate for a small sub-group within a language community takes on empirically unsupportable generalizability here, encompassing widely disparate elements within the entire polity. At any rate, such generalizations may have explanatory power in relatively simple societies and within small populations,[60] but they are unable to clarify the situations that obtain in post-colonial societies which possess rival languages whose written standards (and 'internal' superposition, now visible at least as diglossia) have evolved through more than 1500 years of history.

For Joseph, what makes L prestigious is 'most immediately its use in the prestigious functions that have been assimilated from the H culture, but which heretofore have been performed exclusively in H' (p. 53).

> Indeed, there may be widespread belief that these functions simply cannot be performed in L, because of the supposed inherent inferiority of that dialect. The avant-gardists, having already shown themselves 'genetically' capable of performing the H functions, will next, by performing them in L, gradually dispel belief in L's inferiority.   (p. 53)

---

60.  It is no accident that the contemporary case study of successful standardization undertaken by Joseph focuses on the Greenlandic language spoken by 45,000 Eskimos. The other example discussed in detail refers to sixteenth-century France, the antiquity of which pre-empts arguments alleging over-simplification, were I qualified in any way to make them.

The initial users of H from among the L community are termed avant-gardists because they must first 'learn H with the higher goal of showing themselves the equals of their H-community models, capable of performing in H all the functions which constitute the H culture' (p. 52). Upward mobility is here presented as 'a higher goal', whereas in the case of the 'choice' of 'imitation' *within* the same language of the prestige dialect, the situation is presented somewhat differently:

> Because the intrinsic worth of dialects and of their component elements and processes is well nigh impossible to determine, language is highly susceptible to prestige transfer. Persons who are prestigious for quantifiable reasons, physical or material, are on this account emulated by the rest of the community. These others cannot obtain the physical or material resources which confer the prestige directly (at least they cannot obtain them easily, or else no prestige would be associated with them). But prestige is transferred to attributes of the prestigious persons other than those on which their prestige is founded, and these prestigious-by-transfer attributes include things which others in the community may more easily imitate and acquire, if they so choose. Language is one of these.  (p. 31)

The linguistic reality in my experience is somewhat different. Facility with the so-called prestige dialect is a requirement not merely for upward mobility but also for survival in a variety of contexts. In terms of our work environment at a university, for instance, it is a *sine qua non* for successful completion of the degree at many levels.[61]

---

61. In this connection much work needs to be done to test the hypothesis that non-standard writing (in courses outside English departments) becomes a key index of whether or not an instructor has the licence to come down hard on a student's 'arguments' in a paper. My observation of this phenomenon that I shall call *sanctioned discrimination* (the crucial 'errors' are recognizably 'ethnic', in many cases) is still at the *ad hoc* level, but I believe that the 'same' argument/content in standard dialect and in non-standard dialect will receive different evaluations *as arguments*. I look forward to the forthcoming publications of Chris Abbott at the University of Pittsburgh who is doing doctoral work on this and related aspects of language-based value-systems.

## STANDARDIZING THE 'NEW' ENGLISHES

Perhaps we need to turn to Joseph's brief analysis of creoles in order to determine the special circumstances that concern the standardization of the 'new' Englishes. For him,

> 'the difficulties a creole speech community faces in asserting its linguistic autonomy *vis-à-vis* the 'target' language are considerably greater than those which early proponents of French faced in breaking from Latin, because of '... the greater and more persistent transfer of native speech habits into the learning of the new languages in Africa than is usually accepted in the case of the learning of Latin by Celts and Iberians' [Alleyne 1971: 175]. (Joseph, 1987, p. 55)

Furthermore, we are told,

> 'the "language loyalty" ... of creole speakers varies greatly. While it is perfectly common for the L community in any superposition situation to consider that their idiom is "not a language," but "only a dialect" or "patois," or even "just slang," creole speakers may actually deny that the creole is "human" speech'.   (p. 55)

According to Joseph, therefore, creole avant-gardes tend toward extremist positions, either virulently opposed or excessively in favour of the European H.

> The former position will deprive them of the most readily available model for standardization of their tongue; the latter risks undercutting the creole's Abstand and whatever prestige it may have, or in the worst case, enticing the avant-garde away from creole with the H culture's amenities and international currency. ...
> If a creole or any other L community has chosen the path of standardization, then everything depends on its developing a sense of the autonomous richness of its own culture and language, that these are structurally inferior to none. It should realize that H was itself an L once, and that similar anxieties accompanied its acculturation to an H model, whatever the differences in detail of the circumstances may have been.
> If this sort of cultural security can be established, then the L community should not fear that use of H as a model for standard-

ization entails structural convergence with it. Rather, H furnishes the most convenient source of the universal characteristics of standard languages. Since the L community's disdain of H is inevitably based upon the intrusion of H speakers into L cultural history, the use of H as a model should be seen not as paying tribute, but as exacting payment in kind.　(p. 56)

If one were to present a narrative of the Sri Lankan linguistic situation today, on the basis of Joseph's description of the process of standardization, it would run something like this: Sinhala and Tamil in two relatively separate superpositions were L1 and L2 respectively to English, which functioned as H in the nineteenth and twentieth centuries. At best, such an explanation can be called to account for certain aspects of Sinhala and Tamil standardization, but the fact that these languages had prior standard forms complicates this analysis. Further, the trilingual reality of the Lankan context and the superposition of Sinhala over Tamil produces little empirically, contrary to our expectations after Joseph. Within each of these languages, diglossia also remains to be understood in terms more helpful than its simplistic identification with 'colonial hang-overs'. Joseph quotes Sugathapala de Silva approvingly on this score: 'As Sugathapala de Silva so aptly puts it, "Most diglossic societies suffer from colonial hang-over ..."[1982, 113].'

But what does this say except that virtually every society we can think of had, at one time or another, a colonial encounter? In the case of Sinhala, for instance, the prior diglossia may be traced to periodic Indian invasions and so on. It would seem, however, that Lankan linguists appear to accept the causal relation between western colonialism and Sinhala diglossia, which then becomes a strong argument in favour of Joseph's thesis that standardization is essentially a concomitant of westernization.

Certain historical and cultural factors during the period of the fifteenth and twentieth centuries have been decisive in the inception and continuance of Sinhalese [sic] diglossia. Its beginning is seen in the eighteenth century when a renaissance in indigenous culture – particularly in the religious and literary spheres – was effected in the face of a threat of extinction due to internal decay and the expansion of western culture – mainly Christianity. Since the end of the strong and stable reign of Parakramabahu VI (1412–1467) learning, literary activity and the fortunes of the Buddhist

order which were inextricably bound together had been generally on the decline. The succeeding period of civil strife and the
advent of the Portuguese and the Dutch saw the precipitation of
the decay. In the maritime provinces the Buddhist monasteries
and the seats of learning, which were invariably attached to
them and were manned by Buddhist monks, went out of existence one by one. And in Kandy in the central highlands which
ultimately came to be the last foothold of the Sinhalese kingdom
they continued an existence which was at best precarious, the
energies of the rulers and the populace being almost totally
diverted to the incessant war against the foreigners who had for
all practical purposes surrounded them. When the decline was
near complete there occurred a nativistic revival under the leadership of a Buddhist monk named Valivita Saranankara (1698–
1778) who was actively supported by the first two South Indian
Nayakkar rulers on the throne of Kandy, Sri Vijaya Rajasinghe
(1739–1747) and Kirti Sri Rajasinghe (1747–1782), who it appears
were eager to compensate for their marginal status by being
hyper-zealous in their guardianship of the authentic cultural traditions of the Sinhalese people.

The literary aspect of the eighteenth century renaissance was
characterized by the resuscitation of literary genres which had
gone into abeyance during the period of decline. In their revivalist
zeal the writers of the renaissance period took special care to
adhere to the literary language in use before the decline had set
in. For this purpose a treatise of grammar known as the *Sidat Sangarava* written during the thirteenth century was installed as the
ultimate authority on literary usage. This act of superposition of
an archaic literary idiom over the language of common parlance
at the time – there is a marked divergence between the two codes
as a comparison of the literary treatises of the revivalist writers
and some personal communication of the time indicate – may be
regarded as the beginnings of the diglossic situation in Sinhalese.

The political history and the socio-cultural forces at work during the subsequent era contributed to widen the cleavage
between the spoken and written media and to stabilize the
diglossic situation.[62]

---

62. K. N. O. Dharmadasa, (1975) No. 3. Dharmadasa cites Sugathapala de
Silva in support of his claim for the origin of the Sinhala diglossic situation.

I quote this at length because it provides a fine summary of the context that led to a heightened diglossia of the Sinhala language. However, the argument for the 'beginning' of the diglossic situation remains unconvincing. That this situation was exacerbated and made self-conscious is clear, but there is no evidence that the written form of Sinhala that obtained prior to this was identical with its spoken counterpart. In fact, given the extremely restricted access to education and therefore to literacy, and the near-complete identification of writing with religious instruction that depended heavily on the dead language Pali and on an archaic Sanskrit, it would appear that the diglossic situation was firmly entrenched in the Sinhala language even at the time of the writing of the *Sidat Sangarava* in the thirteenth century. At any rate, Dharmadasa's argument requires corroboration from a *prior* absence of systematic divergence between the written and spoken codes of Sinhala.[63] This issue is of greater significance than its immediate context, however, because it demonstrates how even some of the best of non-western scholarship is doomed to producing alibis for Eurocentric conceptualizations so long as it remains uncritical of their theoretical premises.

## LANKAN ENGLISH AS (COUNTER)EXAMPLE

Generalized critiques notwithstanding, let me explore the implications of Joseph's thesis on standardization as it affects Lankan English specifically in order to see whether it provides useful insights. If we follow Joseph, as regards the standardization of a specific form of English in Sri Lanka, our scenario must focus on, say, the post-colonial period. Here we must posit, counter-factually, that English functions as an L to the Sinhala/Tamil H. Even if we were, for the sake of the argument, to accept this classification, we cannot account for the coexistence of Lankan English with Standard

---

63. The problem is finessed by a move which by now we have seen to be well-nigh universal: the implication that 'educated speakers' provide the exclusive basis for understanding and theorizing a language. My response to this gesture is given in detail in Chapter 1, both from a theoretical standpoint and with reference to practical consequences in the specific case of Lankan English.

(British) English,[64] and for the fact that there is little self-consciousness (defined in conventional ways) on the part of users in the 'avant-garde' as to the proposed role and function of Lankan English. In fact, the schizophrenia of such a counter-intuitive and clearly counter-factual thesis makes it difficult even to imagine a possible scenario in which Lankan English is moving towards standardization in Joseph's terms. We may, therefore, wish to pose the superposition in terms of the 'rival' dialects Standard (British) English and Lankan English, but this abstraction cannot in any way account for the language dynamic of Sri Lanka today, and would thus have a restricted explanatory power.

If we were to incorporate elements of Joseph's argument concerning creoles, though we do not suggest that Lankan English is anything like a creole/pidgin of English 'proper', we begin to understand some of the negative associations of the term among its users. Many users are not even aware that they are speaking and writing a 'different' dialect from the received (British) standard, and once they realize this they translate it into a derogation of their competence in the language. Beyond this we are unable to proceed since the dilemma between a growth in Asbau ('language by development') and a concomitant shrinking of Abstand ('structural difference' from other dialects) does not obtain here since the Asbau of Lankan English results not merely from a transfer from English but also, and perhaps on an increasingly large scale, from Sinhala and Tamil, thus differentiating it more and more from Standard (British) English.

Joseph does not entirely ignore the specific theoretical problems and nuances raised by these 'new' varieties which, according to him, result from 'polycentricity'. In particular, I am troubled by the simple dismissal, as 'nationalistic', of any localized claim for

---

64. I shall use the term 'British' here as a convenient shorthand, though I am well aware of the linguistic imperialism that operates in Great Britain and of which such labels are the consequence. It is interesting that in a language classification of nation states, after Rustow, used by Joseph (1987, p. 47) he appears to be entirely oblivious to the ramifications of this situation! He identifies the United Kingdom with 'the post dynastic states of Western Europe' together with France, Spain, Portugal, The Netherlands, Sweden and Denmark, and singles out 'Israel, the United States, Italy, and the ethnically diverse nations of category (e) [the post-colonial countries of Asia, Africa, and Latin America], [where] the nationalism itself has an imperial dimension' (ibid.).

language specificity because it dissimulates, in the name of an enlightened internationalism, the equally problematic valorization of the standard based in the 'imperial homeland'.[65] In the case of English, for instance, this takes the form of claims for an acceptance of Standard British English (or now, as a result of an equally dubious hegemony, General 'American' English) as truly 'international'. In this manner, the loss of an empire may be actively recuperated through the wielding of linguistic power.[66] The fact that Standard British English is 'acceptable' to all, entirely begs the question of whether this state of affairs should be reinforced or whether it should be actively worked against. The linguist as 'disinterested observer' becomes suspect in precisely these situations where historically marked privileges can be glossed over as 'the way things are'. The alternatives are, therefore, whether linguists should work towards one type of International Standard English for transnational uses (there is no way, however, that use can be restricted to this category because the 'prestige' of such a dialect will be at a premium), or whether International English should become a network of mutually intelligible dialects that systematically enrich and challenge each other through contact.

At no structural level are the standards which constitute Standard English uniform over the many nations in which it is the official or first language: Australia, Canada, India, New Zealand, the United Kingdom, and the United States, to name only a few. To counter such variation would require the existence of a transnational control mechanism which simply does not exist ... . [T]his polycentricity of Standard English serves at least one positive function: the awareness of unique national traits allows for

---

65. See, for instance, C. L. R. James's *Beyond a Boundary* (1984), which can be read as an example of an enabling non-parodic resistance to these norms.
66. Note, moreover, how even this empire is presented in the 'best possible light' through some rather pathetic relativism. The sense in which one can even imagine British linguistic liberality in the colonial period is through a comparison with Spain and perhaps France.

    The British Empire, an administrative entity known for its liberality in encouraging the use of indigenous vernaculars in its colonies ... was reaching its zenith. The OED is itself a monument of linguistic liberality and enlightenment.  [ibid., 5].

satisfaction of the ideology of nationalism, which continues to be
strong. ...

The unique feature of polycentricity is that a new standard is
recognized in spite of an insufficient degree of Abstand for it to be
considered a separate language, and in spite of a desire on the
part of the speech community to maintain a linguistic-cultural
identity with the imperial homeland, even if (as is typical) hostili-
ties with the homeland marked the attainment of independence.
(p. 170)

Joseph has his finger here on an important paradox. On the one
hand, the Abstand of Lankan English (in its 'accepted' standard
form as an 'educated' variety, where education masks a class-based
attitude to the language) is not sufficiently developed to merit a separate language status. On the other hand, however, as productive of
distinctive utterance, Lankan English remains quite different from
Standard British English. This is the essential contradiction that I
pointed to in Chapter 1. In this view, if one were to consider Lankan
English as it is spoken on a widespread basis, then the 'non-standard'
or 'uneducated' use which dominates in terms of frequency and
number forces one to the conclusion that this dialect has achieved a
'sufficient' Abstand. Yet, since this is taboo, the relatively formal registers of 'educated' Lankan English are invoked as a standard
instead, despite the fact that it may not have a sufficient Abstand.
Joseph is quite wrong on more than one count when he identifies
the counter-tendency merely as a 'desire on the part of the speech
community to maintain a linguistic-cultural identity with the imperial homeland'. To talk of the 'speech community' in this monolithic
way (let alone of a collective desire) is even more distorting than
usual in the post-colonial context, and, moreover, the maintenance
of an identity with England (in this case, at least. I refuse to use the
term 'homeland' under any circumstances!) misunderstands the
nature of colonialism as 'epistemic violence' (whether 'enabling' or
not). The point is that there is no real choice involved here since
English is an essential part of the Lankan linguistic experience that
cannot be wished away, nor is it, by and large, an English that is
'pure' either as a reflection of Received Pronunciation or of some
putative English identity.

The development of a polycentric standard does require that the
community which has split off from the linguistic homeland be of

considerable size and importance – a nation, ideally – and produce a cultural avant-garde having a substantial sense of detach-
ment from the homeland culture. On the other hand, if a basic
identity with the homeland culture is not maintained, then polycentricity will not be stable: this is the case in India, a country
whose cultural avant-garde has long been split between those
who violently oppose the use of English and those who support it
less for any intrinsic reason (such as its internationalistic value)
than because promoting the use of an indigenous language would
fuel one Indian people's nationalistic ideology over all others.
Indian English, lacking sufficient cultural-linguistic ties with the
rest of the Anglophone world, will in time develop into a separate
language just as Latin, carried by administrators and settlers to
the various parts of the Roman Empire, evolved from polycentricity into the distinct Romance languages, once the Empire and its
cultural-linguistic bonds had dissolved. (p. 171)

The so-called homeland culture is Sri Lankan more than it is
'British'. In certain élite perceptions it resembles the English at work
*in* Sri Lanka, as well as certain 'literary' and 'dated' notions of
England as it was represented in the height of the old colonialism,
but all this has little to do with the 'homeland culture' today. There
remains much more to be fleshed out around the simplistic dichotomy of alternatives suggested by Joseph as operating in the Indian
context, which must wait for another occasion.[67]

## DE-HEGEMONIZING THE STANDARD

It follows that since Joseph and others have no real sense of
hegemony at work, they cannot theorize resistance to this
phenomenon in any systemic way. I propose here to use the non-
standard as the most sensitive index to this de-hegemonization (or
non-systemic anti-hegemony) that is available to us. Before I examine
the more specifically linguistic implications of this proposal for the

---

67. It is important to mark my agreement with his prediction that Indian
English will diverge into another language, but this depends on the
fraught categories of language *versus* dialect and so on, and reflects a
fairly distinct linguistic future.

debate on standardization, however, I must situate the theoretical apparatus of 'de-hegemonization' within the meta-discourse on hegemony since its articulation as resistance (as distinct from counter-hegemony) may well be the most important contribution of this book.

The concept of de-hegemonization is itself little theorized. Gramsci's critique of the base superstructure model via hegemony is, of course, well known, as is his primary conceptualization of this notion on the basis of an existent political system within civil society[68] that engenders a type of consent and is thereby perceived as opposed to the domination enforced by the state. In the strict Gramscian sense an alternate or counter-hegemony must take the form of an organized and systemic opposition or resistance to domination. Counter-hegemony or alternate hegemony has been explained, therefore, only in terms of organized and systematic, even class-based, resistance to this hegemony. It seems to me, however, that not-quite-so-organized forms of subversion and resistance perform, on the long term, similar functions, though the 'turnover rate' is far greater! Moreover, I wish, strategically, to problematize precisely the distinctions between self-consciously organized dehegemonization and supposedly *ad-hoc*, unintentional protest which even takes the form of imitation. The theory of 'passive revolution' that Gramsci puts forward further exemplifies this systemicity. Here, the dominant classes take the long view and inaugurate various measures in the interest of other groups in order to maintain their hegemony (as moral and intellectual leaders). It would appear then that in a situation where there is a wide space for such appropriation of resistance, the alternatives that remain outside the pale have more fundamentally subversive potential.

This is clearly not the appropriate occasion to work out a sophisticated analysis of the Gramscian project, nor am I qualified to attempt such a task. I shall, therefore, merely confine my remarks to the specific arenas of interaction between the notion of de-hegemonization as articulated in my work and other studies more directly within the Gramscian tradition in order to explain why I think that de-hegemonization is the appropriate conceptualization of the mechanisms at play in the persistent use of non-

---

68.   Walter L. Adamson (1980) pp. 170–1.

standard language by the underclass. Gramsci's own take on language seems, therefore, the most useful occasion in which to intervene:

> If it is true that every language contains the elements of a conception of the world and of a culture, it could also be true that from anyone's language one can assess the greater or lesser complexity of his conception of the world. Someone who only speaks dialect, or understands the standard language incompletely, necessarily has an intuition of the world which is more or less limited and provincial, which is fossilized and anachronistic in relation to the major currents of thought which dominate world history. His interests will be limited, more or less corporate or economistic, not universal. While it is not always possible to learn a number of foreign languages in order to put oneself in contact with other cultural lives, it is at the least necessary to learn the national language properly. A great culture can be translated into the language of another great culture, that is to say a great national language with historic richness and complexity, and it can translate any other great culture and can be a world-wide means of expression. But a dialect cannot do this. (*Selections from the Prison Notebooks*, p. 325)

Here Gramsci is making the strongest case for standard (or in his sense, national) languages where he uses the pre-critical terminology of 'greatness', 'richness and complexity' and so on to represent their 'universality' as opposed to the parochiality of dialects. It is symptomatic that in this celebration of national languages he cannot invoke hegemony but must instead posit a transparency and translatability that transcends class interest.

However, the fact of the matter is that a national language is itself a sometime hegemonic dialect, or a very close likeness of one. Moreover, hegemony in transnational terms accounts for the globalization of national languages as, for instance, American English. Gramsci himself notes this elsewhere in a less celebratory and more analytic passage.

> The pragmatists theorize abstractly about language as a source of error .... But is it possible to remove from language its metaphorical and extensive meanings? It is not possible. Language is transformed with the transformation of the whole of civilization,

> through the acquisition of culture by new classes and through the
> hegemony exercised by one national language over others, and
> what it does is precisely to absorb in metaphorical form the words
> of previous civilizations and cultures.   (pp. 451–2)

Here we see the hegemonic relationship between and among
national languages clearly dramatized. Yet, such an understanding
of hegemony in/through language is perceived only through lexical
and semantic (that is, 'content'-based) transformations and not formal ones.

> It must however be borne in mind that no new historical situ-
> ation, however radical the change that has brought it about, com-
> pletely transforms language, at least in its external formal aspect.
> But the content of language must be changed, even if it is difficult
> to have an exact consciousness of the change in immediate terms.
> (p. 453)

This privileging of the 'content' of language over its 'form' leads to
an exclusive identification of the revolutionary project with changing the content of language, no doubt theorizable as counter-
hegemony here. Yet, within this construction is an ambivalence
toward 'form', since according to Gramsci it is difficult to visualize
these changes, or to form-ulate them, which would not be the case if
what was at stake was a simple reversal of hegemony or a 'war of
position.' There is, of course, no doubt that no 'complete' transformation of language can take place, but in the difficult arenas of the
subversion Gramsci valorizes, a substantial trans-form-ation of
form must also surely ensue and this can certainly be established
even by mainstream historical linguistics.
    Thus, it would seem that even for someone as astute and
theoretically sophisticated as Gramsci, the standard or national
language succeeds in hiding the continuous process of hegemony–
dehegemonization–passive revolution–hegemonization that takes
place in and through language as in the ever-so gradual, yet
bitterly fought, changes in usage and in the widening of acceptable
variation in General American English.
    It seems plausible, therefore, that Gramsci had in mind some
sense of transformation of language that went beyond the purely
lexical/semantic into the syntactic/morphological as well. Moreover, for such a transformation to be possible it would seem to

require not merely strong and systematic oppositions but also nebulous and numerous divergences from the norm. Within Gramsci's own thinking there appears to be just such a realization as identified by Paolo Spriano who cites Athos Lisa's account of Gramsci's rift with the party during the last years in prison.[69] For Spriano what was most instructive at this point was 'his [Gramsci's] insistence on a necessary, indispensable process of *preparation* for action unfolding in society in a "molecular" fashion, before being able to achieve political hegemony'.

The notion of de-hegemonization seems to be a logical development and refinement of this sense of 'molecular' resistance since it does not pre-empt its identification with small collectives or *ad-hoc* groups while retaining the possibility of individuation.[70] Molecules, however, remain uniform and therefore predictable for any given element, as if they represented counter-hegemony in microcosm. Moreover, 'molecular' action may or may not be resistive of hegemony, at least in so far as this term is used by Negri, who cites Deleuze and Guattari as well in support of his usage: '"Molecular" refers to the complex of relations which are developed either in a socializing or antagonistic (but in any case varied) manner, among the plurality of social subjects'.[71]

---

69. *Antonio Gramsci and the Party: The Prison Years* (1979) p. 70. I am grateful to Professor Paul Bové for directing me to this text, and to the work of others, notably Antonio Negri, in the attempt to help me situate de-hegemonization within the Gramscian problematic.
70. See, for instance, Terdiman's excellent book (though focused almost exclusively within literary textual production), *Discourse/Counter-Discourse* (1985), which identifies counter-discourse as follows:

> So no dominant discourse is ever fully protected from contestation. Of course the counter-discourses which exploit such vulnerability implicitly invoke a principle of order just as systematic as that which sustains the discourses they seek to subvert. Ultimately, in the image of the counterhegemonic – conceived now as the emergent principle of history's dynamism, as the force which ensures the flow of social time itself – the counter-discourse always projects, just over its own horizon, the dream of victoriously replacing its antagonist.   (pp. 56–57)

It is precisely this putative alternate order that is structurally absent in de-hegemonization.
71. Antonio Negri (1989) p. 95.

De-hegemonization allows for, even stipulates, a more fluid and less schematic version of hegemony-as-process at work in civil society. In addition, the rubric of de-hegemonization allows us to conceive of multiple hegemonies that are in hierarchical relation to each other, as opposed to the binary model represented by counter-hegemony.

In this sense, then, it is the not-quite subaltern voice that must be effaced if communication is to proceed smoothly. It is important that virtually everything that Joseph has to say about so-called non-standard forms of language have their 'exception' in the Lankan situation, for instance. I shall simply indicate a short list of the functions of the non-standard, according to Joseph, culled from various parts of his book, that I find untenable or simplistic in the Lankan context:

- Matters of regional or local pertinence.
- The context of intimacy.
- Non-national, *non-cultural* functions.
- Symbolic of parochial solidarity and individuality.
  (This is further identified with 'a desire for privacy, a distrust for official institutions, a sense of shame that their native idiom is not the standard language but a "degenerate" dialect' – p. 83.)

These will be examined in some detail in this section to point to the fact that they are true only in a restricted sense, and only if we consider 'educated' users of Lankan English using 'non-standard' variants of the language. In Sri Lanka, so-called uneducated Lankan English is used, typically, *not* in contexts of regional or local pertinence, where in many cases Sinhala or Tamil will be used,[72] but in more general and broader situations.

The context of intimacy provides a curious paradox that I shall identify, albeit anecdotally. In my field work in Sri Lanka in 1987–8, I identified three broad categories of Lankan English speakers in terms of their choice of English or Sinhala words to describe family relationships: those who used English nouns (mother, father, mummy, daddy and so on) as well as terms of endearment (dear, darling); those who used Sinhala terms (*amma, thaththa, nangi, aiyya* and so on) exclusively; and those who mixed both Sinhala and

---

72. See Siromi Fernando's refinement or updating of Chitra Fernando's chart on bilinguals' use of English in Sri Lanka (S. Fernando, 1985).

English. The first category was becoming rare, and comprised the old élite, many of whom would consider themselves monolingual in English, and that too of the purest standard variety. The second category varied widely from the bilingually educated younger generation who spoke 'impeccable' standard Lankan English, to those who hardly used English at all. For the former, family relationships and intimacies remained the domain of Sinhala, at least in this token sense of naming. All this is quite well-known among Lankan linguists. It is the third category, however, that appears counter-intuitive to this researcher. I taped conversations between speakers of non-standard Lankan English, and on many occasions was surprised to find reference to parents as 'mummy' and 'daddy', which, despite the serious tone used, appeared parodic in its incongruity. It is this caricature element that is captured in the popular music that I have discussed in Chapter 4, where the identification of parents by their English descriptors becomes metonymic for the hybridization (often read in this context as 'bastardization') of the westernized subculture.[73] The major argument against Lankan English as a self-sufficient language in its own right has been the fact that it does not fulfil the domestic and personal language role, giving way to Sinhala and/or Tamil in these arenas.[74] However, once we consider Lankan English as less a mirror of Standard English and more a creative mix of English, Sinhala and Tamil, this argument becomes less pertinent, since these 'missing' lexical elements can be seen as 'borrowings' from Sinhala and Tamil. Thus, the 'more natural' use of *karapincha* or *goraka*, the Sinhala words for two important condiments in cooking curry, instead of their English equivalents, becomes proof of the distinctiveness of Lankan English as opposed to an example of its inadequacy to capture the Lankan experience.

All this goes to show that the situation is much more complex and contradictory than Joseph contends.

As regards 'non-national, non-cultural functions', the generalizations become equally untenable. What is at stake here, it seems to me, is the violent breaking down of notions of standard and non-standard themselves. Joseph's analysis holds only for cases where the localized non-standard dialect exists in clear contrast to a well-developed

---

73. See pp. 139ff for specific examples of how this metonymy works parodically through what I would like to term 'deliberately inappropriate imitation as parody'.
74. See de Souza, discussed in Chapter 1 of this work (p. 39).

and geographically diffuse standard. His theory of standardization cannot encompass the peculiar context of post-coloniality where the new 'standard' is itself looked down upon by many as 'non-standard', and where non-standard subvarieties of this new variety are less regional than the emerging standard itself because they reflect language 'interference' at the broadest level.

It is, therefore, not true that non-standard Lankan English is 'symbolic of parochial solidarity and individuality', nor that it can be identified with 'a desire for privacy'. There, is however, a sense in which Joseph's contention that such use is occasioned by a 'distrust for official institutions' becomes valid, though not necessarily self-consciously. The distrust of official institutions, which are, in theory at least, run in the official languages, Sinhala and Tamil,[75] can be expressed more forcefully in these languages. The anger against the *de facto* hegemony of English is perennially articulated in Sinhala and Tamil. Non-standard English is used differently: on the one hand it is used 'as best it can' – that is, speakers do not know that they are, in fact, breaking the rules – and on the other, it is used in a 'devil may care' manner – mockingly, exaggeratedly, to show off, and to poke fun – all the while, it is also used 'to get the job done'.

## POLICING THE STANDARD

I shall also provide an analysis here of the *control* function within the standard, or emerging standard language, as outlined by Joseph (1987, pp. 108–130 *passim*). The articulation of this operation within the non-standard and the response it generates will provide perhaps the most interesting theoretical example of the non-standard as counter-hegemonic in more than a knee-jerk sort of way. Also, in this regard, I shall look at issues such as elaboration and the register-specific domains of the standard (Lankan) and the standard-within-the-standard (British?).

---

75.  And, as of 1988, English.

The tendency toward eloquence, which results in elaboration,[76] and the tendency toward efficiency, which results in the control of elaboration, are always already inherent aspects of linguistic structure, and both become cultural forces in standardization ... Control begins as a manifestation of the inherent tendency toward stability, but once the forces of control are socially established, they begin to do more than oppose new change: they retroactively hierarchize elements already established in the language, leading to reductivistic changes which constitute linguistic change nonetheless. In the development and ongoing existence of the standard language, the forces of elaboration and control maintain an unsteady balance, the scale alternately tipping in one direction or the other.

The histories of standard languages reveal the same pattern over and over: elaboration triggers control. (Joseph, pp. 108ff).

Here control refers to 'that facet of standardization in which new elements threatening to enter the language are limited, and, secondly, variants within the language are hierarchized, and sometimes eliminated' (p. 109). Moreover, the accepted wisdom which Joseph too espouses is that this function of the standard is beneficial sociopolitically. Joseph cites Weinrich approvingly that 'it is part of the process of standardization itself to affirm the identity of a language, to set it off discretely from other languages and to strive continually for a reduction of differences within it' (*Languages in Contact: Findings and Problems*, 1953, p. 396).

This reduction of differences is connected to certain of the mythological and ideological elements that surround the standard: the myth of a Golden Age of linguistic, cultural, spiritual, and racial harmony; the ideology of nationalistic identity and unity. Beyond ideology, however, there do seem to be practical benefits to linguistic uniformity within a nation or other polity. In an impressive statistical study of language use in 133 countries, Pool has determined that among them

---

76. Elaborations are divided into two categories, 'cosmetic' and 'remedial', depending on whether the addition is perceived as filling a lacuna within the standard or as one that is merely a variant (Joseph, 1987, p. 110).

a country can have any degree of language uniformity or fragmentation and still be underdeveloped; and a country whose entire population, more or less, speaks the same language can be anywhere from very rich to very poor. But a country that is linguistically highly heterogeneous is always underdeveloped or semideveloped and a country that is highly developed always has considerable language uniformity.   (Pool, 1972, p. 222)

Thus, Joseph is able to see that standardization takes place toward clearly marked ideological ends, but he does not point to any possibility of subversion or displacement of these objectives. Weinrich's formulation, which is typical, provides standardization with a life of its own as if it were a self-willed process devoid of human agency. In this way, the narrower-than-national forces that impose a national standard through a complex combination of coercion and incentive are let off the hook. Pool's conclusion, on the other hand, does not even have a tenable plausibility because either he must hide behind the relativism of 'highly heterogeneous' and 'considerable language uniformity', or he has to admit to too many exceptions such as Switzerland and Canada, for instance. The more serious objection to Pool's thesis is, however, that he confuses an effect with its cause, or, more precisely, two effects of the same cause are made to relate to each other causally. For Pool is, in fact, implying that linguistic heterogeneity is a necessary but not sufficient cause for underdevelopment, and that language uniformity is necessary but not sufficient for 'high' development. Even if his thesis were empirically true, it is so because the heterogeneous nations were 'created', both in terms of this heterogeneity and their so-called underdevelopment, by the same cause, namely colonialism. Due to a simplistic identification of the standard with the larger-than-national and the non-standard with the narrowly national, Joseph is able to valorize standardization as enlightened internationalism as opposed to the nationalism of non-standard dialects. It is important here, as elsewhere, to note that Joseph is not entirely wrong because there is a transnational element in the standardized form, but the internationalism is itself complicit with the history of imperialism and is bought at the price of excluding too many from participation.

Though Joseph is able to identify control with élite intervention, he does so in a way that vitiates any agency and, hence, culpability.

Control is usually triggered early in the elaborative process, when persons of authority begin to find their language becoming some-what foreign to them. A number of avant-garde elaborations may be firmly entrenched before adequate control mechanisms can be set in motion; cosmetic ones, like other previously established variants, may become subject to retroactive hierarchization when it comes to the controllers' attention. This awareness of variation will come about at the latest when the language is codified, and especially when it is 'ultra-codified' for teaching to foreigners. ...

Control consists of a seemingly infinite but really finite series of individual gestures and decisions. The efforts of many people enter into the process, though the number of those who work full-time at linguistic control is very small. More often, control occurs as a byproduct of other language-connected duties, like writing, editing, and teaching. ...

There is in addition a rather broad group of professions which function as a bridge between the upper-class/urban/cultural avant-garde and the lower-class/rural/vernacular-speaking majority. By acting as both a cultural and a linguistic go-between, members of these professions control the elaborating avant-garde language in such a way that it remains comprehensible to vernac-ular speakers.

These professions include, according to Haugen and Joseph, guilds of merchants and traders, clergymen, grammarians and so on, though teachers have a crucial role in transmitting control decisions. As Joseph aptly describes it, 'Here we see several major threads in the history of language standardization come together: writing is necessary for the recording and initial diffusion of standardization decisions; civilizing institutions such as schools are necessary for their further diffusion' (p. 114). In addition to planning boards, academies and ministries, Joseph identifies editors as the most important controllers of the standard language.

Joseph describes the basis on which limitation and hierarchiza-tion takes place in the standard into two types: 'the "normal", in which the only factor is usage, however the group of standard users is to be defined; and the "extranormal", which I shall subdivide into four categories – economy, logic, purism, and connotation' (p. 117). One cannot, however, dismiss the manner in which the group of standard users is defined because the more restrictive this element, the less normal the 'norm' would be.

Standard languages are characterized by a rather complete hierarchization of their norms, consciously developed, pursued, codified,
and inculcated. This conscious development results in the norms of
standardization moving progressively away from the unconscious
norms which underlie non-standardized speech. The more points
of divergence between them, the more likely the standard will be
perceived as 'artificial.' There are certainly no upper and lower
limits on how many rules a standard language may or must contain that violate the norms of its synecdochic dialect, but it seems
reasonable to assume that unless the great majority of the norms
are uniform, the standard language will be confined to 'classical'
status (p. 118)....

Setting the technical difficulties aside, if we ask whether the
admission or rejection of a norm to or from the standard language
has ever been based on its broad base of usage throughout the
populace, the answer is definitely yes. However, the rejection of a
norm on the grounds that it is 'vulgar' (in the etymological sense
of 'commonplace') may more accurately be classified as aristocratic. The rejection of a norm because it is too closely restricted to
an affected élite is not democratic, strictly speaking, but anti-
aristocratic. Finally, the acceptance of a norm as standard because
of its vulgarity – which has happened in times of strongly Romantic nationalism – is not standardization; it is rather the refusal to
intervene against a change affecting the standard's synecdochic
base.   (p. 120)

Joseph's argument here is vitiated by his use of the connotatively
loaded term 'vulgar' which, notwithstanding his protestations, der-
ogates the norm in question. It is clear that he is on the side of the
'processes of standardization' against all-comers, and this allows
him to quibble about notions of 'democracy' as well as to present
'acceptance of a norm' as 'the refusal to intervene against change'!
In terms of Joseph's own definition of the 'normal' processes of
standardization whose only criterion is usage (p. 117), he contra-
dicts himself when he writes that the acceptance of a norm as standard because of its 'vulgarity' is not standardization.

Because norms are inherent to all language, normal criteria often
seem more basic and endowed with greater authority than do
extranormal ones. The best procedure in analyzing standard languages is to assume that any given control decision is founded

upon a norm, and to treat the use of extranormal criteria as the 'marked' or exceptional case.    (Ibid., p. 120)

Once linguistic standards are formed and accepted, they are liable to a fallacious interpretation ... . The simple fact is that in the common vernacular belief system of Western culture, language standards are not recognized as man-made constructs, built consciously upon inherent linguistic norms. The standards are held to represent the original state of the language, in accordance with the mythology of a Golden Age and subsequent decadence. Any deviation from the standard is taken as a sign of ignorance, or degeneracy, or both.

This is the tyranny exercised by linguistic standards: adherence to them identifies members of the upper social classes; but the standards themselves are largely defined by upper-class usage. The other classes should, logically, resent this practice of exclusion and the sort of measurement derived from it; yet, on the contrary, such measurement is demanded throughout the society. (pp. 125ff)

These standards, albeit defined by upper-class usage, *appear* to be 'neutral' and non-localized, equally relevant to all members of the larger polity (p. 129).

Several of the factors which enter into the making of standard languages, including their social-class associations, their lingua franca function, their use as vehicle of the wider unit of loyalty, and their reshaping by codification and elaboration, contribute to a perception of the standard as non-localized, that is, not belonging to any single area or group of individuals, but rather to the unit of loyalty as a whole.

It is precisely this dissimulation of the standard as politically neutral, socially non-localized and ideologically uncontaminated[77] that must be avoided at all cost, if language is to be seen for what it is, the site of struggle.

---

77. See, for instance, Joseph's reference to the advantages of linguistic uniformity, citing Pool, as an attempt to get 'Beyond ideology' (p. 109, quoted above).

DISCOURSE AND MAKING SENSE

The role of non-standard language as the site of struggle,[78] then, is enacted in Chapters 3 and 4 of this work where a historical accounting

---

78.  This refinement of the piety that 'language is the site of struggle' is theoretically derived from my reading of Derrida's discussion of marginality and parasitism in his critique of Austin in *Limited Inc. abc...* and *Signature Event Context*. I give a summary of this analysis below since it is of importance to the conceptual framework of this argument. I am indebted to Michael Ryan's (1982) analysis from which I draw freely.

According to Derrida, Austin excludes from his analysis of ordinary language, the befoulment of non-normal, non-standard speech acts such as citations in play. It is not important *here* whether Derrida is right in his criticism: the point is that non-standard uses, called infelicities by Austin, leave their mark on the norm of standard speech acts. Derrida argues that any accidental exclusion must be considered as a structural possibility, even necessity, of the system from which it derives, and this explains his concept of parasitism. In fact, for Derrida, non-identical repetition (citation) remains the basis for the functioning of all signifying forms of communication.

The sign must be repeatable, citable, and especially so in the absence of the sender. Therefore, the so-called standard speech act is itself constituted by a more general version of the abnormality Austin allegedly excludes; that is, it is constituted by citation. All speech acts presuppose a general citationality. To be acceptable, to work at all, a speech act must cite a previously established code, convention or repeatable model, and must itself be repeatable in other contexts. Repetition here has a double function of both making identical and altering or making different. Repetition or citationality makes possible and establishes the identity of the signifying form, but equally it makes pure or rigorous identity impossible. Since repetition is the basis of identification, it has to be faced that alteration identifies and identification is always impure. Without a movement of self-differentiating repetition or citation there could be no event, no presence of speech act. This is why the word 'repetition' is replaced by 'iteration', which contains the double meaning of repetition and alteration or difference.

Whereas simple repetition presupposes a 'full' idealization, iteration entails no more than a minimal idealization. Thus, as Spivak notes, Derrida's alternate denomination for the method of metaphysics becomes, here, the graphic of iterability, over the logic of repetition.

In addition, for Austin, conscious intention (and self-identical meaning, of course) is central to the theory of speech acts. This centrality is displaced by Derrida who shows that intention must operate within an already given system and structure that is unconscious, as well as within an imminent possibility of displacement that exceeds its control. Intentional consciousness cannot be anchored on any absolute; only multiple, floating contexts. Therefore, citation, fiction and convention become more important to standard language than Austin allows.

The point is not to write off conscious intentionality, though this for Derrida is the traditional locus of metaphysics, but to situate it within larger structures and movements that allow it to function but without significant power. Conscience intention can never be completely actualized (or made present to itself) because iteration, which would make it possible in the first place, introduces the doubling (dehiscence) that makes such purity impossible. Derrida produces here the non-continuist version of the radical break in intentionality (*Limited Inc.*, p. 202).

What is fundamental to Derrida's critique of Austin is showing that it is illegitimate to exclude even provisionally or methodologically (strategically) such elements as infelicity or citation from the vigorously determined system of speech acts because these are merely examples of the general operation of citationality or iterability that is at the root of the system of speech acts (Michael Ryan, 1982, p. 33).

This does not in turn result in the mere reversal of the hierarchy by the privileging of fictional, theatrical uses of speech acts. It is rather that among the many heterogeneous components of the speech act, the iterable non self-identical intention and context, as well as the parasitic use, are structural moments. The theater does not win over 'real life', the two are indistinguishably and structurally implicated (*Limited Inc.*, p. 232).

Derrida reiterates in *Limited Inc.* that the standard is always *potentially* capable of being affected by the non-standard. Iteration implies the structural possibility that, to occur, an act must already be citational; it must contain the possibility of being repeated and thus potentially of being 'mimed, feigned, cited' and so on. The standard language speech act cannot, therefore, be distinguished in rigorous opposition to fiction, play, convention. This is precisely the point Derrida is making with the 'high class tomfoolery' (Spivak, p. 15) of *Limited Inc.* In being both serious and non serious at the same time, Derrida is problematizing the entire notion of seriousness as ethico-political centralization, the nonserious element is most pertinent (ibid., p. 44). The unquestioning assumption of a natural standard is, therefore, not an impartial gesture. This notion is 'popularized' in *Positions* where Derrida points out that everyday language is not neutral, that it carries with it presuppositions of western metaphysics (p. 19).

Derrida's response to Searle becomes a reiteration of *Signature Event Context*, and he is able to cite all of the earlier essay because he feels that Searle has not really read this piece at all. Searle forgets that his own theoretical statements that elaborate Austin's Theory of Speech Acts are in themselves speech acts. Derrida points out that Searle's justification of Austin's theory rests in an analogy (*Limited Inc.*, p. 208) that is a metaphorical comparison of Speech Act Theory with 'most' other sciences. This non-strict recourse to a resemblance, to a non-literal figure allows Derrida to argue that 'in Searle's terms it is based ultimately on the metaphorical, the sarcastic, the non-literal. And this is rather disturbing for an utterance that purports to *found the entire methodology* (abstraction, idealization, systematization etc.) on the theory of speech acts' (ibid., p. 209).

of language in Sri Lanka during the early British occupation culminates in an examination of subaltern use of non-standard language during the rebellion of 1848 (Chapter 4), and a contemporary analysis of non-standard use of English in the island makes a claim for its institutionalization and legitimization as a 'new' standard (Chapters 3 and 4).

The specific theoretical underpinnings of these chapters are as follows: the historiographic methodology is derived from the work of the Subaltern collective, specifically Ranajit Guha; the strategies of discourse analysis are both narrowly linguistic and broadly influenced by the Foucault of *The Archaeology of Knowledge*, each of which is described therein; the theory of resistance in language owes its origin to a misreading of Wittgenstein via Volosinov and Marx, which I shall spell out in the following pages since it provides the basis for the non-linguistic analysis throughout.

> Don't *for heaven's sake*, be afraid of talking nonsense! But you must pay attention to your nonsense. (*Culture & Value*, p. 56e)

> My aim is: to teach you to pass from a piece of disguised nonsense to something that is patent nonsense. (*Philosophical Investigations*, no. 464).

> Don't take as a matter of course, but as a remarkable fact, that pictures and fictitious narratives give us pleasure, occupy our minds. ('Don't take it as a matter of course' means: find it surprising, as you do some things which disturb you. Then the puzzling aspect of the latter will disappear, by your accepting this fact as you do the other.) ((The transition from patent nonsense to something which is disguised nonsense.)) (ibid., no. 524)

It is clear that Wittgenstein is here talking about philosophy as a personal perplexity,[79] and outlines the means of curing this 'mental cramp' through bringing a latent philosophical problem into the open. Moreover, he has little if anything to say about the standard/

---

Searle's choice in ignoring 'marginal, fringe' cases is problematic in that these always constitute the most certain and the most decisive indices wherever essential conditions are to be grasped. Thus, the most seemingly obvious natural assumption of scientific neutrality is a(nother) fiction.

79.  See F. Rossi-Landi (1983) p. 10.

non-standard dichotomy in language since it probably was not a philosophically interesting issue to him. However, it is also possible to read these passages as pointing to a counter-hegemonic theory of discourse in which we are encouraged to resist the hidden nonsense (as irrationality, arbitrariness, injustice perhaps) of standardized discourse by heightening the nonsense through exaggeration, misrecognition, imitation–parody, literalization (of the metaphoric) and so on. In this view, the standard is disguised as neutral and shared, and it can only come undone if stripped of its camouflage. In working out a Wittgensteinian social theory of knowledge, David Bloor[80] follows an analogous agenda, using the familiar elements of the theory of language games such as functional diversity, finitism, training and translation, the rejection of extensions, family resemblances, the interaction of criteria and symptoms, and the role of needs (which Bloor equates with social interests)(p. 49).

As a prerequisite to changing the language game that comprises the hegemonic discourse in a particular arena, it is, in my view, necessary to render this discourse absurd and self-contradictory so that it cannot remain convincing any more. In my empirical field work and research in this text I map out two distinct moments in which the standards of language and language-in-use are challenged through imitation, excess, misrecognition.[81] This is not to make an essentialist argument (and one that fetishizes the underclass) that every imitation, excess, misrecognition or signal-jamming is dehegemonizing. In each case, the larger context would determine the consequences of the action in question, though I wish to de-emphasize the privileging of individualized intention and self-consciousness that is characteristic of analyses of social protest/resistance. Support for this counter-intuitive position is forthcoming from Wittgenstein as well: his problematizing of private access to intention is a powerful philosophical refutation of personalism to boot.

---

80. *Wittgenstein: A Social Theory of Knowledge* (1983).
81. I must note the influence of Pierre Bourdieu here: 'Symbolic domination really begins when the misrecognition, implied by recognition, leads those who are dominated to apply the dominant criteria of evaluation to their own practices' (Bourdieu and Boltanski, 1984, p. 46). I have moved away from Bourdieu's consensual model of social reproduction, however, as can be seen by my use of 'misrecognition' as a sometime-element of subversion/protest.

An intention is embedded in its situation, in human customs and institutions. (*Philosophical Investigations*, no. 337).

'My intention was no less certain as it was than it would have been if I had said "Now I'll deceive him".' But of you had said the words, would you necessarily have meant them quite seriously? (Thus the most explicit expression of intention is by itself insufficient evidence of intention.)   (ibid., no. 641)

What is the natural expression of an intention? – Look at a cat when it stalks a bird; or a beast when it wants to escape.   (ibid., no. 647)

The possibility of protest that I have outlined here can be read into Wittgenstein's discussion of 'normal' situations and their breakdown, which is what such action precipitates. It is perhaps this sense of 'catachresis' that is used in deconstruction to signal a discursive breakdown, albeit (and this is perhaps a limitation of the deconstructive practice in the hands of literary critics) in the restricted realm of metaphor.

Should it be said that I am using a word whose meaning I don't know, and so am talking nonsense? – Say what you choose, so long as it does not prevent you from seeing the facts. (And when you see them there is a good deal that you will not say.)   (ibid., no. 79)

It is only in normal cases that the use of a word is clearly prescribed; we know, are in no doubt, what to say in this or that case. The more abnormal the case, the more doubtful it becomes what we are to say. And if things were quite different from what they actually are – if there were for instance no characteristic expression of pain, of fear, of joy; if rule became exception and exception rule; or if both became phenomena of roughly equal frequency – this would make our normal language-games lose their point. (ibid., no. 142)

Wittgenstein does not consider what the outcome of a change in the normal language-games of a society would amount to. There is no doubt that certain language-games are more tenacious than others, and that some are well-nigh 'indispensable', but our language-games *are changing* with time, particularly in the areas of science and technology where paradigm shifts reflect modifications in the rules of the game.

Philosophers very often talk about investigating, analysing, the meaning of words. But let's not forget that a word hasn't got a word given to it, as it were, by a power independent of us, so that there could be a kind of scientific investigation into what the word *really* means. A word has the meaning someone has given to it.

There are words with several clearly defined meanings. It is easy to tabulate these meanings. And there are words of which one might say: They are used in a thousand different ways which gradually merge into one another. No wonder that we can't tabulate strict rules for their use.

It is wrong to say that in philosophy we consider an ideal language as opposed to our ordinary one. For this makes it appear as though we thought we could improve on ordinary language. But ordinary language is all right. Whenever we make up 'ideal languages' it is not in order to replace our ordinary language by them; but just to remove some trouble caused in someone's mind by thinking that he has got hold of the exact use of a common word. That is why our method is not merely to enumerate actual usages of words, but rather deliberately to invent new ones, some of them because of their absurd appearance. (*The Blue Book*, pp. 27ff).

The confrontation between élite/standard discourse and underclass/non-standard discourse is analogous to Wittgenstein's dramatization of the individual's conflict with normative description of personal experience.

And we find there is puzzlement and mental discomfort, not only when our curiosity about certain facts is not satisfied or when we can't find a law of nature fitting in with all our experience, but also when a notation dissatisfies us – perhaps because of various associations which it calls up. Our ordinary language, which of all possible notations is the one which pervades all our life, holds our mind rigidly in one position, as it were, and in this position sometimes it feels cramped, having a desire for other positions as well. Thus we sometimes wish for a notation which stresses a difference more strongly, makes it more obvious, than ordinary language does, or one which in a particular case uses more closely similar forms of expression than our ordinary language. Our mental cramp is loosened when we are shown the notations which fulfil these needs. These needs can be of the greatest variety.   (*The Blue Book*, p. 59)

Again, we see the characteristic move which identifies the social basis of individual divergence from standard notation, but having made the identification moves on. It is in this 'greatest variety' of needs (or social interests) that our non-standard speaker must stake his/her claim. It is in this space that the subaltern peasant must turn the standard notation on its head, even for the briefest of moments. It is in systematically opening up the possibility of widening the standard to include this greatest variety that the linguist/language teacher/intellectual can work toward productive change.

## NON-STANDARD LANGUAGE AND 'NON-STANDARD' DISCOURSE

I have shown in the first part of this book that the existing theoretical bases for the hierarchization of language into standard and non-standard forms is suspect. In order to establish this I have claimed that it is necessary to consider the *other* Englishes which for so long were the paradigmatically non-standard varieties of English. I have argued that it is only through taking *seriously* the apparent oddities and deviations of these varieties that one can understand the way language works in its most general form(s). I have proposed, therefore, that rather than treating them as exceptions, however individually valid, it would be more useful to consider these and other non-standard forms as the most general cases of which Standard (British) English and General American are the hegemonic deviants.

It is important to reiterate that this central argument has its mirror *within* these other forms of language as well as *among* the various forms themselves. Thus, the processes of legitimization and standardization within, say, Lankan English tend to marginalize those variants which reflect contestory non-élite interventions that are not so easily appropriated. What takes place at the global level is evident in microcosm at the level of the individual post-colonial context. It is in this contest (which is also always an accommodation and a negotiation) to have a stake in making meanings stick, in having access to the legitimizations of discourse, that language becomes the site of the heterogeneous struggles that now everyone says they are.

Discourse, however, is certainly not identical with language. Yet it would not be unthinkable to say that the only way that language has existence is through discursive practices, if discourse is then defined as the possibility of making sense. Language in this view can be studied significantly only as discourse, only in its use within the context of discursive formations. Hence, what was argued for language becomes equally valid for discourse.

I shall use the term discourse in this section in somewhat cavalier (read pre-critical) a fashion as it operates in the discipline of linguistics, and this usage is deliberate since it seems to me that the generalized notion is the most useful for the concerns of the present study since I have a methodological interest in reclaiming the ordinariness and ubiquity of 'discourse', and since I wish to maintain a relevance, however tenuous, with the study of language in its privileged form as linguistics.

Discourse as used in linguistics refers 'to a continuous stretch of (especially spoken) language larger than a sentence – but, within this broad notion, several different applications may be found. At its most general, a discourse is a behavioral unit which has a pre-theoretical status in linguistics.'[82] Yet, it becomes immediately necessary to modify this definition if we are to distinguish between language-in-use and discourse, otherwise non-standard language-in-use would always produce non-normative discourse: this distinction will be fleshed out further in Chapter 4 where particular historical interventions against colonial discourse are discussed in detail.

Therefore, at least within the linguistic description of discourse, what has been argued for in terms of language standardization can be supported in terms of the *standardization of discourse*. This standardized discourse takes the form of setting the bounds of acceptable variation that includes, for instance, the possibility of protest against its own dictates. If, as has been argued earlier, the non-standard variants of a language provide greater insights into the ways in which the struggles of class, race, gender, age, region and so on take place and are covered over, if also they provide a more useful view of culture as representation and self-representation, then the

---

82.   David Crystal (1985) p. 96.

analysis of discourse that is sensitive to the complex calculus that I have provisionally called the non-standard, the marginal, the deviant, the catachrestic, must provide an example of this struggle in progress.

The users of non-standard language are, in a sense, the subalterns[83] *vis-à-vis* that language context. Non-standard or marginal discourse marks the subalternity of its proponents, albeit in non-uniform ways. My contention is that the effacement of the subaltern as subject operates a social text of far wider spread than its immediate colonialist weave. For instance, even in the relatively decolonized space of the post-colonial societies, there remains the attenuation/reinscription of subaltern resistance as agency, and it does appear facile to lay blame the production of such 'knowledge' entirely on the culture of imperialism, or on the internalizing of colonialist paradigms by national élites.

I am not doubting that such internalization-cum-representation is in fact nearly universal, albeit displaced, but my argument is that the impossibility of providing for subaltern agency is symptomatic of language production of all societies. The colonial histories of South Asia, for instance, have, through the imposition of *another* language, merely made visible what was more or less the case even before the establishment of (variations of) the Portuguese–Dutch–French–English complex.

In this view, language standardization makes élite discourse normative, and marginalizes other voices. There is always a hierarchy and a complex network of accommodations and appropriations

---

83. The concept of subalterneity is taken from the work of the Subaltern Studies Collective, particularly Ranajit Guha, whose radical interventions in colonial Indian historiography I have discussed in *Language and Rebellion: Discursive Unities and the Possibility of Protest* (1990). I refer the reader to this book for a more detailed analysis of the arguments outlined here, as well as for an empirical example of this theory in its treatment of the rebellion of 1848 in Ceylon (Sri Lanka). I draw much of this discussion from the first twenty pages of this book.

   In this text, then, the term 'subaltern' identifies the 'representative' of the (pre)proletarian underclass without necessarily predicating an overt consciousness of itself as a member of a (cohesive) class.

within this standard. As regards the underclass, moreover, this process of standardization has compounded an already attenuated access to power. Standardization creates not merely grammatical/syntactical rules (as criteria of acceptability) but also a value-coding that enables the 'free-play' of world-views.

The analysis of 'non-standard' (or non-normative) discourse is, however, made more difficult by the fact that one must take into account the social-historical limits on the available discourses to the underclass (or any other group) of society at a given time. The point is not to show the difficulty that exists for marginal voices to be heard; not merely to point to the problems associated with the articulation of minority discourse, as 'unpopular' or oppositional discourses; but rather to describe the problematic of articulating the discourses that lie completely outside this spectrum.

It is differentiating and different in that it takes into account discourse ranges that are not static: the terms of the discourse and its ground rules are always being shifted as well as transgressed. There is flexibility as to what can be debated or challenged, and these are dependent on the broadest context of the discourse. Context here becomes a short-hand for class, race and gender determinations in addition to that which more generally comes under the rubric of context such as 'the general historical background'.

I hope to describe the ways available within (and 'without') the hegemonic discourses to sabotage them, to deny their authority and validity, and thereby to work against them. I shall also examine the question of intention in such protest/counter-hegemonic discourse/anti-discourse. I will look at the ways in which the very rules and inner logic of discourse are flouted by those examples of protest to be studied. In each of these cases, the intention to protest cannot be denied, in the broadest sense. It is in the details, the specific situations that the question of intention becomes moot.

I shall also describe the power of imitation as protest, especially when it is manifestly impossible to become, in any pragmatic sense, that which is being imitated. Class becomes the most important determinant here, but in an uncritical fetishizing sense. Exaggeration is another type of protest that will be described. What we will have through these examples, then, is a new typology of protest within the dominant discourses, with special emphasis on the structures of protest that are counter-intuitive, as for instance in the case of intention and imitation.[84]

I would, therefore, locate the most general case of the subaltern within the normative systems of language as used (within discourse in its broadest sense), that make operative certain rules and conditions of validity which, by witting or unwitting design, legitimize specific interests precisely obscuring the fact that they represent only these interests.

*Discourse is the 'originary' system of value-coding since it provides the condition of possibility for the diverse coding of value, and since it must appear to be epistemologically prior to value itself.* Not only is discourse the site of the *naming* of individual values, it is also the arena in which words are made to compete with other words in order that they may become names, which only then are in the *category* of value-terms.

There is a way of reading Marx's description of the forms of value as a justification for the study of non-standard discourse where the 'system' does not work smoothly. The non-standard discourse, or in this sense the *entire* system of discourse, including both standard and non-standard forms, is homologous with Marx's Total or Expanded Form of Value (*Capital*, vol. I, pp. 154ff) where 'the value of a commodity, the linen for example, is now expressed in terms of innumerable other members of the world of commodities' (p. 155). This process is cumbersome and always incomplete, hence an equivalent form is derived, which in turn becomes the universal equivalent or money form. Now, the money form is the most efficient and smooth-running, yet this very efficacy tends to hide the real comparison of human labour expended:

It is however precisely this finished form of the world of commodities – the money form – which conceals the social character

---

84. Access to this different type of discourse is very difficult. It is not so much that the subaltern 'has no voice' but that in order to hear it one has to 'unlearn' so much. Often they are heard only through the palimpsest of citation in official letters and in records of court proceedings, in addition to petitions and pleas. A word of caution: what they say about their actions in general must not be privileged as somehow unquestionably authentic and 'the real thing', which then is the yardstick from which all the other discourses should be measured. Yet, in these fleeting moments we are confronted with a more or less direct glimpse of the self-representation of the subaltern as rebel operating within the patterns and frameworks of discourse available to him/her.

of private labour and the social relations between the individual workers, by making those relations appear as relations between material objects, instead of revealing them plainly. If I state that coats or boots stand in a relation to linen because the latter is the universal incarnation of abstract human labour, the absurdity of the statement is self-evident. Nevertheless, when the producers of coats and boots bring these commodities into a relation with linen, or with gold or silver (and this makes no difference here), as the universal equivalent, the relation between their own private labour and the collective labour of society appears to them in exactly this absurd form.   (pp. 168–69)

It may, therefore, be useful to study this 'defective' form of value – the total expanded form of value – in order to see precisely what gets covered over if the system is to work smoothly. By analogy, the non-standard forms of language are clumsy and defective in the sense that there is no single uniform equivalence: the parameters keep shifting and context is all-important. It is here, moreover, that the struggles for control become evident because there is no 'neutral' form to dissimulate or displace this. Marx was interested in studying general exploitation and thus had to analyse the general system, whereas in the specific case of language it may be therapeutic to examine, selectively, the specific links of the cumbersome chain that comprises the total expanded form of discourse in a given society.[85]

---

85. This argument is my awkward attempt to transpose into a different arena an informal lecture delivered by Professor Spivak at the University of Pittsburgh in early 1989.

# 3

# 'Uneducated' (Sri) Lankan English Speech: A Case Study and its Theoretical Implications

## INTRODUCTION

The two following chapters comprise a prolegomenon towards the identification and classification of a broader 'standard' Lankan English that takes account not only of so-called native-like, habitual or first language use, but also of the speech and writing of 'non-educated' users of the language.[86] This chapter will provide a theoretical framework for the analysis of Lankan English, taking off from the general comments contained in the first chapter, and will concentrate on forms of spoken discourse. Chapter 4 will work with evidence of non-standard use in writing, here conceived in its broadest sense as linguistic material that has/can be structurally replicated ('cited') in the absence of its source.

The point is that there is a variety of English that is alive and well in Sri Lanka today, but it is not the Educated Standard English described and legitimized by linguists in the field. In fact, the 'English' language in use outside of the Anglo-Americanized urban élite bears less and less resemblance to the language imposed/ espoused as a result of British colonialism. Even within the habitual use of 'native speakers' of Lankan English there remains much that has been reduced out of linguistic classification on the grounds of

---

86. The study concentrates on Sinhala speakers since I am not fluent in Tamil, and have had little access to mainly Tamil-speaking areas of the country. This limitation of the work is strongly felt, and will be the major focus of my work in the future.

non-generality, colloquiality and all-round unacceptability. My contention is that these 'deviations' that linguistic purists denigrate are influenced by non-élite usage, whether consciously or not, and as such represent the 'contamination' of élite discourse through subaltern 'misuse' of language.

In this portion of my work I shall point to such 'non-standard' use of English within contextualized conversation, and identify written variants which require a more serious analysis than the dismissive gestures (as substandard) or the patronization (as quaint) that they have received so far.

There are different types of users of Lankan English. The usual classification agreed upon by linguists has been made on the basis of fluency with the language in terms described in Chapter 1.[87]

Chitra Fernando identifies Lankan users of English as falling into three main groups of bilinguals 'who can be distinguished most readily in terms of the character of their English, the degree of Sinhala influence on it, and the domains in which they use it' (C. Fernando, 1976, p. 348). Of these groups, Group Two is distinguished from Group One on the basis of phonology, even though in terms of grammar and lexis they are not significantly different (ibid., pp. 351ff).

> The pronunciation of this second group of bilinguals shows, typically, one or more of three major phonemic features which separate such bilinguals from those of Group One. These three features are of great social significance, since they stamp speakers as having learnt English late and, therefore, not generally using English in the personal domains of family, friendship and religion.

> (a)  Substitution of the long half-open rounded vowel /ɔ for the long pure vowel /o:/ of the Group One bilingual. bo:t, ro:d become bɔt and rɔd.

> (b)  Substitution of the short pure vowel /o/ for the short open back rounded vowel /ɔ / of the Group One bilingual in nɔt, pɔt etc.

---

87.  See pp. 28–40 (Chapter 1), and especially pp. 35ff where Fernando's classification has been summarized through selective quotation.

These two substitutions have the result that Group Two bilinguals will reverse the forms *hall* and *hole*, from the standpoint of the Group One bilinguals:

hall  hɔl – ho:l
hole  ho:l – hɔl ...

(c)   Substitution of the voiceless bilabial stop /p/ for the voiceless bilabial fricative /F/ of Sri Lankan English and vice versa in English words which use these sounds. Sinhala has no /f/ phoneme and *speakers of Sri Lankan English (Group One)* [my emphasis] use a bilabial fricative as the closest substitute to the Standard English labiodental fricative. The same type of reversal noted in (b) between *hall* and *hole* then takes place between words like *pan* and *fan* in the speech of these Group Two bilinguals.

Chitra Fernando's position here is fairly typical of liberal linguists writing on the Lankan situation,[88] not least in her identification of educated Lankan English with the speech of Group One bilinguals. It must be observed, however, that in this view Group Two bilinguals may also use the same grammatical and lexical structures, so Lankan English is not the sole prerogative of Group One. The phonetic 'deviations' of Group Two bilinguals, however, become negative class-markers for the English-educated élite, and are crucial to understanding prevalent language attitudes in Sri Lanka. Fernando's analysis implies that such derogation of Group Two speakers is a thing of the past, and in this she is only partly correct.[89] I shall discuss this in detail when outlining the results of my attitudinal survey in the last chapter of this book.

---

88.  Here, as elsewhere, the exception is Kandiah, whose critique of Kachru's 'cline of bilingualism' (from which Fernando draws her model) is discussed in detail in Chapter 5.

89.  One needs only to recall the popularity of the *Mind Your Language* television series in Colombo in the early 1980s (many years after Fernando's article) and the uproar that went on in the Letters to the Editor page of the *Daily News* when it was taken off the air, as well as, of course, to imagine the reasons for the continued popularity of plays such as *He Comes From Jaffna* and *Well, Mudliyar* which poke fun at the English speech of 'uneducated' rural Sinhalese and Tamils.

Such features, being substandard in terms of the norms of Group One, have attracted a good deal of derision, so much so that Group Two bilinguals were till quite recently referred to contemptuously as 'the *not–pot* cases' by the more snobbish members of Group One. But though they still continue to exist and increase the term is hardly ever used today in view of the growing power of the lower-middle and working classes as social forces. The widespread failure to distinguish /v/ and /w/, although evident to a native speaker of English does not attract the same attention because it appears in the speech of Group One bilinguals as well. (ibid., p. 352)

What makes this observation relevant at this point is the unquestioned primacy of the 'native speaker of English' who is contrasted favourably with the Group One bilingual. The fact that some of the Group One bilinguals are in fact 'native speakers' of this variety of English is not even considered by Fernando. This tendency to devalue Lankan English obtains in the case of most writing on the subject, and results in the uncomfortable forcing together of user-classifications that are in the main based on second and foreign language learning paradigms.

Though the cline of bilingualism as matrix is not without its problems, it is important to reiterate that the usual classification that obtains in the British (and perhaps 'American') language situations does not operate so smoothly here as well as in other post-colonial contexts. Each of these categories appears to be problematic, but it is in the fraught nature of the 'native speaker' that the entire system comes apart. It is the most unarguable linguistic truism that the 'native speaker' is the arbiter of language, that native speakers have intuitive abilities to distinguish what is acceptable and what is not at a given time in their native dialects. If there is a doubt as to the currency of an expression or the viability of a formulation, the educated native speaker provides the linguist with the necessary authority to pronounce judgement.

All this is a little strange since some native speakers are clearly less able to arbitrate than others, and some who are not native speakers are able to correct the 'mistakes' of native speakers. Yet, despite these problems, the discipline has still to relinquish its reliance on the native speaker as the ultimate judge of linguistic acceptability. One of the reasons for this may be that native speakers are easier to identify in the Euro-American contexts, and that difficulties and contradictions can be adduced, therefore, to relatively minor dialectal variations. The necessity for an acceptable arbiter overrides the specific issues of individual acts of arbitration.

In the subcontinent, however, the native speakers of English are much more elusive, much less uniform. Linguists have taken different approaches to this problem: many, like Kachru, have asserted that there are no real native speakers of English in the subcontinent, or that their number is so small as to be negligible. Some argue that even those who may appear to be native speakers do not use English in every aspect of their lives, that they have no words in English to describe certain experiences, relationships, functions, situations, and therefore cannot be considered *bona fide* native speakers.[90] We have noted others who discuss speakers of English in terms of their bilinguality alone, implying that English is always the 'second' or other language, however habitual its use.[91] Yet others wish to mark this contentious category of speakers as habitual, native-like and so on, recognizing that there remains a difference from the native speaker norm. What happens in each instance is that the dialect spoken by these people becomes devalued and requires external justification since it has been labelled a dialect without *bona fide* native speakers.

None of these formulations are completely inaccurate, of course. If this were the case, the problem would be a simpler one, and the simple solution of renaming these users as native speakers would leave nothing much changed, theoretically at least in the larger linguistic picture. While these caveats remain important, many of the group of speakers under consideration use English as their only language of communication and interaction, their language of intimate dreams and conceptual thoughts. They are, in other words, clearly native speakers of a dialect or dialects of English.

What this places at risk, then, is the received notion of native speaker competence itself, the transparency and uniformity of native speaker judgements of usage and misusage. The Lankan context, for instance, figures native speakers who cannot be granted such a privileged status, and some of whose linguistic behaviour does not display the self-assurance of a typical native speaker,

---

90. See pp. 39ff and particularly n. 51.
91. See, for instance, the essays by Chitra Fernando (1976) and Siromi Fernando (1985).

whereas others hold notions of linguistic excellence and purity even above that of Standard English itself.

I shall examine linguistic evidence from the speech (and writing in Chapter 4) of 'native speakers' of Lankan English to show the kinds of attitudinal moves that are made at this level of performance.

Habitual educated users of English still mix and switch more than is allowed for in the literature, particularly in the examples provided by linguists. One of the reasons for this is that examples continue to be abstracted and isolated from the discourses in which they appear. The spoken language is much less 'standard' than it would appear from the sets of grammatical and syntactic rules provided by linguists, and this is especially so in the entire range of everyday non-formal intercourse of habitual users. At least in the Lankan context, the label 'educated' dissimulates, therefore, both in terms of its relatively neutral identification of the commonality shared by upper-class speakers, particularly since it has little to do with education *per se*, or with English education *per se* either, *and* in terms of its bias for an 'educated' (literary, perhaps) form of the language which is only one of its component parts.

Some habitual users and native speakers pride themselves on the quality of their language even *vis-à-vis* the 'corruption' of (Standard) English in England and the United States. This group is not limited to those who are unaware of linguistic debate or are unself conscious of the nature of the language they use. In a semi-formal interview in early 1989 an internationally known intellectual, a sometime English scholar and perceptive critic of Lankan English writing, for instance, admitted with a self-deprecating laugh that he too often felt superior to British users of English!

I will, then, examine certain linguistic data on so-called non-educated users of English to show that their use cannot be restricted merely to the proliferation of mistakes, hyper-corrections, or at best purely limited functional uses in certain specific contexts. I will provide counter-examples of creative use, use as protest, deliberate misuse, travesty as critique and so on. In this analysis, my innovation, which since it is radically counter-intuitive I resisted for so long, suggests that intention (especially at the individual level) becomes not the all-important yardstick but only another element to be "read".

I shall then present an analysis of language attitudes within Sri Lanka that is sensitive to the many different variables at work in the environment. Through this study, I hope to show that schizoglossia, though in evidence, is not endemic to this situation.[92] Hyper-correction and other 'mistakes' can and must be read differently for a more acceptable politics, but not to the extent that the underclass is fetishized. These 'errors' will be less debilitating to users/learners when these practices are on the way to being legitimized. What is very different, however, is the individual contempt and the institu-tional blind eye that is turned upon certain sorts of teaching of English that has gained currency, such as the demand for spoken English in the urban areas.[93] Within the prevailing attitudinal cli-mate this serves in another way to keep out the majority: it would be another matter to make these kinds of Englishes the norm or one of the norms, instead of derogating them by focusing upon common 'errors' that are mass-produced by these means.

As has been noted earlier,[94] non-standard writing is much less accessible outside of the immediate context of its generation than non-standard speech, and has therefore received much less theoreti-cal emphasis by those whose work problematizes notions of stan-dardization. One of the most useful and powerful means of recording such non-standard 'writing' is through popular cultural material such as songs. Though these lyrics are seldom written down in the literal sense in the Lankan context,[95] they are fixed and established in a sense that is analogous to writing and therefore can be taken to represent this form. I shall examine some popular songs in Chapter 4 in order to show the creative and subversive potential of non-standard 'writing' which runs parallel to the more traditional analyses of analogous speech.

---

92. See Kandiah (1981a).
93. Notable also is the cultural insensitivity and plain inappropriateness of 'international' language-teaching programmes, many of which have been given wide-ranging sponsorship and endorsement at the national level in Sri Lanka today.
94. See Chapter 1, pp. 11ff.
95. Record dust-jackets that contain the texts of songs are not available, except in special cases, and these invariably figure the more 'serious', 'classical', or 'high cultural' varieties.

## NATIVE SPEAKERS OF ENGLISH IN SRI LANKA

Here is a complete segment of discourse (only some names were changed) mainly among 'habitual' speakers of English to whom English functions as a 'first language'. The text is transcribed from a tape of a conversation that took place in Bandarawela, Sri Lanka in January 1988:

... A natural girl, no?

That real, that Kandyan, that *Udarata* talk: *'Appachchi Dannawada? Ammai Appachchii awane ...' amuthu vidiyata kathaakeranne, aney.* Not like us ...

That's the thing! Mr Saleem, whom did you think would win?

I thought that, whose that, Miss Bothal, hehehe, Bothal, hehe.

She was a *bothal* [bottle] alright, uncle! [*Laughter*]. ...

She's pretty, ah, very pretty.

She also a very nice girl, no?

She wore a wig for her *reddai hatte*.

No!

Hairpiece.

*Kohomada eka demme?*

*Sumana!*

*Ai ithing*, Special people only dressed her, no! Mrs Dissanayake *eyata* dress *karanna hitiye.* ... Mrs Dissanayake *hitiya nisaa thama mung aawe neththe.* ...

Mrs. Dissanayake stage *eken baagayak gaththa.* ... *ara keli daala thiyenawane* stage *eke* ... How many times that came down ... Yes, she used to like hit against those things. Those things used to collapse ... those big like screens, men. Those are hung by some rope, no, so it used to balance either that way or this way. She goes and knocks against it or she's fidgeting there

I haven't seen this Mrs Dissanayake, no! ...

Who's that girl, men, at the back? Here, we must put this in the papers, no? ...

It must be splashed in the papers. ...

Shaa. Reporters*la kaawahari genneaganne thibunane?* ...

Ah, Kaushalya came and asked, 'is it going on TV?' And we said, 'Sure! About four full hours broadcast or something!'

Maybe they wanted to inform all their friends and relations to see ... That'll be the day, no?

You must tell, men, Karl, that it's worth putting on

Superb ad for them, no, men?

Yes!

I told Karl, I said, 'your [you're?] getting a big plug on this, no? Can't stop talking about Veytex, Veytex, Veytex.' He said,    'Yeah, I told Feroze, not to over do it or something.'

Did he tell you something like that?

Yeah, something like that. ...

Sumana! Sumano! Sumana! *The hadala genawada?*

This, Lalitha. Ask her to make tea and not coffee, Lalitha, please. *Honda the ekak gahanna kiyanna.*

*The, The.* You like tea, no? ...

So when is your trip coming? Your ride back?

I don't know men. This chap has gone to see some friends. ...

*Enna gahamu Aaju thapara.*

What does *Aaju thapara* mean?

I think it's really a Dutch song, no? ... Cafferingha type.

Aiyyo, that girl was killed, Arjuna.

Yeah.

Which?

Really!

You didn't know?

By a boyfriend. ...

He's an up and coming character. ...

He was always a bit of a half-way house, no?

*Eeka nennang*, Arjuna ...

A child like Naomi, I can't imagine Beatrice putting up with it. Naomi is the one who taught me GRC, no! From January to March she coached me, ah. That was the only thing I knew of GRC. So now she was teaching me, then whilst talking she said, 'mama' and she called Beatrice. Now Beatrice was in the kitchen.

Who's Beatrice, Walles?

Beatrice Jayawardena.

Ah! Beatrice, right.

Naomi's mother. ... Beatrice's husband was there in a big way SAARC, no. Yes, yes, yes ... So, wait will you. So, 'Mama' she calls, and she continued. She waited for the mother, Beatrice didn't come. She took some time in coming. Then finally we were going through this, what is this, er, 'Oedipus' or whatever it is, then Beatrice came: 'Yes, Naomi?' 'Ah, forget it' ... Ah, Leilani. can you imagine dismissing Beatrice with a wave of her hand: 'Ah, Forget it.' [laughter] 'What is this, Naomi, I am cooking, no.

You must know these things no.' [*Laughter*] And Beatrice really ...
Baskets with roses and toffees (?) and grapes. ...
[Another person enters]
   What the hell, men!
   No, machang, these things happen, no.
   Circuit visit. [*Laughter*] ...
   I got stuck with her. Coffee, and don't you know, the old ladies.
If they catch a guy, they want to talk. There's hardly anyone to
talk otherwise for her. ...
   Jobless, no.
   So, you have turned pro, no. Put a good show in Colombo and
that'll show them! ...
   What men, yesterday was my first appearance ... my maiden
over. Now I must get into the circuit. ...
   Yeah. *Piliganna* Miss Veytex Kumari 1988. [*Laughter*]
   I did not say *piliganna*.
   Then what did you say?
   When I introduced the Queen I did not first
   No, no, no. I was there ... Before you said that 'Miss' you said
*piliganna* or something like that.
   Arjuna, I said '*piliganna Veytex Kumari* 1988, Miss'
   No ...
   What about 1988?
   Ah, *asu ata*.
   Yes. ...
   Anyway, hats off you did a good job. ...
   See that, I mean, there itself, Amal, we caught him out no? He was
so keen on going and giving Indunil the gift that he forgot everything
else. We spoiled his fun, no. ... *Meyage jinji* piece *eka*. [*Laughter*] ...
   Only Number Two was not too happy.
   Very upset. Cried and all. ...
   She didn't kiss, no, the winner also.
   And I don't think even the contestants expected that girl to
win. ... They never considered her a competition. Because they
even on the rehearsal day, you know, real hoity-toity ...
   Can you believe, Holdenbottle! The tailor fellow said Miss
Bottle should have won, it seems. [*Laughter*] ...
   This buggar read some different number and another name and
   That's the girl he wants to get in!
   Who, Who did I mention?

Kosala. You like Kosala, no. You want her in somehow. So you read the number

Because you know what happened! I said, contestant number five, Kosala. ... Only then I knew I had made a mistake. My God! [*Laughter*]. *Aiyyo, Aiyyo!*

Bandarawela *hindaa kamak ne*. Otherwise you would have been thrown out.

No ... because you could hear *Ado, yako kiyapan kana ehenna!*

Specially when you were milking it out, they gave you some bloody *maara* comments, no?

No, no. Milking, they were very happy. They were saying ah, number 2, number 3, number 10 and all this.

There was a foreigner who thought number 3 was winning, it seems, ah. He had come and told Feroze, next time I hope the judging is fair!

On which side of you'lls chair?

Anyway, three was not anywhere near it no? I can understand somebody fighting for that twelve or for the five.

Who was three? ...

The one who was an English teacher. ...

*Yamuda?*

*Yamu, yamu.* ...

*Ai? api aapu paara hondaine?*

*Ah,* OK then we'll go that way.

This conversation appears to me to be fairly typical of the informal discourse among equals of the 'younger'[96] generation of Sri Lankan adults who are habitual users of English. The participants were three men and one woman, in their late twenties to early thirties, and, briefly, a tailor whose pronunciation, idiom and extra-linguistic attitudes were the unwitting object of their 'harmless' ridicule. The immediate context of the discussion is the beauty contest of the previous night, organized, compèred and judged by them. The setting is a home, there is a little child in the vicinity and, of course, the ubiquitous servant, Sumana. The time is the late morning and the atmosphere is relaxed. Towards the end of the discourse, Keith, another friend appears and joins in the 'good-hearted' banter. The

---

96. Such a term must, necessarily, be ambiguous. In this context, I would say that the users of the language typified are those who were educated after independence in 1948, or more precisely those who 'came of age' after the Official Language Act of 1956 which significantly increased the élites' interaction with Sinhala and, to a lesser extent, Tamil.

obnoxious sexism and callous classism of the discussion must not be vitiated, particularly since it operates upon the text of language attitudes toward the underclass.

The persistent tag question marker, 'no', has been widely noted in Lankan English but has not been incorporated into the 'educated' Standard by scholars who appear to regard this feature as a non-standard or unacceptable element.[97] The fact that in certain contexts, and for certain users this remains unacceptable cannot become the only criterion for its exclusion, even within the most conservative of linguistic practice. Here is, then, an important influence of non-élite speech upon sections of habitual speakers, since use of 'no', for instance, has increased appreciably in the last two decades or so – so much so that the use of 'no' (or its Sinhala source, *'neda'*) as tag question and as an operator that affirms, asserts or invites assent to the truth of the statement[98] can be seen to be less frequent in 'uneducated' speech,[99] even though it is derived from the direct transference of the question-form from Sinhala into English. This feature, as well as the lexical elements 'machang', 'men', and so on have been relegated to the register of slang. Even if we accept this arbitrary dichotomy between the standard and 'slang', it is in the blurring of the formal and informal distinction that the post-colonial Englishes refuse appropriation in any straightforward way. It is true that these and similar words will not be used universally in any given context, but that is so of most others too. In fact, the tendency to use these 'slang' elements is on the increase, and as a gauge of easy familiarity with the language they outweigh any negativity in terms of their 'inappropriateness' for non-standard users.

This observation appears equally relevant about the following words and phrases taken from this conversation:

Special people *only* dressed her, no!
those big *like* screens, men.
About four full hours broadcast *or something*!
husband was there in a big way
Jobless
Cried and all.

---

97. A notable exception in this as elsewhere is Kandiah. See, for instance, Kandiah (1981b), pp. 92–113.
98. Kandiah, (1981b) pp. 93–4.
99. In the conversation transcribed below, for instance, there are twelve tag questions, whereas in the much shorter transcription of 'native speakers' there were at least eighteen examples.

buggar
some bloody *maara* comments, no?
On which side of *you'll's* chair?

It must be noted, however, that no claim is being made for the exclusivity of these linguistic forms to the Lankan context. The use of 'like' in the second utterance above is widespread in informal conversation among young people in the United States, for instance. 'You'll' is, of course, a common marker of certain southern American dialects, though I am not aware whether it regularly takes the possessive form. Both 'bloody' and 'buggar' are vestiges of the old colonial pukka sahib talk which probably exists in Britain mainly in caricature. In this environment, however, it is a sign of familiarity with the language and hence, among equals, an important marker of fluency as well as class, since it establishes frequent use of English at the informal level. It seems to be this understanding that has prompted the teachers of 'spoken English' in Sri Lanka to emphasize such items of slang which otherwise run counter to received notions of the language as a formal instrument of upward mobility.

There is a sense, then, in which habitual users of English in Sri Lanka are appropriating the hitherto unacceptable registers of 'uneducated' speech in order to appear more accessible to their colleagues and subordinates who do not seem to know the difference between appropriate and inappropriate discourse (as designated by these habitual users, of course) in certain semi-formal contexts. This linguistic 'slumming'[100] is again (mis)read by not-so-habitual users

---

100. Siromi Fernando (1985) identifies crucial changes in Sri Lankan English (SLE) today as a result of a growing insecurity among L1 speakers of the language who are less assured of their privileges than in earlier times.

> Educationally, and in terms of status, the English language weapon he [the SLE user] wields, still gives him an edge over this group [the Sinhala speaking élite he interacts with], but the liberalism of his anglicised cultural background, and the ideological and moral framework he has inherited, ironically enough from this very westernization, often gives him a sense of guilt and embarrassment about this slight edge, and triggers off in him an attempt to identify with the other group.   (p. 6)

> Though I cannot agree with the generalization of the SLE speaker as anything like 'liberal,' there is a sense in which her analysis of this insecurity (as perhaps more forced upon 'him' than Fernando would allow) complements my reading of this interaction as linguistic slumming.

to mean that the easy facility with slang and 'bad language' is, in fact, a criterion that the language has been mastered. There is, in this reading, then, a persistent 'mistaking' of the appropriate register in non-standard discourse which requires further analysis.[101]

An example of this 'mistake'[102] can be read in the ways in which 'spoken English', by far the most popular 'form' of the language for prospective learners, provides lists and instances of the use of slang without any mention of context at all. A leading Sri Lankan book-store referred me to *A Short and Sweet Way to SPOKEN ENGLISH* by Reginold Cooray as the most popular English 'text' book in stock. This primer presents phrases for use in conversation together with Sinhala 'transliterations' and explanations. The emphasis appears to be on colloquialisms and slang in order to establish familiarity with the language. Fluency is equated with the ability to use the language in informal settings and casual conversations among friends, finessing the fact that English, for these new learners, is primarily associated with formal contexts such as employment, education and 'social climbing.'

---

101.　There is, for instance, a way in which what is acceptable as 'reasonable' and 'fair', or simply what can be got away with on either side of this somewhat arbitrary educated/uneducated divide is undergoing drastic change in the current Lankan crisis. An empirical work on the operation of language in crisis situations is long overdue, and has been the focus of my post-doctoral work. At this point, it must suffice to indicate the general area in which once acceptable discourse is no longer tenable and therefore is dissimulated in terms of more 'neutral' formulations.

In today's Lankan context, for example, it cannot be said with impunity that prestige entry-level jobs in the private sector are systematically denied to educated Sinhala speakers in favour of often not-so-educated English speakers on the sole basis of fluency in the language, so now arguments are adduced regarding the 'personality', 'intelligence' and 'versatility' of applicants interviewed. On closely questioning the interviewer, one discovers that fluency (and most important in this respect is 'proper' pronunciation) in English provides the surest yardstick of these 'neutral' categories!

102.　The term 'mistake' domesticates a much more complex phenomenon, and, yet, the quotation marks are only another not-even-so trendy gesture which merely points to a problem in the nomenclature. The whole discursive area of imitation as protest is crucial to an understanding of what takes place here. I can find nothing useful written on the subject, least of all within language studies, and refer the reader to Chapter 2 where I make a stab at theorizing this concept.

Whats the hell!
I got damn wild.
I boiled.
Don't raise my anger.
Don't raise the devil with me.
Don't be a bloody rascal.
Don't be a damn fool.
You are a bloody bastard.
You are a stupid.
You are a hell of a buggar.
You go and hang.
Shut up your mouth.
Hold on your tongue.
How dirty fellow you are.
What is that bloody mocking laugh?

This attempt to display competence in the language through an exclusive concentration on informal registers is counter-productive because there is no concomitant sense of *appropriateness* for the use of these sentences. This problematic is clearly marked in terms of the intended audience and the appropriate register imagined for the task at hand. Cooray is selling his product to the 'uneducated' youth who require touchstones of intimacy with English. In this situation, however, a *category mistake* has been made: the heterogeneity of English use and the power relations it operates within have been obfuscated. In other words, what is acceptable in specific informal contexts among equals has been mistaken for universal usage by Cooray, and therefore, its underclass proponents will receive worse treatment than their peers who are unable to speak English at all. The privileged enclave of the élite is being breached here in what can be seen as a most radical subversion, but which is vitiated by its simulation as a desire for upward mobility by the grace of this very élite.

To return to the discourse in question, however, it is apparent that borrowing and switching from Sinhala to English and vice versa takes place frequently. Chitra Fernando describes some of these uses as 'Singlish'.

Ragged switching *together* with extensive transfer of lexical items from English to Sinhala is so widespread that this particular form of bilingualism has been humorously called 'Singlish'. Singlish, of course, would be considerably 'toned down' so as to appear more clearly either Sinhala or English if the interlocutor(s) were unfamiliar as well as being superior in age and position.    (C. Fernando, 1976, p. 354)

'Singlish', then, is associated with ragged switching and extensive transference of lexical items from English to Sinhala, and 'ragged switching' occurs when the bilingual switches codes even within the confines of a single sentence, showing no demonstrable correlation between code on the one hand and interlocutors on the other.[103]

Yet Chitra Fernando does not actually define 'Singlish' in this essay, perhaps due to the assumption that it would be universally recognized as such whenever it is encountered. This remains problematic, since many of its users do not 'know' they are using 'Singlish', and because this somewhat derogatory (and not merely 'humorous') label is itself a way of recuperating an 'educated' standard Lankan English without any theoretical argument to support the exclusion of the linguistic practices that come under the classification of 'Singlish'. Moreover, it only allows for the *strategic use* of 'Singlish' by educated speakers for a variety of purposes such as comic effect, imitation or even liberal conscience-salving/ self-deprecation.

The notion of 'ragged' switching undermines the complexity of speech situations by over-simplifying the reasons for lexical transference, and by making assumptions on the basis of, say, Group One competence about Groups Two and Three. In some cases the code-switching occurs when the most appropriate and/or economical word or phrase is from Sinhala, in others because the speaker does

---

103.   In describing speakers of Lankan English, Siromi Fernando seems to identify ragged switching, by implication, with 'self-consciousness or compulsion,' in the following passage:

> Ragged code-switching and transference of lexical items across languages is also a feature of their [speakers of Sri Lankan English today – 1985] bilingualism, as noted by Chitra Fernando. Ragged code-switching however is a feature for only some in this group. Such bilinguals code-switch frequently and easily, for purposes of translation, stylistic effects like emphasis, humour, sarcasm or no definable purpose. For others, however, there would be an element of self-consciousness or compulsion in the choice of language, and in code-switching.   (S. Fernando, 1985, p. 7)

not know the equivalent in English. Yet, other cases involve a far more complex process. Take, for instance, the utterance,

She was a *bothal* [bottle] alright, *uncle!*

An analysis of the functioning of the word 'uncle' here will show the complex relationship that Lankan English has with its 'parent form(s)'. I am fortunate to have recourse to Kandiah's brilliant analysis of the nuances of this usage, which must be quoted in its entirety:

> Consider, for example, the word *uncle* as it is used in LE [Lankan English]. [The] LE speaker could use it to convey the meaning it would have to a speaker of Standard British or American English. In addition, without any sense of using a different word, they could use it to refer to or address various male relatives who, in the indigenous languages of Sri Lanka, are given at least three distinct names, depending on the nature of the relationship they have (elder brother, younger brother, 'cousin', and so on) to the parents of the speakers, and on whether the relationship is to their mother or their father. What is important to note is that they use the same term ... differently for all these different kinds of relatives. In doing so, they are *not* invoking the meanings of the native terms, meanings that, in two of these cases, involve relationships that are fairly transparently represented in the terms themselves.
>
> To complicate matters further, all adult males of equal social status tend, for reasons of respect and propriety, to be 'uncles' to children, unless their relationship to them is defined in a specific way that requires some other specific term, like 'sir', to a teacher. Perhaps as a result of this use, the syntactic behaviour of the word in LE is, too, very different from that of its homonym in British or American English, talking [*sic*] pre-nominal and post-nominal qualifiers with a freedom that homonym lacks.
>
> Moreover, trading on this last-mentioned use of the word is a further, marginal use that is very Lankan. In this use, speakers simultaneously express through it different attitudes that do not normally sit together. For instance, in a conversation about an adult male in a position of high authority, a speaker (often an adult male himself) who belongs well outside the spheres in which the subject of his conversation operates may, with slight

humour, reassure his listeners with the words, 'Not to worry. Uncle won't allow anything to go wrong.' This use of the word simultaneously expresses the speaker's sense of his distance from the person referred to, his sense of confidence in that person and, also, a certain sense of affectionate identification with him.

Again, the use of the term 'uncle' by adolescents in addressing adult male strangers, particularly when these adolescents are together in groups, sometimes expresses *both* an overt acknowledgement of the respect that society expects them to give him *as well as* a wry indication, arising out of their sense of their own adulthood, that such deference is not really necessary, and, therefore, to be presented in a humorous light – which invariably leaves the victim wondering how really he is being taken.

Significantly, none of the words used in the local languages for the male relatives who are referred to by the word *uncle* in LE is used in quite these last few ways in those languages, so that these uses of the word derive directly neither from its original British English source nor from the native languages.

The conclusion to be drawn from all this is that the word demands to be described fully and properly as a systematic, synchronic element in its own right. Certainly, it cannot be accounted for in the manner that Kachru (1983, Ch. 6) proposes that the words of IE [Indian English] must be, by assigning '[+] or [–] Indian (semantic) features' to entries – that is by adding to or subtracting from the OVE [Old(er) Varieties of English] homonym. Neither can it be described satisfactorily in terms of a target that was originally aimed at but never achieved owing to 'interference' from the native languages and environment. The reasons are as follows: first, as already mentioned, it can, when necessary, pick out exactly the individuals picked out by the British English homonym, and in exactly the same way; second, it picks out a whole set of other individuals who are not picked out in that way by words in either British English or the indigenous languages; and finally, even where the male relatives it picks out are just those who are picked out by the indigenous language terms, the word does not take on the *meaning* of these terms, and there is just no 'translatability' between it and them.[104]

---

104. Kandiah (1987), pp. 37–9. See also Chapter 5 where Kandiah's conclusion is developed further.

In our example, the use of 'uncle' combines more than one of the motivations/practices listed by Kandiah, and this too in a modified form. From the context, we know that Mr Saleem (the older man whose status as employee [tailor] is inferior to his younger interlocutors) is referred to as 'uncle'. The individual who called Saleem 'uncle' is about twenty-eight (hardly adolescent), and the function of the term here is in part to reassure Saleem that he is going to be treated with respect. This is the 'clue' to Saleem that he can afford to be 'informal' with his employers/'social superiors'. Whereas Saleem may be comforted by the term, to the extent that he does not take offence at this mockery, the others read this as a reinforcement of the parody of Saleem's mispronunciation of the Burgher name, 'Holdenbottle'. He is being enticed into greater mistakes by this familiarity, in much the same way that youngsters will 'butter-up' *ad-hoc* 'uncles' either for favours or amusement. In any case, it becomes quite clear that in order to understand the significance of the lexical item 'uncle' in this utterance, one must be aware of the fundamental ways in which its usage differs from that of Standard British or American English.

In terms of the more conventionally categorized Lankanisms that constitute borrowing from Sinhala/Tamil, the lexical items *reddai hette* [cloth and jacket] and *yamuda* [shall we go?] have clearly been selected by the users since they are the most appropriate/economical choices available, whereas perhaps *maara* [fantastic] represents a case where no precise English attitudinal/tonal equivalent is known to the speaker. None of this is very clear here, though, and my instinct is that detailed analyses such as that undertaken by Kandiah for the usage of 'uncle' will prove the rule rather than the exception.

To continue with Chitra Fernando's analysis of mixing and switching, however, we are told that the

The influence of English on Sinhala is much more dramatic and striking than the influence of Sinhala on English. The tendency to introduce English words into Sinhala is much more marked than the reverse. The bilingual who chooses to talk English rather than Singlish or Sinhala will only introduce those Sinhala words (names of local fauna, flora etc.) that have become an accepted part of the Sri Lankan English lexis. ... While ragged switching is acceptable among younger bilinguals, lexical transfers with the exception of the items cited above, are unidirectional from English to Sinhala or Singlish which is as a linguistic system more Sinhala than English based i.e. Singlish would show a higher proportion of Sinhala phrases and sentences than English ones. In other words Singlish is a sub-variety of Sinhala, not a sub-variety of English. (C. Fernando, 1976, p. 355)

This argument for classifying 'Singlish' within Sinhala is entirely understandable in certain specific situations but remains too much within the confines of an acceptance of traditional linguistic description that this phenomenon itself calls into question. The term 'Singlish' itself points in the opposite direction, both in its use and its derivation.[105] I have yet to come across any reference to 'Singlish' in everyday conversation that did not refer to the 'dilution' of English with Sinhala words and phrases.[106] In addition, whether

---

105. I am grateful to Manique Gunesekera for directing my attention to the fact that 'mixed' English in Singapore is also sometimes called 'Singlish', a phenomenon which supports my contention that English is the base language, and not Sinhala.

106. The absence of an analogous word for Tamilized English in Sri Lanka means that these utterances also get lumped in with examples of 'Singlish'. This phenomenon is, of course, no accident and reflects the hegemony of Sinhala in Sri Lanka, since even non-Sinhala speakers use 'Singlish', and linguists classify all such influences in terms of Sinhala if they are dealing with Sinhala-speakers. Halverston critiques this tendency when he writes:

> Most egregious is Passe's complete neglect of Tamil, which has certainly had as much influence on Ceylon English as Sinhalese and possibly more. In most instances it is impossible to ascertain on linguistic grounds alone whether a Ceylonism comes from Tamil or Sinhalese, but Passe gives the impression, perhaps inadvertently, that Sinhalese is the chief or only source. His treatment of 'put' as a verbal factotum is a case in point. The examples he gives, supposed to be derived from damanava, are actually standard colloquial English. On the other hand, he fails to cite the peculiarly Ceylonese use of the verb as in 'I'll put a short walk up the lane,' 'The dog put a shout to me,' 'Thanks for putting me awake.' This construction is Tamil in origin: Athu saththam pottathu, 'He put a shout' (cf. Avar puththahaththai kiilai pottar, 'He put the book down'). There is apparently no Sinhalese equivalent. (1966, p. 64.)

This raises the most important issue of intention/consciousness in general language-use as well as specifically in code-mixing and borrowing. The influences of Tamil on Sinhala speakers is not only unconscious but must also be consciously denied for extra-linguistic reasons. For instance, Tarzie Vittachi identifies 'putting' in four different cases as 'Singlish' ['putting parts', 'putting a break' and so on in his popular newspaper essays on the subject (contained in Trials of Transition in the Island in the Sun, n.d., pp. 25–42). It may be relevant to mark here that evidence of the contradictions and confusions inherent in the problematic of identifying appropriate examples of Lankanisms is to be found in Halverston's dismissal of Vittachi on the grounds that 'The kind of patois collected by Vittachi is sub-dialectal'. (Halverston, 1966, p. 63)

'Singlish' has more Sinhala phrases and sentences than English ones is arguable empirically: my experience is that, in terms of individual utterances, the relative frequency of Sinhala and English is variable, as is their relative importance within the utterance.

> *Ai ithing*, special people only dressed her, no!
> Mrs Dissanayake *eyata* dress *karanna hitiye*.

In the first of the two contiguous sentences, the Sinhala component is subordinate both in terms of quantity and importance, whereas in the second the reverse is true. Yet, by the token of 'popular recognition', this utterance would be categorized as 'Singlish' by many of Fernando's Group One bilinguals.

At the level of the sentence, which is generally used by Kachru and others in their examples of this phenomenon of code-mixing, it is, therefore, unclear as to which language is primary and which is secondary. In many instances, entire sentences and complete utterances are used, and it is difficult with certainty to identify the primary language of the conversation, and hence to mark the 'borrowings' from a secondary one. Of course, as concerns these habitual English speakers, by and large, the use of Sinhala is associated with talking to the servant Sumana, or with responding to the tailor, Saleem, but there still remain examples such as

> *Ai? api aapu paara hondaine?*

which complicates any easy categorization on the basis of a simple privileging of a monolithic English. The 'odd one out' in this discourse in which the habitual speakers were from the Sinhala, (Tamil-speaking) Muslim and, albeit tokenly, Tamil communities,[107] is the tailor, Saleem, whose speech approximates the so-called non-educated language that I am attempting to validate.

If 'educated' implies the creative and sensitive use of language in this context, if it involves the ability to be understood as well as to be misunderstood, if it incorporates a complex and not necessarily self-conscious identity, then everyone is 'educated'. If, for purposes

---

107. Whose 'ethnic' diversity is covered over by their common class position which resulted in old school ties, childhood friendships and so on. The primacy, broadly speaking, of class at the urban upper level in matters of language affiliation in the Lankan context is apparent here.

of analysis and classification, such 'educated'[108] use must also be systematic and non-idiosyncratic, then this too must be established. It is here that the implicit or explicit denigrations of traditional linguists prove most useful, since they have carefully classified the systemic 'errors' and 'deviations' used in non-standard speech. The subdisciplines of TEFL and TESL/TESOL abound with such analyses, which are invariably combined with a brief description of stereotypic behaviour of the 'usual suspects'. Take for instance, a manual for 'Tutoring Non-Native Speakers of English'[109] produced for the Writing Workshop at the University of Pittsburgh,[110] which identifies and systematizes such mistakes in the writing of foreign students. The disclaimer which appears to pre-empt the charge of

---

108.   It is the view of this writer that 'educated' is a displaced class-marker in this context, but one that, given the complexities of post-coloniality, can be read less and less easily now, even by those who use it as a valid descriptor. See Chapter 1 for an example of such use as it concerns Lankan English.

109.   Undated, anonymous mimeograph of sixteen pages which appears to be incomplete. This document is given to all first-time tutors at the Writing Workshop, or, at any rate, it was part of the standard package in the summer of 1987 when I tutored there. The point, of course, is not that this contains absurd over-simplifications, but that it is symptomatic of the lag in linguistics, and that it provides an example of the worst sort of magnanimous cultural relativism.

110.   This manual is most interesting since it re-presents, in microcosm, vestiges of the orientalist move where, despite the now usual disclaimer, foreigners are always taken as representatives of their monolithic and undifferentiated cultures. This too at a time and in an environment that makes such over-simplifications untenable. Culture studies, it seems, does not affect the text of language teaching except in the most knee-jerk deference to diversity which is played out as inferiority.
       Thus, Arabs are categorized in the following terms:

1.   Arabs tend to speak loudly and the tutee may not confine his voice to the tutorial area.
2.   Tutee may be bold about contradicting the tutor.
3.   'Yes' and 'No' may not be used or interpreted as decisive by the tutee. Tutor should clarify that 'yes' means 'yes' and 'no' means 'no'. [For some reason, this one remains my favourite!]
4.   Silence by the tutee may mean 'yes' or 'no', but generally has a negative connotation.
5.   A tutee who is following an explanation will generally ask confirming questions.

homogenization can allow for real diversity and difference most easily in terms of the non-native speaker's exposure to the US! There follows short lists of 'typical problem areas in writing' for speakers of Arabic, Farsi, Japanese, Spanish (Latin Americans) and Thai, which, if nothing else point to the systematic nature of these 'problems'.

## 'UNEDUCATED' USERS OF LANKAN ENGLISH

In the conversation with the tailor, the habitual speakers make 'innocent' fun of his accent, for instance in his pronunciation and abbreviation of the name 'Holdenbottle' which is articulated as *boothal*, the Sinhala word for bottle. His situation as a social subordinate and 'beneficiary' would certainly have affected the tenor of his input. It would seem important, therefore, to analyse also a conversation among 'equals' who are not habitual or 'educated' speakers of English,[111] even though they are both more educated and less

---

Thais, we are told benevolently, have the following taboos, or 'cultural constraints/characteristics':

A.  **Physical Behaviour**
1.  Don't touch the student or sit too close – particularly, don't touch S[tudent]'s head.
2.  Don't point your feet, or the soles of your feet at S[tudent].
3.  Women S[tudents] may be intimated by large men.

B.  **Verbal Behaviour**
1.  Don't talk loudly or shrilly.
2.  Don't say anything negative about the Thai King or Queen.
3.  Don't get personal unless S initiates the topic.
4.  S may have many 'spelling pronunciations' which cause trouble in understanding him.
111.  It is not unrelated to my argument critiquing the politics of policing 'educated' (localized) standards in the name of presenting the 'best' possible alternative that can stand up to, say, Standard British English, to point out that of the seven participants in the following discussion, three were English teachers at that time, one of whom had received specialized training under US teachers, while the others had passed the General Certificate of Education (Ordinary Level) well. All but one were at university or had graduated (one of the requirements of which is English proficiency).

infrequent users of English than these 'interested' descriptors acknowledge, and who, moreover, *make* the language their own. This discussion took place around the same time as the one involving native speakers, in early 1988 in Kurunegala, Sri Lanka. The participants undertook to tape themselves, and to the extent that they were asked to 'speak in English if possible', the context is not 'natural'. No context is, strictly speaking, 'natural', however, and the focus of this study pertains as much to the actuality of 'uneducated' English speech/writing as to its potential. As theorists in the field who are not merely describing language at work but also policing its domain in varied and complex ways, we must recognize that once such diversity is accepted and progressively legitimized, its potentiality increases exponentially through the dissipation of linguistic insecurity.

*Mokakda* topic*eka?*
Now you can start.
*ebuwada*
Yes.
So what about?
Anything you like.
*machang,* my *katahanda* is very *baraarung,* no? What do you say?
Why do you think so? ...
It's just like a *naaki manussaya!*
Of course, it must be! [*Laughter*]
I made a mistake!?
Why?
Because we can't say 'what about,' we must say 'about what'
Yes, 'about what'.
So I have made a mistake.
Doesn't matter. He needs lots of mistakes from us, that's what he's taping. That is his pield, no? [*Laughter*]
That's why I told it. [*Laughter*]
*Machang,* shall I tell you ... shall I ask several questions from you?
That's the best way, otherwise ...
We'll interview each other.
Don't keep silence, *machang,* tell something, tell.
*Ma[cha]ng,* I can't *ispeak* English. I know little bit.
But if I ask several questions, you must try to answer them. OK?
Yes I'll try, but I can't be sure.

Never mind, never mind. What were you doing in your home last month? You get the idea, no? You understand? ... Try to answer the question, don't worry!

Last week I

Last month.

Last month I ... in home. I can't think about ...

Then, you tell something about the political situation in Sri Lanka. Or you say something about yourself.

Yes. ...

Your native place, your family members, and your hobbies and your political view.

*Machang* my father is – my family is very poor. My father is farmer, mother at home. I have

How many sisters and how many brothers?

Yes I have six brothers and two sisters. My elder brother is carpenter. I am *isstudent* now.

Still studying.

Yes. My sister *istudying* external degree, *eyata igena ganna puluwan*, sorry, not like me. Now I try to, but I can't be sure, to get a job.

OK. Thank you very much. This man is in a very happy mood these days, no? Why?

By seeing your face! ...

Don't ask about that!

Why?

How many times did you go to the Lovers' Lane? [*laughter*]

Go and ask

From whom?

Anybody!

We are asking from you, no *machang*.

I don't know.

You should know. You can't remember the times ...?

Aren't you happy these days?

No.

Why?

Because of this situation, [What?] this wonderful situation. Because of the country's political situation. I'm worried about it.

But you don't do anything.

What can you do?

You are running away from all those problems.

I don't like to involved. I don't know how to believe all those problems.

But all those problems have been effective for your future life, no?
Obviously.

So why don't you struggle to

Because they won't listen to me, sometimes they will kill me,
that's why I am silence.

But, if they are wrong, *machang*, if the situation, if the things
going on campus are wrong ...

Have you heard the statement: political gets you nowhere but
into jail or into cemetery, into the cemetery ...

No, *machang*, you have to neglect all those death threats and
such and such things because we should continue our lives in the
campus, no?

We should organize.

Yes.

You should organize. ...

But, I can't do that lonely.

We know that *machang*. Ninety percent in the campus students
are opposing to those ideas, no?

But they are full silence.

Yes, you should do something.

We should overcome all the barriers.

I don't know how can I do that.

You must speak with people – those who are opposed to the situation, opposed to the strikes and exam boycotts and such and such.
No, no, you have to get organized.

I know that last month some fourth year girls, they have written petition.

For what?

Because they are going to sit for the exams, so the JVP threatened
to 'don't do that. If you are doing that we'll kill you.'

So they have given up?

Yes. Because of that situation they were stopped.

Completely?

Yes.

So now it's OK. They didn't present that petition for the
administration, so nothing ... There is no guidance for that.

Why is the medical school is on strike now?

Yes. They're against private medical school. ...

[name], I think that all the medical students are very selfish persons
because they are not involving with the others' problems which are
continuing in the campus. That's why we have left the campus also.

Mmm.

You know?

Yes, already they have gone to their homes. But if they are active students, they should want to continue their struggle.

They have left the campus, no? ...

Other thing is medical students think they are the greatest, they are the students of the greatest faculty and they think medical faculty is the most important faculty, and other faculties are inferior. ... The medical students think that arts faculty and other faculties are inferior.

That's why they are trying to separate from others, no?

Yes. ...

OK shall we talk anything else?

We'll give the chance to S [name].

K [name], is he sleeping?

S [name, abbreviation of K], tell something.

S [abbreviated name], K [name], tell something, *machang*.

*Mama* support *ekata hitiye ne machang*. ...

We are not going to value support.

Not for us, *machang*, for Arjuna.

Now Arjuna also know you are also now in this place, therefore you must speak.

It is not a rag, *neda?*

Show your knowledge. ...

*Mata mokowathma kiyanna barinang mokadda karanne?* [*laughter*]

Speak something that you can speak. ...

*Ithin meeka ne ... mata kadda bae bung!* [*Kadda* – slang for sword in Sinhala which in turn is slang for English]

What is your name?

He can support others.

Yes. ... How old are you?

Twenty-six years old, I am.

What is your name, *machang*?

K [name].

So, how many children have you got? [Laughter] Are you married?

No. *eka ahanna deyak da?*

When are you going to marry? You're about to marry?

*Ehema prashna ahanna epa machang. Arjuna oova dena ganna one ne ehema.* ...

[name] What did Arjuna tell about Vijaya Kumaranatunga's assassination? What is his opinion?

Opinion?

Yes.

As if you don't know his opinion!

I don't know.

*Machang*, you know the general opinion that he is rejecting all those political murders, no?

What about this agreement that JR ... they have made.

I think that he is accepting for certain positions for a certain extent. He is not in accordance with Mahajana Party politics, I think.

What about Samajavadi?

USA?

Yes, United Socialist Alliance.

That's funny, no? USA.

I don't know, I didn't ask, *machang* until this time.

Not only Arjuna, *machang*, also we can agree with them for a certain extent, no?

Yes.

With whom?

USA.

Sometimes, if they contest for the Presidential Election, sometimes, I'll help, not help, I will give my vote.

As a alternative?

As a alternative. I'm still considering about that, I'm not made up my mind yet. ...

You can read, I have brought the paper, *prathipaththi prakashanaya*, policy paper.

Who else you can vote? ...

So you think that party is correct?

Not completely. I can agree with them for a certain extent. ...

You are asking me to vote for the UNP or SLFP?

No.

Then?

You must prevent.

From voting?

Yes.

What bullshit, *machang*!

Then you are going to support the UNP.

How?

If you are not using your vote against them. Who will gain from that?

So that Mahajana Party, they will come to power.

Yes ... I think it is better than SLFP, no? At this moment, *machang*, we have no complete alternative.

Why, the JVP?

I have completely given up supporting the JVP. Actually, I am worried at this moment that I was a JVPer. I am worried *eka gena* ... because I have also contributed to the built that party in the past, I am worried about that. ...

Since when are you worrying about that?

Mmm. Since near past, after they have accelerated their political murders. Even before that I was criticising for certain positions, but about some events that they did, yes we were stimulated by those incidents, but I feel that even that is wrong.

But, sometime, if they are coming to power, they will stop their murders. [Laughter]

How can they come to power, without people? ...

Clearly some, if not all, of these discussants belong to Fernando's Group Three: the introduction of vowels into consonantal clusters that begin with /s/ such as *istudent* and *istudying* are fundamental in this evaluation, as is the pronunciation of 'field' as *peeled*. The discussion itself, which lasted for over one hour ranges, from the playful and personal to the serious political analyses that must form a major component of the everyday life of young people in Sri Lanka today. In short, it runs the gamut of issues, and there is no striking limitation or inadequacy posed by the choice of the medium. In terms of style, there is a curious mix of what may appear to be archaisms and formalisms in the context of Standard English, particularly when more familiar and 'simpler' alternatives exist (that is, *several* questions, *native place, assassination, stimulated* and *accordance*), and 'slang' such as *machang* and bullshit.

The discourse contains many structures that have been described as common Lankan English errors by Passe,[112] but which have been denied validity in more recent scholarship. In this category would be expressions that Passe categorizes as 'Translation Error'[113] since

---

112.   See H. A. Passe (1948) p. 361 onwards.
113.   I am in complete agreement with Kandiah's analysis of the inadequacy of the notion of translation for the purpose of accounting for all (or most) 'non-standard' expressions of Lankan English (Cf Kandiah, 1981b, p. 94), but find Passe's terminology useful in this limited context.

they are derived from direct translation of the Sinhala word or idiom, such as

Siri, *tell* something.
I can agree with them *for* a certain extent.
*Sometimes*, if they contest *for* the Presidential Election.
Shall I ask several questions *from* you?
Go and ask.
From whom?

In each of these cases, the word choice is dependent on the Sinhala equivalent: for instance, Sinhala makes no distinction between 'tell' and 'say', both of which translate to *kiyanna* (cf. Passe, 1948, p. 365).

Characteristic of this conversation, and, by implication, of spoken contexts involving similar categories of 'uneducated' speakers of English, is the frequent use of 'ungrammatical' structures, unacceptable to native speakers of 'educated Lankan English',[114] which, however, do not as a rule interfere with the communication of meaning. Thus, utterances such as

My father is farmer, mother at home.
Don't keep silence, *machang*, tell something, tell.
I don't like to involved.
We are asking from you.
But, I can't do that lonely.
But they are full silence.
I don't know how can I do that.

---

114. Kandiah writes, for instance, that

> the full range of errors that learners of the language, including those who have no opportunities for 'picking it up' as a first language, would make; and a host of examples of the following kind, which, although they may be produced even by some of the very people who use English as a first language in certain spheres of their lives, and, moreover, apparently at times manifest certain operations and processes whose different use elsewhere makes them acceptable within the system, are rejected out of hand by those habitual users of Lankan English whose usage, for non-linguistic reasons admittedly, determine the Lankan standard. (ibid., p. 108)

It would seem that this 'determination' must be worked against, or, more precisely, the workings against it in the form of these counter-hegemonic (mis)uses must be recognized and valorized.

Why is the medical school is on strike now?

*Machang*, you know the general opinion that he is rejecting all those political murders, no?

Sometimes, if they contest for the Presidential Election, sometimes, I'll help ...

I'm still considering about that, I'm not made up my mind yet.

How many times did you go to the Lover's Lane?

Since when are you worrying about that?

As a alternative?

The absence of the article 'a' in the first example, and the presence of 'the' in the twelfth exemplify a very common 'problem' associated with 'misuse' by language learners in Sri Lanka, as well as elsewhere. Kachru writes that 'the deviant use of such function words as definite and indefinite articles is shared by several non-native Englishes' (p. 51).

## THEORETICAL FRONTIERS: BORROWING/SWITCHING/ TRASHING CODES

Perhaps the most important theoretical work to date using the 'new varieties' of English to explain general linguistic phenomena is Kandiah's use of 'syntactic deletion' in Lankan English speech to better understand this occurrence which has been variously described as 'suppression', 'ellipsis', and 'truncation'.[115] Here, Kandiah is able to move beyond the defensive special-case rhetoric to the challenging of dominant linguistic paradigms through a careful analysis of the specific deletions found acceptable by 'educated users of Lankan English'. I have pointed to the general theoretical force of reconsidering language norms through so-called nonstandard English in Chapters 1 and 2, and this specific proof of its validity points to the vast areas of study that such a dehegemonizing of theory itself will open up. In terms of Kandiah's argument itself, the text of 'uneducated' Lankan English transcribed

---

115.  See Kandiah, 'On so-called Syntactic Deletion in Lankan English Speech: Learning from a New Variety of English', unpublished paper delivered at South Asian English Conference in Islamabad, Pakistan (January 1989).

above provides us with at least one example of syntactic deletion as an 'incomplete' sentence:

Because of that situation they were stopped.

in which case the sentence was probably interpreted as if it were something like,

Because of that situation, they were stopped from protesting by the JVP.

It seems clear, moreover, that Kachru's analysis of code-switching and mixing is inadequate to describe the Lankan English users' practice. However, before we decide that new theoretical paradigms are required to understand and explain this phenomenon, we need to examine Gumperz's seminal work in this area as well. In *Discourse Strategies*, Gumperz describes 'metaphorical code-switching', which appears similar to our examples.

The conversational switching described here clearly differs both linguistically and socially from what has been characterized as diglossia in the sociolinguistic literature on bilingualism (Ferguson, 1964). In diglossia, code alternation is largely of the situational type (Blom & Gumperz, 1972) Distinct varieties are employed in certain settings (such as home, school, work) that are associated with separate, bounded kinds of activities (public speaking, formal negotiations, special ceremonials, verbal games etc.) or spoken with different categories of speakers (friends, family members, strangers, social inferiors, government officials etc.) Although speakers in diglossia [*sic*] situations must know more than one grammatical system to carry on their daily affairs, only one code is employed at any one time. ...

In conversational code switching ... where the items in question form part of the same minimal speech act, and message elements are tied by syntactic and semantic relations equivalent to those that join passages in a single language, the relationship of language usage to social context is much more complex. While linguists, concerned with grammatical description as such, see the code alternation as highly salient, participants immersed in the interaction itself are often quite unaware which code is used at any one time. Their main concern is with the communicative effect of what they are saying. Selection among linguistic alternates is automatic, not readily subject to conscious recall. The social norms or rules which govern language usage here, at first glance at least, seem to function like grammatical rules. They form part of the underlying knowledge which speakers use to convey meaning. Rather than claiming that speakers use language in response to a fixed, predetermined set of prescriptions, it seems more reasonable to assume that they build on their own and their audience's abstract understanding of situational norms, to communicate metaphoric information about how they intend their words to be understood (Gumperz & Hernandez-Chavez, 1971; Blom & Gumperz, 1972).   (Gumperz, 1982, pp. 60–1)

For Gumperz, code switching can be distinguished from loan word usage and borrowing because they 'can be defined as the introduction of single words or short, frozen, idiomatic phrases from one variety into the other. The items in question are incorporated into the grammatical system of the borrowing language' (p. 66). On the other hand, code switching 'relies on the meaningful juxtaposition of what speakers must consciously or subconsciously process as strings formed according to the internal rules of *two distinct grammatical systems*' (p. 66).

Thus, code-switching comprises two standard strings of at least dialectal difference whose juxtaposition is what creates the nonstandard utterance. Some of our examples do not conform to this description, as can be seen from the following:

> My sister *isstudying* external degree, *eyata igena ganna puluwan*, sorry, not like me.
> *Ai ithing*, special people only dressed her, no!

It must be noted that both these examples come from 'uneducated' speakers of English, and their relative position on the cline is reflected by the level of acceptability of the English strings in these utterances. By and large, however, it can be seen that the second group of speakers did not code-switch as often as the first, and that code-switching in the former discourse generally conformed to Gumperz's paradigm.

What code-switching cannot explain is the use of *structures* from one language in utterances made in the other language. When these are systematic and repetitive they are described as 'interference errors' but I suggest that this is a simplistic rationalization, and one that is politically suspect. For Gumperz, for instance,

> Whereas borrowing is a word and clause level phenomenon, code switching is ultimately a matter of conversational interpretation, so that the relevant inferential processes are strongly affected by contextual and social presuppositions. This raises a further problem since, as our discussion to language usage suggests, norms of appropriateness with respect to both borrowings and code switching vary greatly.     (p. 68)

The problem arises when these norms of appropriateness are somehow held to be universal for every subgroup of communicators, who, moreover, are not described in any useful way. We are told, for instance, that 'Depending on such factors as region of origin, local residence, social class and occupational niche, each communicating subgroup tends to establish its own conventions with respect to both borrowing and code switching' (p. 68). Of the 'factors' identified clearly not all are going to be the same for everyone in any but the most artificially designated communicating subgroups. This means that the factors themselves operate in a hierarchy of sorts, and that there is a dynamic of struggle (which may not appear as such, of course) taking place within these so-called communicating subgroups. In addition, the relationship between these subgroups and the larger, hegemonic groups also determines the nature of the linguistic conventions in place. Gumperz is, therefore, correct in saying that 'To judge a bilingual by any *a priori* standards of grammaticality can therefore hardly be satisfactory.' He does, however, bring back grammaticality as the test of acceptability in the very next sentence:

> The best that can be done is to establish a range of interpretable alternatives or communicative options and thus to distinguish between meaningful discourse and errors due to lack of grammatical knowledge. Rules of productive control within such a range of options are always context bound so that generalization becomes difficult. Acceptable usage is learned through constant practice by living in a group and varies just as control of lexicon and style varies in monolingual groups.     (pp. 68–9)

There are two main objections to this thesis, both of which are dramatized in the discourses analysed above. First, the existence of 'interpretable alternatives or communicative options' does not presuppose so-called grammaticality. That is to say that 'errors due to lack of grammatical knowledge' can and do also provide 'meaningful discourse'. Nor is it the case that grammatically correct utterances always produce meaningful discourse. The absence of shared meaning in certain cases may have little to do with grammar as such. Second, the notions that 'acceptable usage' is acceptable throughout a group, and that all that is required to learn acceptable usage is to live in that group, is to efface both conflict and resistance in/through language. These idyllic communities are symptomatic of linguistic wish-fulfilment, and have little basis in empirical fact. Here is a typical example of the liberal linguist's inability to push beyond surface explanations which tends, therefore, to valorize the status quo:

On further questioning, participants referred to their own metaphorical switching [between Standard Norwegian and a local North Norwegian dialect] as lapses of attention, or failures to live up to village norms, and 'promised' that only the village dialect would be used in subsequent discussion sessions. Yet tape recordings of these later sessions showed no significant decrease in the amount of switching. ... In interview sessions where conversational code switching is discussed, speakers tend to express widely differing attitudes. Some characterize it as an extreme form of language mixing or linguistic borrowing attributable to lack of education, bad manners or improper control of the two grammars. Others see it as a legitimate style of informal talk.   (Gumperz, 1982, p. 62)

The crucial factors are not so much the perceptions of the speakers as the reasons for them. The alibi of descriptive neutrality only serves here to obfuscate power relations that militate against a sense of security in mixing/switching. Notions of linguistic purity should not be considered in isolation, nor are speakers' perceptions to be valorized simply because they are valid as perceptions. Not only are there issues of ideological interpellation and reproduction, these perceptions are also firmly rooted within the present reality. It is no accident that in none of these 'neutral' interview sessions, which purport to get at the unmediated language attitudes, is a question asked about attitudes in the ideal situation. In other words, would those who felt that code-switching was a failing in today's context have felt that it would be so in the best of all possible worlds as well? In addition, the interview sessions are presented as so neutral as to be class/gender/race/region/age/education blind, so that we do not know what kinds of speakers felt positive towards code switching and what types felt negative. If there was no correlation between any of these 'demographic' variables and language attitudes, then this is important too. As it is, however, these neutral descriptions are worse than useless since they are misleading. Take, for example, this: 'In Texas and throughout the American [sic] South West, where code switching is common among Mexican Americans, the derogative term "Tex-Mex" is widely used' (ibid.). Surely, the crucial questions are, used by whom, and with what motivation? There is a subtle shift from the Norwegian case of self-evaluation of code switching to the 'classed' and 'raced' derogation of someone else's use of it here, and it would not be too much to identify such a move as symptomatic of the homogenizing tendency in linguistic attitudinal studies.

Let us return to our array of non-standard usage now in order to pick up other 'infelicities' and marginalities which may produce more theoretical problems. The transcribed conversation contains an example of code-mixing that would be unacceptable to educated speakers, and would, therefore, be classified as 'odd-mixing':

*Machang*, my *katahanda* is very *baraarum*, no? [Friend, my voice (mouth-sound) is very gruff, no?]

Yet, on reflection, such utterances appear to break new ground in creatively combining Sinhala and English, and, moreover, do so without violating the spirit of either language. I cite this example as one of many in which the 'uneducated' user of English displays greater freedom of movement in and out of English.

Another productive feature of 'uneducated' speech (and writing) is its 'travestying' of accepted meanings and appropriate connotations of English words and phrases. In a casual 'mixed' conversation with a tour guide, the following English lexical items were used in 'innovative' ways:

send, pit [fit] *vei*, *hari* p[f]rendly, guest*la*, satificat [certificate], madical [medical certificate], joint *venna*, ponsor [sponsor], contac[t], palo [follow], sure, pull set [full(y) set?], isstart, salu[te], pull kit [full kit?], towerlers [travellers'] cheque.

In a brief dialogue among rural youth in the remote village of Madithiyagolla, Sri Lanka, where the participants were unaware of being taped, and where there was no outsider present, the following English code-mixings were recorded:

Dope *daala*, Bajaar (?) *eka*, caterpill*an*, p[f]ull try, support, master, gemper (damper?) *eka*, supervisor, Good Morning Sir!, cigarette, tv *eka*, fit *ekak nae* and *konthraath* (from contract).

In this latter case, the conversation was clearly in Sinhala, and therefore it can be argued that these 'borrowings' do nothing for the English language in Sri Lanka, though they undoubtedly enrich Sinhala speech.[116] I have evidence, however, that lexical items thus used in Sinhala are 'brought back' into English with shifts in connotation and reference. Many users first hear the word in question in its Sinhala setting and only then transfer it to English. Let us consider as an example the English word 'diet', which appeared in colloquial Sinhala around two decades or so ago as 'dite.' In the Sinhala usage 'dite' referred to the hearty intake of food, as in the frequently heard expression,

*Machang, mama ada maara dite ekak demma!*
[Friend (literally, brother-in-law), I had (put) a great meal]

The English use in Sri Lanka was predominantly in the sense of reducing the amount of food eaten, as in 'dieting', which was absent in the transplanted word. This word which had a restricted usage in English before, now appears to have a somewhat wider application both in sense and frequency, though its currency in Sinhala remains unchanged. Much work needs to be done to identify similar occurrences in order to theorize on the repercussions of 'borrowing' and 'mixing' upon the source language itself, since linguists have con-

---

116. The vast majority of Sinhala scholars and linguists will not agree with formulation, seeing this phenomenon as a dilution of Sinhala. As a result, when new words are brought into Sinhala by official and academic sanction, they are invariably neologisms of Sanskrit derivation that heighten the spoken/written diglossia.

centrated on the consequences of borrowing only on recipient languages. Such an analysis will seek to understand 'borrowing' neither as anomalous nor as unidirectional, with the dynamic of borrowing inflecting, albeit non-schematically, all the languages/dialects involved in its process.

An important and relatively unexplored theoretical arena that the 'uneducated' 'non-standard' (post)colonial Englishes can help broaden is the concept of *antilanguages*, after Halliday.[117] Notions of antilanguages, which have been pursued mainly as 'pathologies' among criminals/lumpens and so on, can be rethought in the light of much more widespread resistance to normativity, in which the 'pathology' is the (standard) 'language' in terms of its origins and impositions. From the (post)colonial "other" Englishes can be derived the ubiquity (not, as is current with work on antilanguages, their localization and specificity), flexibility and range of antilanguages, as well the nexus between antilanguages and society (not antisociety as Halliday would have it). This work, which ultimately ties in to the over-arching project of resistance/subversion in/through language, has been long overdue in linguistics.

It may, therefore, be therapeutic to end where we began, with the problematizing of the authority of the habitual speaker, by mischievously reborrowing the word 'habitual' from its non-standard Lankan English currency. Of all the nearly fifty 'Singlish' terms identified by Vittachi, 'hapichole' ('The Singlish version of "habitual" Means: good-for-nothing, vagabond, parasite, hanger-on – *Trials of Transition*, p. 34), was one of the only two or three that habitual speakers of English had no clue to at all! Yet, all the Sinhala speakers I interviewed knew or at least had heard of the word before, even those who did not know what 'habitual' meant in Standard English! The habitual speaker so valorized in Lankan linguistics may yet live to regret his/her habit if 'hapichole' has its day. Thus, in yet another way, a cherished linguistic paradigm of 'good' authority, the habitual speaker, may be stigmatized as being in 'bad faith' like the *habichole karaya*, vindicating our theoretical analysis, by the travestying of the 'original/parent' referent by its 'derivative/parasite', and providing us with a powerful metonym for the de-hegemonization of language standards.

---

117.   See M. A. K. Halliday (1978) pp. 164–82.

# 4

# Non-Standard Lankan English Writing: New Models and Old Modalities

Non-standard forms of writing in print are less prolific and less easily accessible than spoken varieties. In addition, when non-standard structures do appear in writing, wittingly or not, they often represent speech situations, creating a sense that these are merely imitations of non-standard conversation captured on the page. This fact, which has perhaps more to do with the politics of publication and the gatekeeping role played by editors and academics than with self-conscious choices made by individual writers, has led many scholars to make too sharp a distinction between these two functions.[118] Non-standard writing, when recognized,[119] is all too easily reduced to 'ignorance' and 'error' that must be corrected/avoided. Thus, much of the evidence for non-standard writing that is non-idiosyncratic remains outside the archive. When examples are found in print, they are invariably unselfconscious in that the writers are not aware that the rules of grammar and good taste have been broken. In this sense, therefore, in most cases, these examples are, in fact, 'errors' that are made from 'ignorance'. Hence, the impossibility of quickly dismissing the derogations of conventional

---

118. See, for instance, Chapter 1 where I discuss Cowley's position legitimizing Standard Written English on the basis of an absence of serious alternatives.

119. There is an urgent need for an empirical study that ties the recognition of certain non-standard forms of English with the licence to derogate/stigmatize the writer. This phenomenon of *hyper-perceiving* certain 'errors' and *legitimizing* others, a practice that appears to cut across diverse positions of authority – whether by teachers, (prospective) employers or government officials – functions as a means of policing the language, particularly since, anecdotally at least, it appears that the hyper-perceived 'errors' are race-marked and class-marked.

linguistics which relegates these to the realm of the 'unacceptable'. To treat these 'errors' seriously, then, what is required is a overhauling of the very theoretical framework within which 'acceptability' and standardization itself takes place.[120]

I have argued elsewhere in this book, however, that this absence of 'intention', narrowly defined, cannot militate against the existence of these alternate forms of writing, and, in fact, that this difference (from, say, the 'authentic' use of the non-standard in certain creative contexts, framed within the 'well-written', that is standard, narrative) is a strength since it cannot be quickly appropriated within an enhanced standard.

A striking example of such non-standard writing comes from a teacher of English whose textbook on 'Spoken English' proved to be one of the most popular of its kind in Sri Lanka.[121]

---

120. The basis for linguistic acceptability has been, for those 'whose heart is in the right place' at least, non-idiosyncratic intelligibility and frequency of use; in short, general social acceptance. In this way, by appearing merely to record whether a particular society considers an utterance acceptable/sensible, after the fact, the linguist is provided with an alibi against taking sides, against making value-judgements about the utterance in question. However, to legitimize such a claim of good faith, we need to consider some assumptions inherent here. The first and most difficult to swallow is the homogenizing of 'society' in this formulation, making it appear cohesive and comprised of members whose self-interest/group interest is identical for everyone. Not only is this manifestly not the case in all of the societies that we know, it is also true that 'social acceptance' is not even determined by the majority of users of a language. The concept of social acceptance is, therefore, a legitimization of specific, though complex, classed/raced/gendered/regioned interests through making these interests neutral ones. Once these 'norms' are enforced, however, both by 'society' (read élites) and by the educational apparatus, many others subscribe to them for specific reasons such as upward mobility as well as through the ideological consensus created by linguistic legitimizations which, in a circular argument, are predicated on 'social acceptance'.

      This means that linguists who argue from already existent social norms of language practice without paying sufficient attention to the nature of conflict within these practices as well the nature of the 'resolution' of these conflicts, are in turn reproducing and legitimizing these normative practices, thereby cementing the status quo.

121. See Chapter 3, for an analysis of this book. I have emphasized the main 'errors' to be found in this passage. Unless otherwise stated, I shall follow this practice of highlighting the most obvious non-standard usages in the texts cited simply to facilitate my discussion of these elements.

Although *amidst of* financial difficulties, the first edition of this booklet was published in 1981. Two thousand copies of the *books* were sold within *a* short period of six months. When considering the difficulties of the readers due to *high printing cost* it can be regarded as a considerable achievement; in a society where the trend of *reading rapidly disappearing*. But owing to financial difficulties *from the first edition I was compelled to idle another three years to publish another edition with necessary amendments.*

Being experienced as a teacher to train the students from every corner of the country for ten years I have been compelled to publish this book specially for the benefit of the rural students, who face immense difficulties due to their inability to speak in English.

*A great enthusiasm of learning English has been arisen in spite of age, with the implemantation of liberalised economic policies.* Those who only *knows* to use their mother tongue feel inferior and *compelled* to play a subordinate role in the society while *possesing* high educational qualifications.

There is *no any exaggeration* to say an *intolerence* dominates in the minds of scholars and clerical employees. So the students strive hard to achieve a sound knowledge of English as a way of upgrading the quality of life year by year. Hundreds of Institutions and teachers emerge as mushrooms to meet the demands of the students. But it is a matter *to* regret that the facilities, and opportunities are not adequate at all to make the dreams of the students a reality.

*I am no under illusion* that I myself or this booklet is perfect to serve the present purpose, *hundred per cent*. In Sri Lanka *we have been experiencing a new trend*. A new approach is necessary. The time has come to say *good bye to out dated* methods of teaching thousands of grammatical items, and their exceptions to frighten the students. Our *motive* should be 'Learn to use Use to learn'. As a consequence of teaching a lot of grammatical items without showing avenues to use them in *day today* purposes, *the students have become as dumbs who swallowed a bitter decoction.*

We are in a transitional period between the old method of teaching to get through *from examinations and practical purpose of speaking*. Every English teacher *should be dedicated to find out* ways and means to make the students speak. When I wrote this book *always i kept in my mind* the beginners. *I started from very simple things to breed self confidence and improved little by little to enable the*

*students to understand the expansion of the sentence. Deliberately repe-
tition* has been used to improve the *students* memory.

*Success* of this publication is not an individual triumph of mine
but a tribute to all associates including my students. I owe a special word of thanks to Amal Shantha Munindradasa for his beau-
tiful *couer* page and *also* Sathsara Printers for their excellent job.
Your criticism is highly appreciated.

Reginald Cooray[122]

I have emphasized the more glaring non-standard usages contained
in this passage, and even if one were to allow for the fact that typesetting and editing may have been responsible for some of the
'problems', this text remains remarkable in the extent and variety of
its 'deviations'. Yet for all its 'ignorance' the linguistic sentiments
expressed by Cooray seem more enlightened than that of 'scholars'
such as Professor D. C. R. A. Goonetilleke whose 'intolerance' is
contextualized in Chapter 5 of this text.[123]

Many of the difficulties that the 'educated' user of English in Sri
Lanka would have with this writer are fairly typical: questions of
agreement, (mis)use of articles, prepositions, spelling and punctua-
tion. In addition, Cooray uses 'big words' wherever possible, prefer-
ring the archaic or formal expression to the more familiar one, as in
the use of 'decoction' instead of, say, 'pill'. This is surely a device to
display his command of the language, and just as surely reflects an
insecurity as to his credibility among his readers. At this level, one
of the proofs of fluency in English is precisely the ability to use polysyllabic and uncommon words, to be able to complicate simple
ideas. The structures are very formal and some of the sentences
awkward because they are too long, and this is not accidental. There
is a great deal of embellishment and even redundancy as in,
'another edition with necessary amendments' or 'specially for the
benefit of the rural students', though these are not 'ungrammatical'
or non-standard utterances.

In fact, the pressures placed upon this writer to produce the 'educated' variety of English have resulted in much less satisfactory
utterances, though grammatical in the narrow sense, than those that

---

122.   *A Short and Sweet Way to Spoken English*, 3rd edn, 1986, preface.
123.   Please see p. 175 *passim*.

are clearly unacceptable in élite Lankan usage. The use of 'no any' to negate the adjective 'any', which provokes laughter in educated circles in Sri Lanka today, is both logical and concise. At the same time, the image of institutions and teachers 'emerging as mushrooms' to meet student demands is a grammatical though inappropriate use of the commonplace metaphoric descriptor, 'mushrooming', which would be acceptable only in terms of the sudden appearance and growth of the institutions, the tuition classes. The 'unacceptable' sentence, 'Those who only knows to use their mother tongue feel inferior and compelled to play a subordinate role in the society while possesing high educational qualifications', admirably captures the predicament facing the Sri Lankan learner of English. Educated speakers would prefer 'feel inferior and *are* compelled', in addition to the plural verb 'know' in the first line. However, if one were to give this 'error' a generous reading, as one might be prone to in a creative context, one can argue that the non-reiteration of the verb ('are') serves to jam the two actions together in a disharmonious way. Thus, the feeling of inferiority and the compulsion to play a subordinate role become connected as part of the same complex phenomenon, and not as two distinct/separable reactions. There is a sense in which these feelings of 'inferiority' are also 'compelled' upon this group of Sri Lankans by the very socio-economic factors that ensure them a 'subordinate role'. I am aware that too much can be made of such analyses, but I think that examples such as this abound, in which the 'mistake' is more appropriate than the 'corrected' form of the sentence in order to convey the tensions and conflicts of the context within which the 'mistake' was generated.

Cooray's predicament, then, is not so much his use of non-standard structures, but his desire to show off how much of the language he does know. In sharp contrast to his excessively formal style is the rest of his book, which attempts to teach informal speech patterns and vocabulary to students.[124] Here again, Cooray's most unfortunate interventions have been when formal structures have displaced semantic considerations: such as the utterances, 'May I know the

---

124. See pp. 97ff of this text where I identify some of his examples as inappropriately informal for the linguistic and extra-linguistic tasks for which they are conceived.

queue'[125] and 'May I know the temple', which are presented as well-mannered forms whose politeness has overridden their lack of use/ sense to the point to which even their function as questions is negated by the absence of question-markers. The crux, then, is to show how polite one is, to display this ability to be polite, and not to obtain any information!

Cooray's (mis)recognition of the formal/informal diglossia in which he signals his knowledge through 'the formal', but wants his students to display fluency through 'the informal', can be read against the manifestation of its direct opposite on another level[126] which is excessively preoccupied with mimicking *generic examples* of the accepted standard. The *Sri Lanka News* of 14 December, 1988 contained the following advertisement for Malinga H. Gunaratna's *For a Sovereign State* published by Sarvodaya, the much acclaimed grassroots development organization which is said to incorporate Gandhian principles:

The thrilling sensational but true story of Sri Lanka's separatist war unfolding a vivid picture of events, facts and information

---

125. This example can serve to illustrate the criteria of acceptability for the 'new' use (including teaching) of Lankan English (or any other language, for that matter) advocated in this book,

'May I know the queue?' is unacceptable (without a supporting context, at any rate) because it is ambiguous. Is the speaker asking for the location of the queue or for the reason for the queue? Contrast the sentence above with 'May I know where is the queue?' or 'May I know what for is the queue?' neither of which are in Standard form, but both of which are semantically clear and therefore 'correct'.

I am suggesting that the new sets of rules should privilege the semantic, and, of course, this would mean that some syntactic rules would follow. The rules, however, can then be explained (thereby facilitating both acquisition by children and learning by adults) and even contested since they would not be arbitrary structural ones. This is a crucial difference between the rules I wish to valorize and those that are currently in place. It is not the case, then, that non-standard Lankan English can have no rules, nor that these rules must be absurdly flexible.

126. The difference is clearly marked in terms of the intended audience and the appropriate register imagined for the task at hand. In the first case, Cooray is selling his product to the 'uneducated' youth who require touchstones of intimacy with English, whereas the second example targets the 'educated' Lankan residing abroad who is to be wooed through an advertisement of the 'established' kind.

never before made available. It is the story of man, land and water, of power lust, espionage, betrayal and intrigue; a story every Sri Lankan should know.

This description is clearly inappropriate to the content of the book, and even more so to the objectives of the organization that published it. It is written in Standard English. The message has been sensationalized, and clichés such as 'thrilling sensational but true', have been borrowed from the genre of adventure stories and popular movies. The attempt to approximate the received standard, both in form and content, has here resulted in a grotesque parody which cannot have been intended by the user. The desire here was to adhere to a (mis)perceived norm which was so alien to these users that questions of appropriateness or sensitivity did not surface: it seems that this became purely a technical exercise. Here, then, is a user of English who 'knows' enough to want to speak and write the Standard, which becomes an end in itself, over and above the expression of his/her ideas.

Contrast this with the underground newspaper of the JVP:[127]

The UNP of Junius Richard Jayewardene who calls himself the local Hitler and who is responsible for destroying the country politically, economically, and culturally, and also for ceding the country to India is cracking and tottering from its very foundation. The cracks are widening daily and it is impossible to close them now. There is no doubt that the vain attempt made by certain people to close these cracks, will be futile. ...

The whole UNP including J. R. Jayewardene and Gamini Dissanayake who are suffering from Election-fear (Election *Bayalitis*) objected to this [the (ex!)Finance Minister's remarks that the government was wrong to deprive the people of the 1983 general election] ...

---

127.   The Janatha Vimukthi Peramuna or People's Liberation Front, a quasi-Marxist terrorist organization, which was proscribed by the Sri Lankan government in 1983, and which had been involved in an armed struggle for about four years until 1991, though now it has been virtually wiped out by the state. This passage is excerpted from *Redpower* the 'central organ of the JVP', No. I (1988), and appears to be a translation of *Ginipupura*, the Sinhala original.

In the meantime, those that are hiding in 5-star hotels in Colombo with their families, being unable to go back to their electorates, are questioning as to how long they are to be in hiding like this and are murmering behind the big-chief's back.

It is not necessary to relate how the country has fallen to zero, economically. The fact that 75% of the population is suffering from malnutrition is sufficient evidence.

On the other hand, it is no secret that Sri Lanka has now become a *full-pledged* colony of India. The Indian army that has been brought to Sri Lanka to vanquish a handful of Tigers now exceeds, 100,000 soldiers. It is clear to everyone that these Apes will go back in the same way the Yankee army did in Vietnam after getting a bellyful from us, *only*. ...

At the Party Conference held at the Sugathadasa Stadium and at several other meeting, what he said was, 'kill, kill, kill; I am Hitler. I declare war'. The people he intends killing are the opposition [*sic*] and the people against whom he declares war are those of the opposition.

From all these factors, it is clear that Sri Lanka has now come to a decisive cross-road. The masses of Sri Lanka have now realized that the *meak* and senile Jayewardene, his coterie of bootlickers in the UNP and the Indian agents in the SLMP, CP, NSSP, EPRLF and the PLOTE and the LTTE are all responsible for *the said situation* that Sri Lanka has been placed in. The masses have, therefore, come forward to sweep them out of power.    (Emphasis added)

This text is hortatory and does not have the same agenda as the discussion above, but within its 'relative' standardization there can be adduced certain 'deviances' of form as well as structure. The use of 'only' at the end of the third paragraph from the bottom is a recognizable Lankanism, for instance. The description of Sri Lanka as a 'full-pledged' colony of India is an interesting case of the 'p' for 'f' substitution which has been noted by Chitra Fernando as an indicator of the second level on the cline of bilingualism. The paragraph that begins, 'In the meantime, those that are hiding in 5-star hotels', which is, in fact, a single sentence, presents perhaps the clearest example of an unacceptable idiom to habitual users of English in Sri Lanka. The repeated use of the continuous form, the misspelling of 'murmur' and the awkward construction provide the 'reasons' for its unacceptability. Nothing really major, here, but an 'awkwardness', none the less. The approximation of the standard at the 'sentence-level' takes it toll on the sense of the excerpt, however: the attack on Jayewardene as Hitler is contradicted when he is described in the last paragraph as 'meak', a contradiction so glaring that this 'mistake' requires further analysis. The mixing of registers too is noticeable, as in the sudden shift to the legalistic/business Lankan usage in the last paragraph, 'the said situation'.

In other issues of the same journal there are clearer examples of non-standard usage:

No one should forget that Jayewardene has so far, not dissolved his undeclared Military Junta. His armed goons, the Green Tigers are still armed and are continuing with the business of murdering innocent people. Jayewardene's armed forces, the army, navy and Air Force and Police are on red alert.

So Mr Athulathmudali, THE BALL IS STILL *IN* YOUR SIDE although politics is not a GAME whatsoever for us. Everybody can remember still, how Mr Jayewardene who calls himself HITLER defined the word politics, at a public meeting. According to Jayewardena, 'POLITICS IS A BLOOD GAME.' He is practising what he preaches.

We also remember that Mr Athulathmudali had been the mediator in the previous strike launched *by* Public Service United Nurses' Union. While being *at the verge* of getting their demands Mr Minister took them for a ride and that was the end of the strike and *end of demands*. ...

It is of course, weak leadership ... that is responsible for *swallowing this dead rope*. ...

Everyone is now aware that Tissa Balasuriya (said to be a Roman Catholic priest) has played a very important part in deceiving the people of Sri Lanka and the *world over*. What right has he to do so, when he preaches to *whole world* that people should not tell *the untruth*.

A layman can be pardoned. But can a priest *be*?

We are waiting to see what action the Vatican is contemplating against this *obnoxious* conspirator. ...

The Government is now thinking of filing action against *the so-called Senanayake*, making him totally responsible for the whole fiasco.

We say that is very unreasonable. All the conspirators should be brought before the law. If this is not done, the people have the right to decide what action should be taken against *them, the dirty crooks.*[128]

The 'righteous' anger of these reports is in no way vitiated by the use of Lankanisms, though the paper is, in part, for circulation outside Sri Lanka. Here, as elsewhere in the examples provided, there is no self-consciousness among the users that anything but the accepted Standard is being used, and yet it is in moments of intense feeling that the 'deviance' both in tone and syntax is most clearly felt to a native speaker of another dialect. In fact, the standard idiom in the hands of these writers produces mainly clichés and facile expressions, whereas the non-standard usage breathes fire!

We ask the people not to *be harbour* any anxieties, suspicions or doubts about us on occasions like this. ...

You would have, by now realized that the vain attempts, the intimidations, the repression, and *the loud talks* of the UNP Government and their boot-licking scavengers of the United Socialist Alliance to annihilate us, have all gone down the drain.

Here is an example of such a passage which nine out of ten native speakers would turn their nose up at, and yet which remains more effective than *the same writer's* use of the standard in the analogous concluding section 'From all these factors ... sweep them out of power' quoted above.

Policing the language through newspaper columns, pamphlets and textbooks has become increasingly popular in Sri Lanka today. There are even magazines devoted entirely to teaching English, and the publication of books and teaching aids is an important part of the English industry in the country. General interest magazines and daily newspapers carry tips and instructions for writing 'good' English. In the journal *Taprobane*, for instance, there is a weekly column, 'Mind your language!', which provides sentences 'with assorted mistakes, some of them taken from recent reports in the local media' and corrects them, providing explanations for the corrections. Such nuances of usage as the following are explained here:

---

128. *Redpower* (1988) pp. 2–4.

Two persons were found cut to death at Sea Street, Colombo, *yesterday* morning. [Though we say *last night* and *last evening*, it is incorrect to say *last morning*.]

Corrected sentences include the following:

As the coach whizzed along, stopping abruptly at halts with screeching brakes, plummetting the passengers forward, it filled up.

In its report to the Aid Group, it says that there are reasonable grounds for suspecting that the tariff schedule has been fine-tuned to provide higher than average levels of effective protection for specific enterprises.

The need to emphasize syntactic rules overrides other considerations such as clarity and simplicity, in much the same way that Cooray did, although with far greater sophistication. Occasionally, however, even the 'neutrality' of the rules of syntax and semantics are transgressed as in the 'correction' of the newspaper headline, 'India the chief benefactor in [the] Peace Accord' which becomes 'India, the chief beneficiary in [the] Peace Accord'. This change is explained by the fact that '[a] benefactor is a person who does something good to you. A beneficiary is the person who derives gain or benefit'. The two 'alternatives' are, therefore, clearly not semantically similar. We would, of course, need access to the larger context before we could decide which 'sense' was more appropriate! A more felicitous non-standard usage is provided by the chapter title of a recent publication on the crisis in the north-east of Sri Lanka, *Genocide in Sri Lanka* (1987),[129] which reads, 'Genocides Galore.' The

---

129. The author, M. S. Venkatachalam, is a South Indian Tamil, but since no claim is being made for the exclusivity of the non-standard forms described in this section (except in so far as the languages in conflict differ in each case), I do not consider it illegitimate to cite examples from this source, particularly since he has used 'a mass of testimony by [Lankan] eye-witnesses' in the text. My other rationalization for recourse to this material is the relative difficulty of access to examples of Tamil influence on English writing, given the civil war situation.

'unacceptable' pluralization of genocide is effective because it points to the repetition of the horror of genocide, allowing, moreover, for the incongruous post-positional adjective 'galore' which evokes the grotesque pleasure derived by some from this awful history. The writer, a journalist, who was warmly endorsed in Forewords by Tamil United Liberation Front leaders Amirthalingam and Sivasithamparam, is not always this effective, however. Consider, for instance, the following diatribe against then Sri Lankan President, J. R. Jayewardene:

> A traditional *treacherer* as he is, *the Tamils* have to carry on conciliatory talks with him – *No other go!*
>
> JRJ, a fragile old man, has been volatile in nature – vociferous always against the Tamils. He is vile-minded, venom-tongued, *villainy-eyed* and vulture-nosed *always too ready* to pounce upon the Tamils and suck their blood. In arrogance he is an equal to Herr Hitler, in cold-bloodedness he is comparable to the Czars of Russia, in demagogy and *deceipt* he is capable of excelling even Goebels. He is diabolically cunning like proverbial jackals combined with the cruelty of blood-thirsty panthers! He is a demogogic, double-tongued, unscrupulous and blood-thirsty politician. In short he is the hardest nut to crack! (p. 63)

More important than the obvious 'errors', which do not affect the tone of the passage too much, is the piling up of mixed metaphors, which produces in the reader a comic effect from sheer overkill. This response is reinforced by the utter anti-climax of the last sentence: we are given a list of derogatory compound adjectives that leads to the promised summary in the last sentence, and we expect something pretty nasty. Yet, 'in short' JRJ is merely a difficult customer, even someone who is hard to get the better of. This, then, is clearly a 'malapropism' and/or a kind of linguistic premature ejaculation!

It is appropriate that the next example comes from a recent publication by a Sri Lankan 'popular historian', (the latest euphemism for Sinhala chauvinist!), Rohan Gunaratna, whose credentials are greatly enhanced in mainstream circles by strong recommendations from Cyril Ponnamperuma and Ralph Buultjens, figures of some international repute. It is important to note that Gunaratna's (mis)-use of language here cannot be considered 'educated Lankan English' in that he does not display in any systematic way the recognizable characteristics of this variety.

Sri Lanka must be saved. The future strategy must essentially
be two pronged. While the government concentrates on solving
the deep rooted socio-economic and the political grievances of the
people ... security forces should prevent the resurgence of violence. *Government* has to make certain modifications in the
National Security apparatus. *In context* the first move should be to
revamp the intelligence apparatus in the country and to formulate
a network truly national in character. *It should be national in the
sense that there should be personnel from the civilian sectors as well as
officers and men from the army, navy, airforce, and police should become
a must.* ... This will also enable the *hard core types* to be isolated.
Constant surveillance should be maintained on covert radical
supporters, intellectuals and institutions of learning. This is of
prime importance. Covert induction of intelligence personnel *to*
public and private sector establishments and the reorganisation of
the essential services to *ensure guaranteed functioning* during critical times is imperative. ... Intensive propaganda to reach the
grass roots and to stabilise the military successes is now timely.
This will help to convert the *peripherals*    (1990, pp. 363–4)

It is perhaps important to mark here the fact that not all non-standard usages can be seen as resistant or de-hegemonizing. Nor are all
such non-standard forms of equal 'heinousness' for the educated
writers of a given language. Many linguists have provided empirical evidence as to the acceptable range of variability within the
(emerging) standard, notable among whom is Labov who is cred-
ited with formalizing the concept of the variable rule with reference
to 'creoles.'[130] These case studies point to the fact that such acceptability is fundamentally context dependent, and in itself not static.
The 'educated' Lankan standard (or at least that form of the English
language which Lankan educated élites arbitrate upon) is flexible
enough to accept much variation of a non-threatening kind. Particularly in the print medium, 'typos' become an oft-invoked alibi for
unacceptable errors, or for those that some local purist uncovers in,
say, the newspapers. As Kandiah emphasizes, the final arbiter in
case of a controversy is the dictionary or reference works such as
Fowler and Daniel Jones, so oft-invoked that the authors' names
suffice to resolve an argument!

---

130.  See particularly Labov (1971).

The reasons for the existence of such typesetting errors is that those working on transferring the edited copy into print are not 'educated' users of the language. As a result, the uninitiated reader of the English daily newspapers in Sri Lanka, for instance, will come away with the impression that 'educated' Lankan English is far more divergent from Standard British or 'American' English, and far less systematic than in fact it is. On the contrary, an excellent recent study of newspapers in Sri Lanka (as well as elsewhere in the region) undertaken by Manique Gunesekera[131] has shown conclusively that specifically Lankan elements of the language are minimal in editorials and front-page news stories, which approximate Standard English.

An example of such non-threatening 'deviance' from the standard which borders on acceptability is near at hand:

> This does not, in *actual fact*, mean that they have forsaken their own norms; for, after they have procured the phonological information *sought for*, they would proceed, in their usage, to 'reinterpret' it in terms of their own inbuilt phonological system, realizing the form involved in terms of their own phonemic and phonetic counters.   (Kandiah, 1987, p. 34)

More interesting than these relatively minor redundancies is the typically Lankan use of 'proceed ... to ' which, in this case, adds nothing to 'reinterpret'. In Kandiah's usage, however, interference of the unrestricted modifier lends some credibility to the need for the circumlocution in the eyes of the standard. More disturbing to the English or 'American' user would be utterances such as 'I proceeded to blackguard [far more commonly used as a verb in

---

131.  See Gunesekera's (1989) dissertation. Her findings reveal that

> the language used in the texts investigated reveals only very minor traces of the new Englishes. While this finding is somewhat unexpected in terms of the observations of other scholars, it is not completely surprising if seen in the context of the 'standard bearer' role taken on by editors of the quality press, and the prestige accorded the two genres [editorials and lead stories]. The interesting contrasts with other genres such as advertisements, obituaries and marriage proposals, which do use the new Englishes, suggest that there is a continuum of different Englishes amongst the different genres of newspaper discourse.

Sri Lanka than in Britain or the US] the buggar.' Yet, semantically there is a nuanced difference in meaning with the addition of this prior process in order to begin the action of, say, reinterpreting or blackguarding.

Here is a final example of non-standard usage that remains idiosyncratic at best, and therefore cannot be productive of resistance to hegemonic norms, however sympathetic we are to the reasons for its genesis. This paragraph is taken from the editorial of the *Royal College Mathematical Society Magazine* of 1986, a fact that says more about our changing times than any of the others cited so far: Royal has remained for over 150 years one of the élite educational institutions for boys in the country, and for a long time the bastion of Standard English. Its perceived decline in this respect has been tied to the rise of free education which led to a 'different kind of student' entering its halls. I have shown this passage to many 'old Royalists' who are habitual speakers of English, only telling them afterwards where I found it. Without exception, the initial reaction was one of amusement at the 'howlers', but this soon turned into a derogation of the present educational system and an uncritical nostalgia for the past, once they learned of its source.

> Being a third world country[,] Sri Lanka does not *posess* scientific and technical know how as advanced as the developed countries. [W]ith the 21st. century getting ever closer, the need to do something about *the backlog* is *urgent than ever*. So we must *realice* this and rise to the *tax* [task].

There is contextual evidence that both 'realice' and 'tax' are not 'printers' devils' but attempts at pronunciation-spelling. Earlier in the editorial, the *Oxford Dictionary* is written as 'Oxpord' which is a common 'error' referred to elsewhere in this work. The verb 'teaches' is misspelt 'teachers' in an analogous 'mistake'. In addition, more conventionally difficult words such as 'mathematics', 'physical sciences', 'knowledge', 'realm', 'souvenir', 'development', 'undoubtedly' and 'miraculous' have been reproduced accurately. The four words misspelled are ones that the writers would have heard frequently, which means that they would have been inclined to rely on their intuitions, whereas in some of the other cases they probably looked in the dictionary.

## POPULAR MUSIC AS PUSHING AGAINST STANDARD LANKAN ENGLISH

I am your one and only one
I am your ever-loving one
I am your one and only Kandy *lamissi*
I am your *vate murunga*
I am your *lassana kella*
I am your one and only Kandy *lamissi*

*Ethakota* don't say *palayang*
I've got ten acres *goyang*
I am your one and only Kandy *lamissi*

Sweet Marie, Come to me,
I am your one and only Kandy *lamissi*
*Ethakota* what *maiiokka*
I am your *sudu bonikka*
I am your one and only Kandy *lamissi*

This song, which seems at first to be a traditional rendering of a woman's subservience and devotion to her lover, undercuts its conventional gender-stereotyping through the mixed idiom which caricatures the entire convention. The clichés by which a woman's undying love must be conveyed to her man are juxtaposed with the ridiculous similes in Sinhala which compare her to the *murunga*, a clearly phallic vegetable on a fence! It also critiques the dowry system by warning the man that he should not chase her away since she has 10 acres of paddy-land as her dower, thus implying that all the man really wants is her property anyway. Linguistically, the 'borrowings' function in a fundamentally different way than identified in the literature generally. In '*Ethakota* don't say *palayang*' it is not quite clear which language is primary and which is being borrowed from. And yet this example does not remain a far-fetched one which would not be encountered in a 'real' situation. It is of a category of utterances which has currency in contemporary Sri Lanka, though not at the 'higher' levels of the cline of bilingualism.

Very innocent young girls*la keruva nithara follow follow*
Wife*lawa patas gaala dikkasaada kalo kalo*
Man *thamai* Uganda*we* murder king, hullo hullo

Mister Idi Amin *thaama hangilalu* hullo hullo

The verse above, taken from a *baila* which presents vignettes of notoriety such as Al Capone and Hitler, has as its chorus a claim that entrance into the 'history' books, which depends upon shaking the world, may not be as good as being lulled into an untroubled and untroubling life, described by the 'uneducated' Lankan use of the 'English' word, 'shape'. The expression 'hullo' (or 'hello') too takes on a different connotation here as it can stand for a person's name as in 'Hey, mister'. An utterance such as *'kohomada* Hullo?' would translate across cultures to something like 'How are you doing?'

> *Chudamaanike balaala yanawa mei api*
> *Lobha nethuwa panduru daala yanawa mei api*
> *Chuudamaanike balaala yanawa mei api //*

> I'll H-O-L-D hold your H-A-N-D hand
> And T-A-K-E take you to the P-A-R-K park
> I'll K-I-S-S kiss you in the D-A-R-K dark
> And then you will be M-I-N-E.

> You'll be M-I-N-E mine and …
> And I'll L-O-V-E love you all the T-I-M-E
> You're the B-E-S-T best of all the R-E-S-T rest
> And I'll L-O-V-E love you all the T-I-M-E time.

In this case we have a song that becomes a way of learning English and of showing off this knowledge at the same time. Yet it is quite different too from the drills that are constitutive of language learning, even in adult contexts. There is a sense of play here that works against the mindlessness of such repetition and spelling out. In addition, the fact that this set of English verses is in sharp contrast to the rest of the song further accentuates the incongruity of these lyrics. On the one hand, then, it points to the ways in which English is learned, and on the other, it identifies the contradictions inherent to such situations.

> Trouble in the junction honey
> Shut up when you see my daddy
> He's a real *thadi bidi sando*
> Double-barrel *apey* mummy

Get out *kiyaa* kicking ...
*kekka nethiwa kadanawa* mango.

The song above as well as the one below point to interesting ways in which English is used to parody the élite users of the language. One of the quick tests to discover near-monolingual users of English, that is those who have very little fluency in either Sinhala or Tamil, is by their use of English terms to describe and identify family relationships. Thus, those who call their parents 'daddy and mummy' are, almost always, among this group, whereas in the majority of cases the Sinhala or Tamil equivalents will be used instead. Of course, such use does not guarantee anything, since some Sinhalese who call their parents 'thaththa and amma' (or variations thereof) are near-monolinguals too. Here, however, the terms 'mummy' and 'daddy' are used self-consciously, and become a metonym for a 'westernized' urban lifestyle.

Daddy military*yata bandi*
Daddy *nethiwa* Mummy*ta hari* worry //

Release *velaa ennako* dear
*Apey* mummy *nithara nithara liyum liyanawa.*

Don't be silly *aiyyo mummy*
*Monawa kalath* I'm your Sonny
How to marry *nandagé dooni?*
That girl is really funny
*Eyagé hati danno danii*
*Karata nagi* without a *goni*
Sunday morning saw her running round the Cabana
Some Yankee Johnny chasing with a *baila rabana.*

Here the merging of traditional and anglicized values is shown in the son's refusal to marry his first cousin, who according to custom is his *evessa* or 'necessary' cousin, necessary that is for marriage! The mother, who is clearly 'westernized' and thus appears as 'mummy' and whose son is equally so (hence, 'sonny'), expects him to accept an 'arranged marriage'. The 'girl' is, however, of similar stripe, according to the song and has been seen on the beach with an American tourist in tow. It is important to note here, as elsewhere, that the English phrases and sentences describe what may be termed the 'English-like' experience component.

No one on the veranda
Can I kiss you Marinda
*Oya magé* lozenger*ey*
When I was in Uganda
Got your snap from Metilda
Can't you see my fancy *aaderey!* //

This lyric is instructive since it points to the ability of non-standard usage to be self-critical and satiric. The juxtaposition of 'fancy' with the Sinhala word *'aaderay'* (or love) de-sentimentalizes the emotional baggage associated with love. The blithe sexism of the singer is thus highlighted by this 'code-mixing'. In the only other example of mixing, the function of the combining of both languages is further clarified: that line describes the woman as the singer's lozenge! The reference to Uganda contains a shorthand for the class and context of the singer whose knowledge of English and social status is located succinctly.

*Heenen* I see you night and day
*Api penala yamuda* lovely *magé paney*
Crazy crazy girl – you are my lovely pearl
*Oya magé* hope in all the world.

Kollupitiya junction – you all had a function
I saw you kissing *aayagé kolla*
That *nondi* fellow Johnson – who stole your mother's pension

Had a rocking time *natamin* Baila.
Cheers darling want a devilled coconut brandy
*katakapalaa wakkarapan mokatada* shandy?
Early morning ... train to Kandy
*Ehema kiyala umba pewwalu* Johnny*yata mandi!*

These *baila* lyrics are important examples of non-standard language that appear in a fixed form that we can analogize to writing. *Baila* remains popular and in other contexts appears to respond to the Lankan crisis: there are songs about the civil war, about terrorism and acts of violence, as well as those critical of changing values, political doublespeak and the liberalized economy, though all these are exceptions to the major theme of romantic love and paeans to drinking, dancing and being merry. This genre is frowned upon by 'serious' musicians and both Sinhala and English intellectuals, whose opposition is quite vocal and widespread.[132]

The language of the *bailas* excerpted here is 'jarring' to the 'educated speakers' of both Sinhala and English, and yet to imagine that these are simply unself-conscious and apolitical (or worse, reactionary) gestures is to ignore the complex ways in which subversion and resistance take the form of imitation and parody in public culture. One way of establishing this phenomenon is by comparing it to a 'song' (or rhymed poem) written in the received standard which fails miserably as a result of its use of entirely alien and archaic syntax and lexis.

### Wake Up Lanka

Wake up Lanka, to the sound of the drums:
The sun is rising, and the birds are crowing.
Wake up Lanka, and call for your sons:
The rivers are flowing, and the paddy is growing.
Wake up Lanka, to the sound of the bells:
The monks are chanting, and devotees meditating.
Wake up Lanka, and march to the dells:
To gather the harvest, for merry-making.

Come out ye damsels, and lend in your hand:
To make this country, a prosperous land.
Come out ye men, and put in your weight:
To enrich your country, by increasing its freight.
Take to the plough, and keep tilling the land:
There is no better work, that will suit your hand.

Burn not your money, but collect your dime,
Casting away your habits, one at a time.
Throw off your cigarette, and try to be frank;
Save your penny, and store it in the bank.

---

132. Sustained popular cultural analysis is sadly lacking in Sri Lanka, and linguistic work does not exist in this area. One must, therefore, reinvent the wheel here, as it were, and anticipate all the old prejudices that similar work in, say, the US can now take for granted.

Listen to the elders of your governing clan:
They are out to help you, as much as they can.

The use of archaisms and excessive formalisms contribute towards making this song pathetic in its attempt to imitate an outdated metropolitan model. The end-rhyme and metre are responsible for some of the 'infelicities' of idiom, but the use of 'dime' and 'penny', of 'damsels' and 'dells' are symptomatic. The pseudo-Elizabethan conceit and pastoral echo of 'merry-making' in the fields is singularly inappropriate to describe the hard labour associated with harvesting, thereby marking the writer as a phoney urban romantic. The non-standard prepositional use 'lend *in* your hand' and 'throw *off* your cigarette' as well as the entirely odd 'put in your weight' do not work here, either through the bringing of standard forms to crisis or by stubbornly resisting discursive norms, since the entire frame is of idyllic contentment and 'innocent' acceptance of the status quo.

## ENGLISH WRITING AND HISTORY

The *Administrative Reports of Ceylon* provide some evidence as to the general state of English education in the country during the last century.[133] Here, for instance, is an account of English students in 1872 written by the Inspector of Schools who administered the local examinations and evaluated their performance.[134]

---

133. The histories (and other paraphanelia) of Royal, S. Thomas' and Trinity College, for instance, provide us with more material on what privileged students learned, but these are hardly typical of the rest of the country. See Sarathchandra Wickramasuriya's essay (1986), for an account that is curiously uncritical of the larger project of English studies but argues vehemently against the specific literary choices made by the authorities in Ceylon.

134. This account is contained in the *Administrative Reports, Ceylon 1872, Colombo*, printed by W. H. Herbert, Government Printer (Ceylon, 1873) as Appendix A – II of Public Instruction. The copy I examined was in the Colombo Museum Library. I am grateful to Lakshan Fernando who assisted me with the selection and analysis of this material.

The chief feature of all the paper-work in the examination was the lamentable want of appreciation of English idioms, and the construction of English sentences, betrayed by all the candidates. This is abundantly evidenced in the answering of candidates wherever they were unable to rely upon memory. It is well known that the capacity of Sinhalese and Tamil youths is prodigious for taking in and retaining a mass of crude matter, which being too often bolted without any attempt at intellectual mastication, is, when reproduced, naturally in a undigested state: but it is almost incredible that a student should be thoroughly grounded in grammar, and yet at the same time unable to correct on paper gross grammatical errors.

As an instance of this, I append here below, in juxtaposition, certain sentences given to the candidates for examination, and their amendments. I should mention that several of the candidates whose answers are given, did excellent papers in English grammar.

*For Correction*
(1)   Before some time there would be plenty coffee grown in Southern Province.

*Correction by Candidates*
'Before some time there would be plenty coffee grown in the Southern Province.'
'Before some time there had been plenty coffee grown in the Southern Province.'
'Before some time there was plenty coffee grown in Southern Province.'

*For Correction*
(2)   I see, you went for sport, did you enjoy?

*Correction by Candidates*
'I see, have you gone for sport?'
'I see, you going for sport, do you enjoy?'
By another candidate I was informed, with regard to the last sentence, that 'It is right, if you put the question immediately.'

The above appear to me to point very strongly to the necessity, which I suppose will be acknowledged some day in Ceylon, for the teaching of English as a language. The introduction of this into the higher schools of Ceylon is, it seems to me, one of the points demanding most attention at the present time. It is now difficult to believe that the knowledge of English possessed by the average Ceylon youth is such as to enable him to read, either with pleasure or profit, English books (If he does not do this, the result of his schooling is, I need scarcely remark, of little value) ...

It is in these English schools, where many of the boys are of English-speaking parents, that the anomaly of a boy being fairly grounded in the subject taught, and yet unable to write an original sentence in English decently, or to appreciate any ordinary English classic, is especially prominent. ...

E. A. Helps
Inspector

Yet 'before some time' is widely used in Sri Lanka among 'uneducated' speakers, and derives from the direct translation of something like the colloquial Sinhala *waedi kaalayak yanna kalin*. The other non-acceptable phrases, 'plenty coffee' and 'did you enjoy?' are much less troubling to today's speakers of US English, for instance.

This phenomenon – the difference between a knowledge of grammatical rules and the ability to write grammatically – is the mirror image of the 'native-like' ability to produce grammatical utterances without a knowledge of the underlying rules or explanations. In 115 years, so much has changed and yet nothing has changed if one were to apply Helps's standards to rural learners of English, or indeed to any but those whose parents are 'English-speaking', and if one subscribes to the same notions of 'decency' in English. The echoes of our present context can be discerned from this account of English teacher trainees of the 'Normal School' in 1871:[135]

Object Lesson: All failed miserably (except 2). The lessons given were of too ambitious a character, the language used was not simple enough, the sole aim of the students in some cases being to air some uncommon word, which of course misapplied, and conveyed no meaning whatever to the class, in whose face he

---

135. *Administrative Report of Ceylon, 1871. Report of the Examination of the English Class of the Normal School on 25 March, 1871 by E. A. Helps, Inspector of Schools.*

brandished it, as it were, triumphantly. They also did not recapitulate enough, and examination and explanation were mixed up together. The English of the students admits, of course, of great improvement, the absence of the articles when a question is put being continual.

## SUBALTERNEITY AND NON-STANDARD LANGUAGE

This section attempts to relate the more specific/narrower arguments concerning the resistance-function of non-standard language to the more general/broader realm of non-normative discourse, where discourse is seen as the self-representation of systems of signification (verbal and non-verbal) which present relatively closed world-views. Discourse used in this Foucaultian sense 'is best understood as a system of possibility for knowledge. What rules, for instance, allow the construction of a map, model or classificatory system?'[136] In terms of our analysis, then, what rules govern the classification/identification of resistance to colonial authority, and how do these rules operate? If we can get under the skin, as it were, of these systems of rules, then we would have learned a great deal about both the possibilities and limitations of resisting them. Unfortunately, these systems are so pervasive and so much the bedrock on which we judge/evaluate/explain/understand/criticize our world that we cannot easily unlearn them. In this sense, it is only if we have had no access to these discourses and their embedded systems of rules that we can 'bring them to crisis'. If we act as if we do not know the rules, or if we break some of them *rhetorically*, it does not have the same effect since our deliberate rule-breaking can be accommodated within the rules themselves. Paradoxically, then, only the genuine misrecognitions of these rules serve to undermine them.

---

136.  Ashcroft *et al.* (1989) p. 168. This book is an important event in (post)-colonial studies which valorizes, however schematically, hybridity/syncretism in language, which is analogous to the treatment here. For an extended critique of the weaknesses of this text in its effacement of hybridity-as-struggle, its essentializing of (post)colonial resistance, and its homogenization of the (post)colonial moment through a blindness to economic (and cultural) exploitation, see Neloufer de Mel's dissertation, 'Responses to History' (1990).

All this is radically counter-intuitive, even polemical at this stage and requires a great deal more work by others if it is to be generalizable as a theory of discursive de-hegemonization. I offer the following case study of this process at work, therefore, not because it is exhaustively thought-out, but because I am convinced that this insight is the major contribution of this section, in embryo as it were.[137]

The peasant (or subaltern) voices are represented in this analysis in translation. The assumption here is that these translations of subaltern peasant interventions in the context of the rebellion of 1848 stand in some relation to the 'actual' peasant voices. This relationship between the 'translations' and the 'originals' does not, of course, constitute a simple identity, but it is none the less not an arbitrary or untheorizable connection that obtains. In fact, it is all the more important to consider these representations of peasant discourse since it was in precisely this form that they entered the public domain of linguistic struggle, and it is here that they bring the hegemonic discourse(s) to crisis. Since we are not about to make some mystical or fetishized connection between the peasants and their discourse, and since subalterneity is constituted by the structural exclusion of access to 'acceptable' discourse, the following argument still remains valid:

> Subaltern linguistic intervention (in translation in this case, but 'translation' is the rule in language not the exception) represents (most clearly in a time of crisis) 'inappropriate' or 'unacceptable' discourse which cannot be taken account of by the normative standard. In fact, the 'proper' discourse (of the rebellion of 1848) must systematically exclude these 'mistakes' or 'deviations' (or ridicule them as illegitimate, mistaken, deviant and so on in terms of its own criteria of acceptability decided upon by those élites who can make their 'meaning' stick) which travesty preconceived standards of coherence, good reason and causality, if it is to remain coherent and viable.

---

137. Moreover, in the current crisis in Sri Lanka (and elsewhere), where social groups traditionally perceived as conservative, even ideologically backward (such as the Mothers' Fronts), are effectively in the vanguard against oppression, whereas progressive organizations remain strait-jacketed, such a re-evaluation of the role and function of resistance to authority is fundamental, both to a better understanding of discursive realities and to a more meaningful politics.

It is, therefore, from the study of these marginal and 'ill-formed' discourses that one can evaluate the cost of equating hegemony with making sense in the processes of language-as-action.

Some background is necessary to understand this context of these texts.[138] The rebellion of 1848 in Ceylon (Sri Lanka) lasted only three or so days, at least in terms of its overt opposition to the British administration, and its major acts of aggression were the meticulous destruction of the Matalé and Kurunegala Kachcheris [Government Agent's offices] as well as the freeing of prisoners. The immediate cause of the rebellion, according to élite sources, was the introduction of seven new taxes by the government, including dog, gun and poll taxes. There were no British casualties during the rebellion, but many rebels were killed and their property destroyed/confiscated. Under martial law, many alleged rebels were sentenced to death and others 'transported' to Malacca on the scantiest of evidence. The British could understand neither their motivations nor their strategies of protest, unlike on the previous occasions when local élites plotted to oust them (the British) in order to re-establish their traditional power over the peasants. Nor did the colonial administrators know who the popular leaders were, since there seemed to be so many, and since for the first time no one was seriously claiming royal birth. Yet this was the only rebellion in which a king (or 'pretender' in the British imperial discourse) was actually crowned. As a result of their inability to *read* this rebellion in terms of the discursive patterns available to them, the administration was utterly brutal to all concerned, and this strategy backfired: questions were raised in the British Parliament where for the first and only time Ceylon loomed large in the affairs of the imperial centre. A powerful select committee was appointed to inquire into the matter and Lord Russell's administration came within a hair's breadth of collapse. The Governor and many of his senior staff were changed, however, and the obnoxious taxes were repealed. If this was a victory for the rebels, it also showed the limitations of such struggles, and no further rebellions were recorded after this.

---

138. The following is of necessity an over-simplification. The reader is invited to read my book *Language and Rebellion: Discursive Unities and the Possibility of Protest* (1990), for a more nuanced account of this complex network of events and its representations by contemporaries and others.

Using the few extant subaltern texts among the hundreds of documents on the incidents of 1848, I shall now examine some of the ways in which these rebels brought the entire discursive apparatus to crisis by their stubborn, because unwitting, refusal to play by the rules. The military officer in charge of the region, Colonel Drought's statement [Appendix I] describing the 'epitome of the pretender's career and capture' sets itself up as factual/objective and 'most authentic', at furthest remove from conjecture and sentiment as possible. However, despite its own claims to veracity, this account lacks any kind of corroboration and presents 'evidence' for which there is no support in any other text that I have seen on the rebellion. The very first statement concerning the claim to lineage from Rajasinghe (the last king of Ceylon who was captured by the British in 1815) on behalf of Gongalagoda Banda [the supposed rebel leader] is unsubstantiated. The belief that he is in fact 'a low-country Sinhalese' is also controverted in the text of Gongalagoda Banda's petition[139] which identifies his house with the village of Udunuwara in the Kandyan heartland.

The obvious differences between these two documents are heightened by the tonal antithesis between them. In marked contrast to the self-confessed 'authenticity' of the former is the lack of a sense of facticity in the latter. Gongalagoda Banda's petition appears incoherent and inconsequential, as a series of *non sequiturs* strung together. For instance, as opposed to pointed reference to his lineage, the petition begins with the pointless allusion to Gongalagoda Banda's sojourn with his father-in-law's elder sister and to the disagreement at his home that precipitated this move. We cannot but wonder at the significance of all this, but our expectations of some explanation are never met. In place of royal lineages and larger-than-personal motivations, we are told about everyday domestic details and the immediate situational constraints of peasant life.

Next we are introduced to the issue of the new taxes, here presented as the singular act of Buller, the Government Agent, and as an institution of 'thirty two taxes' instead of seven. This articulation of the taxes in terms of its localized determinations is fundamental in the characterization of the subalterneity of the leadership. The

---

139.  See Appendix II for the complete text of this document (see p. 171).

issues have their central epistemological status as it affects the immediate locality. In terms of the relevant elements of local knowledge, Buller is the force to reckon with, and not so much the colonial government in far off Colombo.

The 'definitive' account by Drought presents the pretender as a self-conscious agent and powerful protagonist of the rebellion, whereas the pretender's account denies agency by presenting himself as the powerless victim of the 'real' rebel leaders. Moreover, Gongalagoda Banda's account denies, by implication, virtually everything contained in Drought's statement, except, ironically, for the most damaging admission, and the only one that could ensure his conviction – the coronation! Yet, for Drought, he has denied precisely this!

> Since his capture he has had every opportunity given him to make a voluntary statement, but he says little or nothing of himself. ... He denies in toto being elected king by the priests, or that they performed the Perit or any other ceremony when he was made king at Dambool; although the priests have, since his capture, been confronted with him, and swear to his being the identical person who was crowned at Dambool.

Gongalagoda Banda cites Dingiralle (another candidate for 'pretender' according to the colonial administration) as the prime mover who has imposed upon him and misled him, but offers no explanation as to why he, of all people, should have been 'nominated ... as their head.' In contradiction to his own description of himself as a puppet, Gongalagoda Banda provides details of incidents in which he single-handedly prevented 'the people' from destroying and plundering public property. His account invests himself with the very agency that is denied at the outset. In fact, his refusal to continue as leader derived only from their non-acceptance of his absolute authority. He nowhere states his opposition to rebellion as such, only to *this one* and that too after it involved plunder and unnecessary physical violence. We may even read the reference to 'false and fraudulent stories' (which, by implication, enticed him in the first place) as a measure of his disappointment against the ultimate direction taken by the rebellion.

Gongalagoda Banda actually identifies his crime in terms of his deserting the cause of rebellion, for which his reason is to save his life. It is almost as if he regrets this act of justifiable selfishness!

Having come to know that in consequence of my having prevented them from committing all these aggressions and chastised
the people of their own party, and thereby prevented the plunder,
that they intended to take away my own life, and conspired
together to constitute some one else as their Head I deserted
them. This is all the offence or wrong I have committed.

As if to add insult to injury, immediately after having represented
his crime in such a way that it may only refer to his desertion,
Gongalagoda Banda makes a *pro forma* plea for his discharge and
pardon 'for the sake of charity'.

The prior invocation of the 'name' of God, of his doctrine, of the
queen, her crown, the church, of its priests and officials, of the 'name'
of the Governor, of the Chief Justice's father and mother, and finally
the Chief Justice's own 'name', accentuates the whole parody of naming that is played out in this rebellion. This rebellion dramatizes the
bringing to crisis of naming itself by always laying bare its propria-
tions. Just as within the colonialist legal-epistemological framework
the 'proper' name for rebellion is treason, and the appropriate title of
a king is pretender whose occupation is invariably that of vagrant, so
too all the other proper names in this context have no proximate referent. This can never be a proper rebellion because none of the names
can really fit, since the rebellion is in fact about trying to make a different scheme of names stick. It is fitting, therefore, that all the appropriate names invoked by Gongalagoda Banda ensure the denial of the
pardon, enacting a repetition of the denial of the propriety of these
very names that constituted the rebellion itself.

In what can only appear as a carefully orchestrated anti-climax,
'besides' the pardon on his life, Gongalagoda Banda asks for the
return of the buffaloes that he had bought with his father-in-law's
money! All the household property of his father-in-law has been con-
fiscated by the authorities, in addition to the burning down of their
home, but Gongalagoda Banda emphasizes the loss of the buffaloes,
thus denying for the listener/reader any lasting sense of the rational
or normal. This final insult seals the absurdity of his fate at the hands
of the authorities and sanctions the reading made here to the effect
that the pretender is not serious about his request for a pardon.

The beginning and ending of Gongalagoda Banda's petition are
highly stylized and ornate, a typical example of what Halpé
describes as the situation that obtained 100 years later at independence in 1948:

Remote villages were signposted in English and hapless seekers for redress were at the mercy of professional petition-writers whose productions were of the 'most humbly beg' variety addressed to a 'most gracious Honour's kind, merciful and sympathetic consideration'.[140]

---

140.  'Creative Writing in English' (1950) p. 447, where Halpé quotes Halverston in support of this description. This claim for the excessive floweriness of Lankan English is commonplace among linguists today. Kandiah, for instance, cites Halverston approvingly on

> his remarks on the predilection of Lankan users of English for eloquent Latinate expressions. This is to be traced partly, no doubt, to the influence of the elevated Victorian notions of style that the earlier teachers of English in the island entertained and passed on to their pupils, whose usage was to determine the nature of LnkE, and to the kind of reading that Lankans who aspired to social recognition by the rulers were encouraged to cultivate as representing the best models (see Gooneratne 1968). At the same time, such usage may also be considered to reflect a typically oriental predilection for ornamentation and stylization, something which makes this kind of language 'right' for the expression of Lankan sensibility.   (1981b, pp. 65)

Much of this analysis is dead-on, and, after Said's influential work in the area, others far more qualified than me have dealt extensively with the problematic of generalizations such as 'a typically oriental predilection' which constitute a kind of internalized 'orientalism.'

I merely wish to caution against the attribution of uniform motives and strategies for the 'same' use by widely divergent categories (as measured by class, 'fluency' location, age and so on) of people across wide ranges of time. For instance, in the case of 'excessive' formalization and the elaborate coding of letters (of the 'most humbly beg' and 'I remain, Sir, most respectfully yours' variety), there has to be the element of parody on the one hand, as well as that of necessity on the other (where the recipient, who wields power over the sender, expects the 'proper' form).

Granting the exigencies of legal petitions and the rigidity of legalese, for example, there still remains a non-fit between Gongalagoda Banda's 'humility' at the beginning and the rest of his petition. It is as if this exaggerated bowing and scraping allows him to be deceptively rebellious in the body because the reader has different expectations (namely that this will be simply another long-winded plea for mercy, which in one sense it also is!).

The humble beginning sets the reader up, however, to misread the lack of any kind of humility in the substantive account of his role in the rebellion. In fact, tucked away in all the hyperbole of the end is the arrogant (at that time even outrageous) claim to equality and challenge to debate:

> Both your Lordship's soul and my own were created by one God. ... Your Lordship's soul and mine will have to communicate with each other before God.

And this too from the self-confessed leader of a rebellion against the British, one of the reasons for which was the degeneration of Buddhism in the country (see below)! Aside from the list of co-conspirators, many of whom the government never charged for want of evidence, Gongalagoda Banda's statement has a crucial empirical verification. His prevention of unnecessary plunder and bloodshed is a testimony to the amazing discipline and organizational control of the thousands who stormed the towns of Matalé and Kurunegala. One only has to look at the recent history of Sri Lanka to see how difficult it is to control large groups of angry people, even with the most careful of orchestrations. If the government was right that Gongalagoda Banda was indeed the leader of the rebellion, and his own evidence does nothing seriously to contradict this claim, then the conduct of the rebellion is itself extra-linguistic evidence that our linguistic/discursive analysis is not simply 'much ado'. He was using here the only discursive structures/strategies available to him as a complete outsider to their rationalizations (that is, how these structures made sense to those who inhabit them), and in doing so he was doing the only thing he knew, thereby problematizing received notions of intentionality and self-consciousness in the domain of protest.

Gongalagoda Banda's entire narrative must be further framed within the confines of two other 'confessions' of the so-called pretender, the first on the day of his capture and the second on his death-bed at Malacca, neither of which I could find in the archive. These 'missing' documents have been repeatedly alluded to by the administration in order to support the contention that the real leaders of the rebellion were the influential chiefs.[141]

The alleged Kurunegala Pretender, Dingiralle, cited by Gongalagoda Banda as the motive force of the rebellion, has recourse to the identical strategy of disavowal and disclaimer based on his own powerlessness. In the evidence at his court martial' conducted in Kurunegala on 31 July, 1848, Dingeralle (*sic*?) states:

I am a poor man who came from Kandy. Why should the Headmen and population of Seven Korles obey me[?] I had no army with me to compel men. I am not the man who knows the strength of this Government. The witnesses are natives of Seven Korles without their concurrence the people could not have assembled – they knew the Government would catch the real King and allowed him to escape and took me. Is it possible for me to raise the people of the District[?] Why did not the Headmen give information if I was doing this mischief[?] It is a false accusation that I pretended to be a King – I pray I may be released for the sake of God. The Raté Mahatmaya consulted to allow the real King to escape to Gopallawa and from thence to Dambool from thence to Tambancada. I was forced to join the rebels. It was the King that did all this. He ordered me to take the office of Adighar which I refused, he then punished me and compelled me to take the office and join his cause. I am a Doctor. Even my pills and medical book was taken from me. I am a beggar. I beg in the name of the Queen and in the name of God I may be set free.    (Public Record Office, London: CO 54/263, pp. 202ff)

---

141.  See especially Torrington's Despatch to Grey of 10 March, 1850, in which he refers to both confessions:

... the writer alludes to having seen and conversed with the pseudo king, who was transported to Malacca before him. He states that he died that very morning (as is reported, of dropsy), having previously made a complete confession upon the subject of the Kandyan rebellion. ...

It will be remembered that on the first day of the capture of the pretended king at Matale, he made a long statement tending to show that a vast number of kandyan chiefs were implicated in the conspiracy, which afterwards, however, he thought proper to withdraw.

In his last words before execution Dingiralle, reiterates the same theme, outlining his coercion and the fact that he is a scapegoat.[142] Again, he does not explain why he was picked for a position of influence by the 'real rebels', the chiefs. The plausibility of his tale of woe is further weakened by his self-contradictory 'professional' claims, as doctor (*vederala*) and beggar, which though not quite as polarized as they are today, are none the less incompatible and call attention to their disparity. As a beggar, he then begs for mercy, and this ritualized invocation of clemency in the 'name' of god and queen takes on a parodic quality when the pleader is charged with taking the name of king in vain, echoing Gongalagoda Banda's virtuoso performance.

Yet, the chief witness for the prosecution and in fact the only native recipient of a medal of honour for his role in crushing the rebellion, Doratiyawé Raté Mahatmaya, quotes a conversation with Dingiralle that is the only one on record in which a (alleged) protagonist describes the rationale and significance of the rebellion. This dialogue is instructive, moreover, as a rebuttal of the widely held view that the chiefs and priests were in tacit if not open support of the exertions of Dingiralle and Gongalagoda Banda.

> I was admitted to his presence. The Prisoner said, 'As you have come to me you are under my protection by my grace.' He said, 'the religion of Buddha has degenerated on account of the improper conduct of the British Government. I, in conjunction with all the Headmen and the people must expel the enemies the low caste English. We must then improve our religion and when we die we shall inherit blessings'. I explained the impossibility of overturning the Government. He answered, 'I do not care what you say you must obey my orders.' I appeared as faithful to him, – I gave him a blow on the back of his neck, and he fell down, and I called my attendants to assist in securing him – his attendants ran away, deserting him.

Dingiralle's last statement exists in at least two forms which display some difference in detail, pointing once more to the vexed question of translation (see Appendix III). I offer here only the most blatant of divergences in the text in which the 'real' king is

---

142.   See Appendix for full text.

described as 'he is a fine young man; he has mustachios' in one version, and as 'a red-coloured man, with cat's eyes' in the other. The
initial difference provides an insight into the function of power relations in the making of meaning, since, as a direct result of centuries
of colonialism, the terms for light-coloured skin and beauty became
synonymous (much like the relationship of 'fair' to 'pretty' in Standard British English) in Ceylon.[143] Light skin colour is invariably
described as being 'red' (*rathu* in Sinhala), hence the 'interchange-
ability'/confusion of 'red-coloured man' with 'fine young man.' The
second divergence can be explained through the conflation of *balal
ravula* (cat's whiskers, or cat-like moustache) with *balal as* (cat's eyes,
used to describe light-coloured eyes even today),[144] again reiterating
the extent to which connotative difference and contextual determinants must be grasped in order for meaning to be conveyed
adequately.

Evidence given by other rebels and the general populace establish
that the rebellion was systematic and rational, though both the systems and rationalities employed were radically different from their
hegemonic varieties, such as those espoused by urban-based élites
in their opposition to the new taxes. Here is a set of statements
culled from rebel testimony which are self-explanatory:

I have gone through the evidence taken by myself, for the purpose of seeing what the people themselves called it; and amongst
others, I find the following expressions used with reference to
their proceedings, viz.:
[1]   That they must go to Kornegalle, and make 'rebellion' with
the troops.
[2]   Why don't you all rise, join together, and drive the English
out of the country ?
[3]   He directed me to go to his house 'for the purpose of proceeding to Kornegalle to make war.'
[4]   There is a rebellion in Matalle. The people coming in on the
Kandy road on the 30th July, asked 'who got the victory?'

---

143.   See R. A. L. H. Gunawardena's brilliant essay 'The People of the Lion:
Sinhala Consciousness in History and Historiography' (1985), in
which he shows that 'light skin' was neither a necessary nor sufficient
criterion of physical beauty in pre-colonial Ceylon.
144.   I am grateful to Kithsiri Jayananda for pointing out this connection to
me.

[5]   English gentlemen got, or Cingalese got?

[6]   All the people should go to Kornegalle to see the king tomorrow.

[7]   The people said, the king was coming towards Kornegalle, and they must take the place for him.

[8]   The people were being collected for the 'insurrection' by beat of tom-toms.

[9]   Our king has come; we will take away all your things; we are afraid of no one now.[145]

While the 'content' of these utterances points to self-consciousness and active agency in the most straightforward way, their 'form' vitiates this by appearing awkward and clumsy. On the one hand, this awkwardness can be put down to 'translation' of idiom, but even this explanation is hardly satisfactory when we compare them with the translations of the so-called Pretenders' speeches above. If the reason for such difference is adduced as the relative formality and structuredness of the speeches, then the counter-argument becomes irrefutable with the evidence of the court proceedings cited below which is identical in form and occasion to these examples. We need, therefore, to look elsewhere for explanations of this lack of fit between what these statements say and how they say it.

The first indication that we have that these are not faithful representations of what the rebels themselves said is the selective use of quotation marks. It is hard to imagine the peasants referring to their rebellion as a 'rebellion' (or for that matter an 'insurrection') with all that such citationality implies. It is conceivable that they thought of this act as a riot or even something less than that, but surely not by, say, curling up their fingers at the appropriate time to signify a quotation. This clue marks for us, then, the fact that for the utterance to be authentic, only the quoted word must be the rebels', while the rest is the reporter's. This would certainly explain some of the oddness which can be put down to the rules of reported speech. Yet utterance [9] is clearly in direct speech, and so too is [2]. In fact, it is

---

145.   Statement made by T. L. Gibson, Esq., District Judge and Police Magistrate of Kornegalle, quoted in Tennent, p. 59.

no accident that these two sentences are the clearest statements of the objectives and strategy of the rebellion:

Why don't you all rise, join together, and drive the English out of the country?

Our king has come; we will take away all your things; we are afraid of no one now.

In the first sentence this mixing of reporting with citing leads to the confusion of rebels with those they are rebelling against. Thus, we have the chosen structure in which it is unclear whom the rebellion is to be against since it is to be made 'with' the troops. In [3], on the other hand, we have a well-turned sentence that is not authentic because it is excessively formalized and out of place in contrast to the radical informality of the others. This sentence resembles the quasi-Victorian effusions that were noted among some 'educated' Lankans both in the past as well as today: it is more like the old letter-writers than the 'illiterate' peasant rebels of 1848. To demonstrate this one has only to compare the phrases 'directed me to go' and 'for the purpose of proceeding' with the directness of 'who got the victory?'

Sentence [5], however, is distinctly 'odd' since it is difficult to imagine an appropriate context where the object of the transitive verb 'got' is unrequired. In fact, I cannot even formulate an equivalent sentence in Sinhala without setting up an elaborate prior discursive sequence, which led me to question Judge Gibson's *bona fides* in including this in such a form here. The point of all this, then, is to show that even when the subaltern is represented 'verbatim' by non-subaltern (and in this case linguistically far-removed) reporters, such representation is suspect and must be read confrontationally, as if one were cross-examining a hostile witness. The (mis)quoting of the subaltern rebels here serves, therefore, to show the contradiction involved in the administration's position which simultaneously wishes to provide evidence of active and shrewd agency with malicious intent, but also incoherent and ill-informed/misguided bumbling. The narrative would (and does even today) run something like this: the rebels are cunning and vicious, requiring the strongest possible counter-action and preventive tactics, but at the same time they are misguided and unintelligent because otherwise they would never think of rebelling against our administration, which is doing all it can for them.

## THE PRIEST'S OLD CLOTHES

Perhaps the most vexed single issue of the rebellion was the shooting of the Buddhist priest Kadahapola Unanse, which raised a storm even in the British Parliament. The discussion of this incident is instructive since it dramatizes at once both the range and depth of various arguments as well as the ultimate narrowness of perspective within the hegemonic narratives. Moreover, this detailed example reinforces our sense of the travestying of discursive norms and standards even within the most rigorous/narrow of confines that demarcate legal codification. Whereas the previous examples were from the relatively autonomous discursive space of individual statements, prepared beforehand and/or edited, here we have access to the relatively constrained yet unrehearsable arena of a courtroom.

As de Silva points out, the execution of the *bhikku* became the central focus of the growing opposition to Torrington's administration.

> The incompetent Torrington succeeded in attracting the attention of critics in England to the more notorious episodes of his administration. Two incidents in particular drew severe criticism. First, there was the shooting of a bhikku, Kadahapola Kuda Unnanse, on a charge of treason; while the bulk of Torrington's critics concentrated on the charge that he had hurt the religious susceptibilities of the Kandyans by executing *a bhikku in his robes*, a more perceptive critic asked the more pertinent question whether the whole business had not been a gross miscarriage of justice.

The perceptive critic referred to by de Silva is Forbes, who condemns the killing of the priest on 26 August particularly since it is his contention that the rebellion was over by 29 July.

> But for me it is sufficient that he was tried, convicted and killed, as 'an influential priest'; his crime being, if I understand it, the aiding in the concealment of the pretender, and administering unlawful oaths – these being dome about the

17th August, whereas on the 29th July the rabble had entirely dispersed. (Forbes, p. 24)

Forbes, however, is one of those who also feels that the execution of the priest in his full robes served as an insult to Buddhism itself which could have been prevented by providing him with 'the dress of a layman' (p. 25).

Henderson provides the fullest and most sympathetic description of the incident among the contemporaries writing about the rebellion. He emphasizes the fact that the two charges against the priest at his court martial 'certainly seem to be of the strangest I ever read' (Henderson, p. 81). The charges are, '1st. Directly or indirectly holding correspondence with rebels, and not giving all the information in his power, which might lead to the apprehension of a proclaimed rebel; he, Kaddapolla Unanse, professing to know his place of concealment on or about the 17th August, 1848.' And '2nd. For administering, or conniving at the administration, of a treasonable oath to one Kiri Bandi [*sic*], on or about the 17th August 1848' (CO 54/263, p. 121ff).

Henderson's analysis of these charges is very perceptive:

Whether, during an insurrection, a priest's holding direct or indirect correspondence with the insurgents merits death or no I will not pretend to say, but this I will venture to remark, that it is the first time I ever heard that it was so highly punishable not to *volunteer* 'all the information in one's power,' whether to enable the government to catch a rebel, or accomplish any other object. With regard to the second charge, it seems extraordinary that the treasonable oath the priest was charged with administering is not stated; and we find the Queen's Advocate stating, to the House of Commons committee, that in his judgement the charges are not sufficiently definite to warrant a sentence of death. Some of those present at the trial, and among others one or two lawyers, felt convinced that the prisoner was innocent, chiefly from their not believing the principal, or only two witnesses – a father and son – whom they knew to be candidates for government appointments, and consequently anxious to appear very active and energetic in its defence.

Henderson also provides a copy of a 'Statement on Oath as to the Innocence of the Priest Shot by Sentence of a Court Martial', written by the proctor J. A Dunuwille on 17 December 1849, which spells out precisely this concern about the truthfulness of the evidence against Kadahapola. Dunuwille's argument is that the priest was made a scapegoat, first in order to lend credibility to the claims of Palemecoombore and son that they had access to the whereabouts of the king, and second as compensation for the fact that the raid on the supposed cave abode of the king proved abortive.

> Mr. Buller was given to understand by Palemecoombore that all his information was derived from a certain jungle priest of Budhoo [*sic*], who was in the immediate confidence of the pretender, and who was acquainted with all his movements. This gave Pale-mecoombore's story a colour of truth; and in order to be able to give up the author at once in case of necessity, some days before the day on which the expedition went out, Kadahapolle Unnanse, who was then living at Koralle on the charity of the people, and who was quite an obscure person, was invited by the Palemecoombores to come to their house upon important religious business. (p. 317)

That the official charges are ridiculous is incontrovertible. The 'innocence' of the priest in terms of his participation in the rebellion is another matter, though it must be emphasized that the court martial did not deal with this issue at all. It would appear that the trial was simply a formality and that a verdict of guilty as charged was inevitable. The adequacy of the court martial is vouchsafed by the administration in general, but Tennent, in his statement, carefully avoids any reference to the nature of the charges themselves, focusing his attention on the question of the priest's innocence and on the absolute red-herring of his execution in full robes. This approach clearly provides the 'best' case for the administration's handling of the issue and deserves a full hearing:

> With regard to the trial and execution of Kahalle Unanse [*sic*], the priest, I never heard one word of remark in Ceylon, till at least seven or eight-months after his death, when the report reached the colony, of dissatisfaction having been expressed in the House of Commons, at his having been shot in his robes.
> Up till that time, the only notice taken of his trial by the press, was a brief notice at the time, to the effect that he had made a qualified admission of the charges adduced against him.

The point relative to his execution in his robes, was susceptible of easy explanation, by every individual in Ceylon, when it was notorious, that a priest had no other dress in which to die, without submitting to the degradation of laying aside his robe, and covering himself with any other dress or cloth.

Had the priest expressed the slightest wish to divest himself of his robe, or to go to execution in any other, his wish would have been instantly complied with, but he made none; and Mr Parsons, the fiscal ... state[s] that, although daily visited by him, and invited to mention any request which he had to make, he thanked him, and said he had none, except to desire that the regulations of the gaol as to food might be altered in his favour, so as to enable him to have his rice at the particular hour at which alone a Buddhist priest is permitted to eat. The request was of course complied with – and it shows that he still clung to his priestly character, which he would have lost by exchanging his robe even for one instant. Such a request he never made; and Mr Parsons adds, 'that from what he knows from the character and feelings of the natives, he does not think it likely he would have desired to be disrobed, and, had he been, it would have added to his disgrace.' ...

And a paper has been voluntarily placed in the hands of the Governor by the priests of the two great temples at Kandy, to explain the laws of Buddhu and the practice of Buddhist sover eigns as to executions and the disrobing of criminal priests, and expressly declares that it had been the custom for Buddhist kings to put priests to death in the robes, and that no insult to their religion was felt by the Buddhists from the recent execution of Kahath Unanse [*sic*] in his robes.

The question of the robes thus disposed of, the parties active in getting up these charges were reluctant to abandon so fertile a subject as the execution of a priest under any circumstances.

And a story was then revived which had never before attracted a moment's attention to the effect that the witnesses against the priest were corrupt and perjured – that he was innocent of the charge imputed to him; and that Lord Torrington had rejected, in offensive terms, an application made on his behalf by Mr Selby, the Queen's Advocate.

In every one of these particulars, this new story is as insubstantial as the former one.

The trial of the priest is one of the few records of the courts martial that have been preserved in the archive, and this too despite the fact that Drought strongly urged the destruction of all such records for reasons of propriety. We are extremely fortunate in this since the trial itself presents in microcosm the entire problematic of the rebellion. It is in this manner that I shall attempt to read the text of this trial.

To begin with, none of the legal luminaries present, whether English or local, was willing to appear on behalf of the accused, Kadahapola Unanse.

Major Lushington the President of the Court asked the Prisoner if he wished that any one should defend him. He looked towards Mr Wilmot the Advocate for prisoners as his material protector, but that gentleman touched his hand and asked for the *kasie* (money). He said he had none and as no one would take up the cause the trial proceeded. The priest then commenced his defence. When he had finished and while the Court was closed several of the Gentlemen present said 'his own defence convicts him.'[146]

Evidence was supplied by 'Pahleme Koombure Basnaike Nilleme', Charles Buller, Government Agent, Kiri Banda and 'Koodawattegedera Kangahn' for the prosecution, while Kadahapola appeared in his own defence. It goes without saying, of course, that Buller's evidence served as an unimpeachable character evaluation of the principal witnesses, and that he was not subjected to any kind of cross-examination at all.

The witnesses present a well-corroborated picture of the alleged incidents that took place on 17/18 August. The basic claim is that Kadahapola was invited to visit the Palemekumbures through the agency of 'one Goonamalla' on which occasion he is tricked into

---

146.  CO 54/264. It is important to note that this trial was held in Kandy, and was one of only two that led to the death penalty there. The other unfortunate was none other than Puran Appu whose trial records are unavailable. The audience at this trial comprised, in all probability, the entire legal profession in Kandy where the thriving business of lawyers was notorious, in addition, of course, to the curious members of the élite. In this respect it was in sharp contrast to the other courts martial at Kurunegala and Matale, which were relatively private affairs.

admitting that he is in contact with the king. Subsequent to administering an oath upon the Bana book, he agrees to take the witnesses to meet the king. Yet, it is in the detail of their evidence that they betray themselves to the questions raised by Kadahapola. At first reading, it appears that he is asking, by rote, a set of trivial questions of the witnesses. Rather than focusing on his innocence, he appears to be obsessed with the timing of his visit and with the Bana book upon which the oath of allegiance was taken.

On closer examination, however, we can discern how the careful orchestration of evidence comes apart in the detail of the Bana book. Palemekumbure states in his evidence that 'my son Kiri Banda was sworn. He took the Banna [*sic*] Book in his hand and said "I will be faithful to any of the kings that reign in this country." The Prisoner gave the book into his hands.'

Kadahapola asks of Kiri Banda, 'How did the Banna Book come into your hands[?]' Kiri Banda responds, 'I did not take the book into my hands but laid my hands upon it as it lay on the table or cot.'[147]

In response to a similar question, the 'Kanghan' replies, 'Basnaik Nilleme handed the Book to Kiri Banda.'

Thus, the Bana book was handed over to Kiri Banda by the priest who swore upon it, while the same Bana book was not in his hand but on the table or cot at the moment of taking the oath. Moreover, the selfsame Bana book was also given to Kiri Banda by his father according to the third witness, while in Kadahapola's own testimony Kiri Banda was nowhere near the blessed tome since he never took an oath!

The conspirators are secure in their 'evidence', however, since the court martial is both incapable and unwilling to identify inconsistency at this level. As regards the questioning of timing, it would seem that the record has itself filtered out the significance of this component. I can only hope to point to some of the obvious incongruities that the self-evidence and coherence of the evidence covers over as they are highlighted by the interventions of Kadahapola.

If the catachresis of the Bana book marks the limitation of rational cross–examination by a subaltern in a hostile discursive unity, then the extravagance and absurd irrelevance of the 'gun fire' question

---

147.  Elsewhere in his evidence Kiri Banda refers to the Bana book as being placed by Kadahapola upon a cushion or table!

calls attention to itself as being an intervention that mocks this very discursivity.

The initial question posed by Kadahapola of each of the witnesses concerns the time of the alleged meeting and treasonous conversation: 'Was it after or before gunfire[?]' To this the father responds, 'It was about twelve o'clock at night.' The next witness, Kiri Banda, says that Kadahapola's visit took place 'Long after gunfire at night', while the Kangani replies, 'Between eleven and twelve at night I think but am not certain.'

Though each of them is asked to specifically situate the meeting in terms of the gunfire, only Kiri Banda does so. We are unaware of any skirmish around 17 August, so the reference to gunfire is intriguing. Perhaps the issue will be clarified by Kadahapola in his defence. But, no, his submission mentions nothing of the time of his visit, nor does it connect in any way to this line of questioning. We can surmise from the alleged lateness of the meeting that it could hardly have taken place for purposes of 'religious instruction'. Nor does it seem plausible as asserted by all concerned that the messenger (who incidentally is surprisingly absent from among the witnesses) persuaded the unsuspecting priest to visit the Basnaike Nilleme at midnight for no more definite a purpose than the Nilleme's anxiety to speak with him.

The timing of the conversation points to another agenda than that disclosed by the evidence, or at any rate to a closer connection among the protagonists than is admitted. Or else, the time itself has been fictionalized. And what of this stubborn insistence on 'gunfire'? The plot thickens when Kadahapola admits to receiving a pistol from the 'Panditya' (scholar or wise man) which he apparently returns to its owner, Palemekumbure, when they meet. We have, then, the classic symbols of colonialism in the form of the 'Prayer Book and Gun', though the prayer book is of the wrong stripe and the pistol is possessed by the weaker side. The discourse seems to have turned the symbols upon their head, but such a discursive displacement is never complete, is never successful. Catachresis as the potential for resistance-as-disruption remains intangible, quicksilver, since it is catachrestic only in so far as it lies outside of hegemonic meaning, and the potential victories of the subalterns are always renegotiated as failures.

In this respect it hardly matters that in order to entrap the priest, the local chief had to lie precisely about his honesty and trustworthiness, while his son had to bear false witness to his allegiance.

Palemekumbure said 'I am not a man to utter two things, and ... spoke to his faithfulness.' Kiri Banda admits, 'I swore that I would never be unfaithful to any King that reigned in this country. I meant in my heart to be faithful to the British Government, but I intended the Prisoner to believe that I was faithful to the rebel King.'

On has only to compare these statements to Kadahapola's account which is at once playful and parodic. It defies the spirit and the letter of the colonial law and it is hardly surprising that this was considered an admission of guilt. Not to consider it as such would be to accept the full brunt of its ridicule, to feel the weight of its scorn.

I observed to him I am not searching or looking after Kings but I am looking for a little boiled rice. I said, don't ask a King from me but if you want a King I'll tell you where you'll find a King. And if you like to go to see that King, any time you like you might come. Then he questioned me as to the distance where the King lived. I said sometime at a distance. I said I'll show you the road whether he is near or at a distance. Then I told him, if you like to take the road through the Katugastotte ferry and come to Kandy through Booladgamme or through Kaigalle district, and proceed to Colombo – and there you could see the King of Ceylon. And you can accompany him and raise any rebellion you like – I threatened them to give information against them if they continued asking questions about Kings – There ended the conversation.

Much has been made of the priest's 'confession' moments before his execution. According to Captain Fenwick, when asked if he had anything to say, 'He replied in the presence of several people who understood both English and Singhalese "I am guilty of being with the King. I am a poor man and meant no harm as I was a friend so I went."'[148] Though this hardly ranks as a confession, it seems that there is no doubt that Kadahapola was involved in the rebellion. It is interesting that those who fault the administration on the handling of his case do so mainly in the romanticized conviction of his innocence, his poverty and helplessness. Tennent is therefore able to refute them with the 'new' evidence collected from Colombo which confirms the long-standing commitment of Kadahapola alias Kahalle toward working for the forcible removal of the British.[149]

---

148.  CO 54/264, p. 518.
149.  See the letters quoted by Tennent, pp. 118–20.

The issue of the priest[150] raged on, however, and like the issue of the rebellion for which it was a metonym, it became central only once it had been domesticated into a question about the propriety of his execution in robes, which in turn is analogous to the focus upon the duration and consequence of martial law as opposed to the nature and substance of the rebellion itself.

## SUCCESS AS FAILURE

One of the most important things about the rebellion of 1848 is perhaps so obvious that it has received scant attention. 1848 represents

---

150. This priest's discursive predicament involves resorting to an 'irrational' and 'illogical' defence of his actions, taking a distance from the principle of good reason because the colonial logico-legal apparatus structurally de-legitimizes him. He *must* explain himself, in this sense, because any 'reasonable' explanation will let him down. Whether all this is self-conscious or not is not strictly relevant.

If Kadahapola Unanse is irrational because rationality has been systemically denied him by definition (as 'traitor', 'pretender' and so on), then the following extract translated from a public speech by an influential priest on 1 August, 1991 in Manampitiya, Sri Lanka provides a complementary example of 'irrationality' which originates in the speaker's political power that renders reasonableness redundant.

> These Sinhala terrorists [JVP detainees who, he suggests should be settled in war-ravaged areas in the north and east of Sri Lanka where they will, no doubt, be massacred] say they have worked for the country. They say they have worked for the race. Yet, they have acted only to destroy their own race and hand the country over to foreigners. ... We should get the maximum benefit from them [derogatory personal pronoun]. If they die we can look after their children. ... We bring them and put them, we bring the forces and we incite [*Kotawanawa*] them to violence. ... We shouldn't give them guns. ... We should get work out of them. Either they must be put into the earth or they must be made to work. What? What? We can't just waste our money like this. [*Laughs Heartily*] If that happens [the youths are killed], its not a sin [for Buddhists].

This 'high' priest can travesty logic and good reason in a cavalier fashion because he has access to the power that arbitrates these matters. Strangely, then, in both these cases rational arguments are a waste of time, in the first case because no one is listening, perhaps, while in the second, because reasons are merely a game.

the culmination of thirty years of virtually uniform unrest, though I have attempted to show elsewhere that these 'eruptions' of 1818, 1823, 1824, 1834, 1843 and 1848 represent neither an easy continuity nor equally uneasy discontinuities. The indisputable fact, however we see this phenomenon, is that there was an abrupt and final cessation of such hostility (in the form of insurrection) after 1848. Yet, in terms of the supposed demands of the rebels, none of its predecessors were as successful as this rebellion. The taxes were repealed, with the exception of the Road Ordinance, the administration was hopelessly compromised and all those involved suffered permanent career setbacks. A 'profound impact' was experienced with reference to the colonial policy on Buddhism, resulting in a shift away from the evangelical to the liberal approach, much to the disgust of the missionaries.[151]

The most visible changes took place in the top administrative capacities. Torrington was recalled, as was Tennent, and this clearly marked a victory for the rebels. Surely, this bade well for future insurrections? Here, one must make the crucial distinction between the 'urban'-based liberal component of the 1848 rebellion and its peasant (subaltern) element. I have focused almost exclusively on the latter since it is to me the more interesting aspect, but an examination of the discursive production of this 'other' Colombo rebellion and its peculiarly parasitic relation to the Kandyan insurrection should prove an especially rich field of study. If one is permitted in this summary to bring these heterogeneous narratives together, however, one is struck by the succes of *the* rebellion despite its equally apparent failure.

The insight of this rebellion, then, is as much a result of its clear victories as of its defeats. Unlike in the other cases, where it was possible to derive the possibility of future success from the present failure, this rationalization is unavailable in 1848. Here we are confronted with the limits of the non-élite rebellion in the midst of its fulfilment. The rebellion was able to dislodge the structures of violence that constitute the immediacy of colonialism, only to have them replaced by another, perhaps more benevolent and less wasteful, but colonialist and exploitative all the same.

This contradiction, productive of subalterneity perhaps, is nowhere more liminal than in the final outcome of the struggles in Ceylon in 1848. True, the 'Supreme Being' in the colony was defeated and had to

---

151.   de Silva (1965) p. 30.

return to his previous appointment in the Queen's Bedchamber, but he was simply replaced by another supreme being. Moreover, the discursive unity that produced him and that he helped reproduce, covered over his public loss as a personal inadequacy: he was asked to resign since he could not get along with his fellow administrators in the colony. The correspondence among Torrington, Tennent and Wodehouse proved, in the end, more telling than anything else! Grey writing to Torrington explains, 'after the disclosure of the private letters and what passed between yourself, Wodehouse and Tennent, it is impossible that you should with advantage continue to hold the government of the colony.'[152]

Why should this be so troubling, since it is so patently a covering over, since it is so much a subterfuge? The question becomes, for me, whether this constitutes a discursive displacement, or whether, in fact, discursive displacements are merely convenient fictions that can only almost-happen on the way to being legitimized.

# APPENDIX

## I

I here give the following epitome of the pretender's career and capture, which may be interesting.

Gonegallegoda Banda, the pretender, is stated to be a descendant of Rajah Singha, king of Kandy; but there appears to be no real foundation for it, as he is believed to be a low-country Singhalese, whereas the kings of Kandy were of Malabar descent, but his mother is said to be a Kandian woman. He has figured in two former rebellions, and was tried for high treason at Badulla in 1843, by the district court and acquitted; previous to the present occasion he was residing in the house of one Dotta pulla Pihemarale [sic] with his wife, and acting as a wederala or doctor; he was in Kandy five days previous to the assemblage of persons on the 6th July to protest against the taxes, and was the chief leader of the people; he lived while in Kandy at the temple called Dallada [sic] Maligawa, whose priests provided him with

---

152. Grey to Torrington, 24 July 1850, quoted in de Silva (1965) p. 30.

food; when the crowd of people left Kandy, he remained one day in a jungle called Danha Golla, and received the homage of the Kandians as their king. From this place he proceeded to Dambool [sic], where he remained in the forest. Golahella Ratemahatmeya sent armed men to him at this place, who escorted the pretender to a cave in a portion of the forest Dahe Yatte Madda Gallinna [sic], to await the arrival of more men; upwards of 400 of the Maha Nilleme's followers, well armed and carrying provisions, joined the pretender at this place. On Tuesday, 25th July, Paldema Aratchy came, when Ingura Watte Banda wrote an ola by order of the pretender to Gopallahella Ratemahatmeya desiring him to state why he had not sent the cloths for his use, as he had sent all the other things; an answer was sent the next day with various articles for the pretender's use, stating they were for my 'lord and king, until such time as you pass Ballacadua [sic], where I shall join you with the Maha Nilleme and cloths for five kings;' the day after (Wednesday) the pretender came with his armed followers to Dambool Vehara, and at half-past 11 A.M. was invested with the sword of state and proclaimed king of Kandy. The next morning the whole force proceeded to Selleman Galla [sic] to fire volleys and make rejoicings where a palankeen [sic] was brought, and the pretender and followers proceeded on to Pallaputwelle where they remained that night. On Friday the pretender came to Wariapulle [sic], where the palankeen was deposited, but he left during the night, and with four of his followers went to the house of Ettepulla Banda in Doomborka Owelle, leaving the charge of his army to Pahalluweare Wongodde Samy, his prime minister (now residing at Dambool). After the affray at Wariapulle on Saturday morning the pretender with a few followers went to Eleadua Jungle (to the very spot where he was afterwards secured), and remained there until Sunday, when he received an ola and some provisions from Dulledewe [sic] Maha Nilleme, and immediately left for Kurnegalle, where he arrived in time to lead on the second attack along with Borker Aratchy (one of the four men last tried and executed at Matalle). Being there defeated also, he made for Dambool, but was prevented by some cause or other, when he entered the forest of Maddaoelputta [sic], where he remained some time closely watched and pursued by the several detachments sent in search of him, but upon the withdrawal of the troops from Dambool an opening was made for him, which he took advantage of, and was on his way to join his old adherents in Doombera and Hangrankettee [sic], when he was seized in the cave.

On the 21st September, the pretender king was taken on the information given by a man who was in the habit of taking him his curry and rice, and who at last became so much alarmed for his own safety, that he came to Captain Watson and informed him that he would show him where the king was, provided he would give him assistance, but that no European could be of the party. Captain Watson sent six Malay soldiers dressed as natives, two modeliers, and a headman with the guide: the party left Matalle so as to arrive at the place of concealment just at dark, which was his feeding time: the guide went in first and took him his curry and rice as usual; the Malays crept in afterwards, and when in the middle of his meal they seized him; he struck and struggled with effect and got up on the side of the rock, but was soon pulled down, thrown on the ground, bound and conducted into Matalle at nine o'clock the same night. The cave in which he was, is described to be in a very large rock, situated in a very thick jungle about eight miles from Matalle, leading to the Elkadua district, so high as to command a view of the surrounding country. There was only one follower with the king at the time of his being captured, and he was stationed on the top of the rock to keep watch; it is supposed that he must have fallen asleep, and was awoke by the noise occasioned by the king's arrest, and then made his escape. The pretender had a worn and jaded appearance, from the harassing he had experienced from the several detachments in pursuit of him.

Since his capture he has had every opportunity given him to make a voluntary statement, but he says little or nothing of himself; and the two headmen he mentions are the most influential men in the Kandyan provinces. He denies in toto being elected king by the priests, or that they performed the Perit or any other ceremony when he was made king at Dambool; although the priests have, since his capture, been confronted with him, and swear to his being the identical person crowned at Dambool. His statement goes on to implicate innumerable headmen throughout the country, which can only prove valuable if supported by corroborating evidence; however, from what has come out before the courts-martial and the Supreme Court, his account tends to establish a fact of which I have had but little doubt ever since the 6th July last, that almost all the headmen, chiefs, and priests, were the originators of this movement, and that the new taxes had very little to do with it beyond being a good pretext for urging on the people, who, as a body, I do not think were altogether willing to encounter the consequences of rebellion, but were worked on by superstition and the influence of the priests, and driven by the despotic control which unfortunately those chiefs possess, who decidedly bear a most inveterate and hostile feeling to British rule.

Description of the pretender Gonegallegoda Banda, otherwise Alluemlena Banda, otherwise Denees, now in the goal of Kandy, and committed for trial before the Supreme Court: – height 5 feet 5½ inches, complexion light brown, eyes hazel, hair dark brown, beard and mustaches dark brown; marks, slight scar over the left temple, age 40, well proportioned and intelligent countenance.[153]

## II

### Translation

I Gongalagoda Banda prostrating myself before this High Tribunal and making my obeisance one million times, most humbly beg leave to submit to the Judge who presides over the administration of justice in the Supreme Court the following circumstances viz:

In consequence of some disagreement at our house at Gongalagoda in Oodunuwere, I was induced to go and live with the elder sister of my father in law who lives at Cadoewela in Matale, and whilst living there, persons who were in office acquainted the poor people, that Mr Buller had established thirty two Taxes on which account the people of the four provinces formed themselves into a rebellion.

At this time I was living at Matale and it is true, that one Dingiralle of Hangoorankette, and the people of Matale collected themselves together, having imposed upon me by false and fraudulent stories misled me and went with me to Dambool where the following persons namely Lenadora Aratchille, Pallegamuwa Aratchille, the Priest Giranagama Unnanse, Elleherra Corale, Aratchille of the same place, Cottuwegedere Mohandirame, Warapitiya Coonammadoowe Lekamralle, Ettipola Banda of the same village, Bowatte Holeapelle Coralle, Ookuwela Kiry Banda, Capuralle of the same village, Neyarepola Adikarame of

---

153. Colonel Drought's letter to Torrington, dated 23 September 1848.

Cadoowela, Badalmohandirama of the same village, Melpitiya Corale and all others of Matale (having conspired together) presented to Lenadore Aratchille three cloths, one jacket, and a silk cloth to be used as a turban and requested him to dress me with the same (which being done) they then procured a Palaquin and nominated me as their Head, notwithstanding my refusal and conducted me from Dambool to the Estate of Wariapola.

The people attempted and wanted to set fire to the Tappal stations between Dambool and Gongawela, to destroy the people therein living and to plunder, but I did not allow them to commit those wrongful acts, but those people came foremost to Gongawela and plundered the property there – I hastened after them and directing them not to plunder property, flogged them with five Rattans until they were smashed to pieces, but seeing that they could not thereby be prevented, I cut two men in their hands with a sword which put a stop to it. The people likewise wanted to destroy the houses, the Court House, the Cutcherry [*sic*] and the people, but I allowed no opportunity for carrying those intentions into effect. I was requested by them to come to Kandy, but I refused, saying 'you have acted according to your own will without listening to what I said, that no injury should be done to anyone.' saying so, I went to the Estate of Wariapola. A Gentleman was then brought there by them whom they wanted to kill, but I saved him and did not permit him to be killed. Having come to know that in consequence of my having prevented them from committing all these aggressions and chastised the people of their own party, and thereby prevented the plunder, that they intended to take away my own life, and conspired together to constitute someone else as their Head I deserted them. This is all the offence or wrong I have committed. Both Your Lordship's souls and my own were created by one God. Your Lordship is a Supreme Being over this Island. Your Lordship's soul and mine will have to communicate with each other before God. I therefore implore in the name of the God who created your Lordship, in the name of his Doctrine, in the name of Her Majesty, in the name of Her Crown, in the name of all the Churches established in different countries subject to British Dominions, in the name of the priests who officiate therein, in the name of His Excellency the Governor of Colombo, in the name of Your Lordship's Royal Father, and Royal Mother, and in Your Lordship's own name that I may be pardoned for the said offence or wrong, and that I may be discharged for the sake of charity.

Besides this having got money from my father-in-law Gongalagoda Menickrale I bought Buffaloes for him. These Buffaloes together with his household property were taken by Government and his house set on fire. I pray that the same may be restored to him.

Signed/ Gongalagoda Band

Kandy. 1st.December 1848

Translated by me
Signed/ D. A. de Alwis
1st Interpreter and Translator of the Supreme Court.[154]

### III

Statement of Dingerale, who was shot at Kornegalle, on 5 August 1848, by Sentence of Court Martial; made to me, Henry Templer, within a few minutes of his Sentence being carried into execution.

I was taken up by the mob who were rising for rebellion; I saw the king; he is a fine young man; he has mustachios [is a red-coloured man, with cat's eyes].

The king was sent away to Adepane Wihare, and I was taken up for him.

I was with the king; the way I came with him was, that I was forced to join the rebellion.

I have received an appointment; I was promised the situation of adigaar.

The Ukkoowelle Ratamahatmaya was the adigar also; he was to be the chief. I do not know whether he was in the action at Matalle; I could not escape; I was surrounded by the people; I am a man of Hangeraucatty, in Hewahette Corle.

I have been practising as doctor.

By all the headman having joined and assisted, the proper king has got away; I was left behind.

The Doretiawe Ratamahatmeya and several others assisted the king to get away, and caught me.

The seven Korles people called me Vederale. My name Dingeralle [right name is Dingeralle].

---

154.   CO 54/252, pp. 263–5.

# 5

# Attitudes to (Teaching) English: De-Hegemonizing Language in a Situation of Crisis

## INTRODUCTION

The local élites' attitudes towards English in Sri Lanka (Ceylon) have varied across the entire spectrum, from unqualified acceptance and valorization above Sinhala and Tamil, to outright rejection as colonialist and discriminatory. In this sense, over the past 150 or so years, these polarities (if not their relative importance and the more widely held positions in between) have remained roughly the same, a factor that allows me to treat the contemporary situation as metonymic of its history. My intuition is that the non-élite perceptions on English, have, however, changed considerably in its favour, as a result of increased exposure/use and appropriation, though I do not have 'hard' evidence of this change in the form of historical data.

In this final chapter I shall examine received notions and attitudes on (varieties of) English that obtain in Sri Lanka today among language planners/teachers and students, habitual speakers and infrequent users, as well as among élite and non-élite groups in the country. By this means I want to analyse the various options available to the language-planner-cum-teacher-cum-linguist in the Sri Lankan and global contexts. Otherwise, the arguments and theoretical positions outlined in this book can be accepted yet invalidated through appeals to the immediate political reality, both local/national and external/international. It is by responding to these objections that I wish to transform the theoretical project of this work into an interventionist programme whose scope is both narrowly localized and broadly transnational.

Here, then, is the credo of an influential Lankan in the field, a professor of English (one of three or so in the country) and head of the English Department of Kelaniya University, who dabbles in matters linguistic and serves on many important national committees on curriculum development and planning. In a much-reproduced essay, 'Language Planning in Sri Lanka',[155] Goonetilleke writes:

Sri Lanka needed and still needs, *English as an international language* for several reasons: to have access to world knowledge, especially in science and technology; to move into the computer age; and to engange [*sic*] in international trade and commerce, diplomacy, [*sic*] international relations in general. Sri Lanka also needs *English as an intra-language*. English has to be promoted nationally for at least three reasons: to serve as a 'link-language', to develop a cohesive multi-cultural society; to serve as a means of bridging the generation gap; and to provide equality of opportunity in a country where English is still the preserve of a privileged minority. The encouragement of English is a politically sensitive issue: it could be construed as belittling and harming Sinhalese [and Tamil?], and could be so exploited by political opponents. *The attitudes of [our?] society to English are complicated: everybody wants to know English for a variety of reasons (for prestige, even for the sake of snobbery as well as for enhancement of personality and its utilitarian value in education and securing employment) but those who do not know it, hate those who do* [my emphasis]. Thus society maintains a kind of love-hate relationship with English. ...

... It is possible to argue that English should be taught to all pupils because there is an important educational value in the intellectual activity entailed in language learning. But the fact is that not all pupils will need English. Is it possible to choose, at an early age, those pupils who will need and benefit from English? Has anyone the right to choose for a child whose future is unknown? How can we make provision for those who develop late in life? Rural children will not need English if they remain in villages, but if we were to stop teaching them English, we would restrict social mobility and employment opportunities. Is it right not to equip rural children with English which will be useful if

---

155. First published in *Navasilu*, vol. V (1983). I examine a reprint which is contained in *Between Cultures: Essays on Literature, Language and Education* (1987).

they migrate to the towns? But can a small country with scarce resources afford to finance an all-embracing programme of English teaching? Is such an investment worthwhile? The questions are numerous but it is to practical considerations that we must pay head, [*sic*] In the 1970s, Thailand tried the experiment of making English optional, but it failed; competition is rife in society; if some students genuinely wish to learn English and opt for it, others follow suit; if one student knows English, others want to learn it too. The Government will have to decide to whom it is going to teach English, leaving out students from the decision-making process, but his may raise political problems. *A fair solution is possible when a country reaches the stage where good teachers of English are available in all the schools, both urban and rural. Then, a Government can offer English-teaching during primary school and allow only those who perform well in the language, to proceed in their studies in this field. Students of English in secondary school are thereby chosen by a process of self selection* [my emphasis]. Yet this process is expensive.[156]

Many 'progressive' sentiments are expressed here, and the fact that this statement has remained unchallenged even by radical linguists such as Kandiah makes it more than likely that there is general agreement on this score.[157] In positing an elitist and self-aggrandizing 'fair solution' to the problem of English language teaching once sufficient teachers are available, however, Goonetilleke betrays his hand. Much of the current debate about who should be taught English in Sri Lanka is mediated by the lack of teachers, and in the immediacy of that context provisional 'solutions' have to be made. Here, however, Goonetilleke is imagining an ideal situation, and yet wishes to reserve English for the 'best'. In this view, then, performance in English is evaluated independently from general performance, as if the language is too precious to waste on all-comers! Moreover, this evaluation is to take place at the primary school level at which stage such a 'weeding out' process is

---

156. Ibid., pp. 25–7.
157. Goonetilleke's position on the variety of English to be learned is another matter. Many have taken issue with him over his unsupported claim that Standard (British) English should be taught in schools since 'too much has been made of the differences between Sri Lankan English and Standard English' (ibid., p. 26).

without precedent in any of the other subjects. One can imagine a situation in which ten-year olds who are within the top 5 per cent of their class, and, therefore, prime candidates for the limited university slots in seven or eight years' time, being deprived of further English education because their English marks were not up to that of some others with access to the language at home.

The reason why such an aggrandizement of the language can go unnoticed is because English has been mystified by its élite practitioners who confuse the classed benefits it confers on them with an intrinsic value in the language. It is symptomatic, for example, that Professor Yasmine Gooneratne, reviewing Goonetilleke's book in *Navasilu*, would pick this essay as exemplary of his clear formulation and frankness.[158] She cites the first paragraph quoted above as a 'succinct outline of our national hang-ups about language' (p. 87), where English becomes identical with language in the multi-lingual Sri Lankan context. In addition, the three reasons outlined by Goonetilleke for the promotion of English nationally, all of them suspect, are implicitly valorized by Gooneratne. It has been argued that as 'link-language' English operates only among the urban educated middle/upper classes, whereas the cohesive multi-cultural society envisaged by Goonetilleke requires socio-economic and political changes of a drastic nature. The notion of English serving 'to bridge the generation gap' is merely a measure of the parochiality of Goonetilleke and his ilk, who blithely equate their own generation of anglicized, educated, urban (upper) middle-class peers, comprising far less than 1 per cent of the population within that age group, with the entire nation. Moreover, by and large, within the same extended family units, where the 'older generation' is English-speaking, the 'younger generation', though more bilingual, speaks English fluently too.

Perhaps more troubling than even this parochialism is the quick generalization on why students wish to learn English. If one were to ignore the gratuitousness of specious arguments that confuse questions of social justice with economic viability, one is still left with his 'holier than thou' attitude towards learners' motivations. The variety of reasons adduced to 'everybody' is clearly unequal. On the one hand there are those who 'genuinely' wish to learn English and others who 'follow suit' for some non-genuine reason that Goonetilleke is privy to. It would seem, therefore, that these non-genuine types

---

158.  See Yasmine Gooneratne (1987) p. 87.

may merge with those who learn English 'for prestige, even for the sake of snobbery'. On the other hand, there are those who learn the language 'for [the] enhancement of personality and its utilitarian value in education and in securing employment'. These are clearly the genuine learners.

Yet, by implication, all of these reasons seem to be achievable. English confers prestige, creates snobs and is instrumental in providing better jobs. The identification of fluency in English with an enhanced personality is the clearest evidence of Goonetilleke's aggrandizement of the value inherent in the language. We have seen elsewhere in this text that one of the ways in which a knowledge of English is valorized is through its ability to transform people. In a language context where it is no longer possible to get away with arguments for the superiority of one language over another, or to insist on a superior knowledge of English over and above other qualifications, the hegemony of English is dissimulated through 'neutral' arguments about 'personality' and/or 'intelligence' of, say, applicants for certain privileged categories of employment.[159]

---

159.   Another way of seeing this situation is dramatized by Kandiah (1989b):

> Among the most important of the questions asked [at a workshop on Problems of Unemployed Arts Graduates' held in Colombo in 1980] was whether there were cultural factors operating against Arts graduates in matters of employment. Again and again, the answers drew attention to these graduates' lack of knowledge of English. But what most significant was that this disability was repeatedly associated, almost as a matter of necessity, with others that were specifically cultural: 'a good command of English, poise, confidence, leadership, sports, team spirit, good schools, personal recommendations, ability to start from the bottom, a dynamic personality, innovative thinking are the other qualities the private sector is interested in.' The ideal, then, is the English speaking public school type of what, until the last couple of years, was believed to be an earlier era in the history of this country.

> My sense is that this association, 'almost as a matter of necessity', needs to be unpacked in order to discern whether 'specifically cultural' is a helpful description of these other attributes perceived as essential by the private-sector in Sri Lanka. It would appear from my discussions with private-sector executives who hold such views, albeit in less blatant a form, that the surest measure they have of such characteristics as 'confidence', 'dynamic personality' and even 'innovative thinking' is through the classed access to fluency in the English language which also reinforces these judgements since it engenders confidence and so on in a typical interview situation.

As for the appropriate variety of English for teaching in Sri Lanka, the late Professor Doric de Souza presented all the conventional arguments in favour of the conventional distinctions between written and spoken forms, and conventionally advocated the British standard. These rationalizations are so stereotypical and socially conservative that I feel a little uneasy that de Souza, the quintessential radical in the eyes of all those who had the privilege of knowing him, is being somewhat playful here.

If I am asked what kind of English such persons [those who require a knowledge of English: candidates for higher education and/or the professions] *need* to be taught, I should answer that it is 'utilitarian' English. This includes the idiom of academic exposition and of formal correspondence and a certain amount of colloquial English, also of a formal rather than an intimate character. We should not treat English as a language to be used for all purposes.

I strongly disagree with those who think English should be introduced at a very early stage in school. This is not only because of the wastage I have referred to, but because the language is ill-adapted to our local culture, particularly so far as children are concerned. ...

English should be introduced, as it is in Japan, at the stage when the child can be taught to think of another culture, and this is about the stage at which he [*sic*] goes on to secondary school. ...

I now turn to more technical standards. Here we must distinguish between the standards of written English (of a utilitarian character as defined above) and spoken English. Standards of English in utilitarian written English are uniform and universal – I ignore the small variants in orthography, grammar, syntax and vocabulary that occur with American English, because generally speaking, a formal letter or a work of academic exposition can be read without difficulty by people anywhere in the English speaking world. We should enforce the standards of written English without permitting any local variants, which do not in fact occur in the fields I have referred to. Spoken English is another matter. Our English speaking élite in Sri Lanka have evolved their own pronunciation which differs on one side from the British or American English and from local 'sub-standard' English. The distribution of phonemes (boarder, border, go, court, fort, lord, stay), the phonetics and phonology of our pronunciation, unaspirated

initial p, t, k, a clearly variant w etc and features of intonation distinguish standard Ceylon English, and this kind of English pronunciation should be taught in schools. The stressing of polysyllabic words should follow the English pattern. As to vocabulary and idioms in colloquial English it is more difficult to draw the lines between permitted and unacceptable 'Ceylonisms'. Since I have in mind colloquial English of a formal rather than intimate character, few deviations from standard English grammar and syntax should be allowed.
Teaching materials should be prepared ... and teachers should be trained in terms of these standards. I don't think this training can be had abroad.   (1977, pp. 41–3)

Professor de Souza, however, knew that his arguments begged certain questions about linguistic and social inequality. He points to the very kernel of this problem with characteristic directness:

I repeat that these suggestions rest on an impractical assumption. Some compromise will however have to be found, to save the enormous waste of the current programme and also produce the limited number of competent users of English we need. I ignore also, though I am wrong in doing so, the fact that English is a status symbol in Sri Lanka and that it serves as a social barrier. This is unfortunate, but true.   (p. 42)

This means that all language planners who ignore these issues are wrong, according to him. Moreover, if one is to consider how English functions as a 'social barrier', then one would be forced to problematize the variety of English to be taught as a means of broadening access to the social benefits of English. One cannot agree with de Souza's conclusions in terms of the central arguments of this study, but at least here there is no mystification of the role and function of English, as in Goonetilleke's account. Be this as it may, in concrete terms, de Souza has not moved beyond Passe's 'Modified Standard English' as the variety most useful for teaching and encouraging in Sri Lanka. By now we can see that this is the most we can expect from the academic/language planning establishment in the country.
It is left, therefore, to Kandiah (and perhaps non-linguists such as Reggie Siriwardena) to offer a more direct and concrete intervention in the realm of language teaching:

Given these facts LnkE could conceivably play a role in the writing of course material for rural students, if not others, particularly in the lower social classes, where considerable emphasis would fall on everyday rather than formal situations. At the very least, it could be used to help overcome the disadvantages that St E suffers from in trying to handle such situations. However, it is in the language teaching classroom that the notion of a standard raises itself with the greatest insistence; and, given the considerations described earlier, this ensures that, except as far as pronunciation goes, the Lankan system is rejected in favor of BrE. But, owing to the remoteness of this system from the experience of, particularly, the rural pupil, this only helps impose on him [*sic*], in addition to the problems he already has with the code itself, the further burden of grappling with the mysteries of the unfamiliar experiential modes the system embodies. No doubt, as the pupil's knowledge of the language gradually develops and his foundations in it grow more secure, he will have to make an effort to acquire control over at least some of this alien matter. But, especially in the lower classes, the challenge of trying to do so might endanger his acquisition of the language altogether.   (1981a, pp. 72–3)

Though not perhaps radically different from de Souza's position in theoretical terms, this view opts for teaching informal Lankan English structures to those whom neither Goonetilleke nor de Souza would wish to be taught English at all. The importance of the everyday/non-formal register in learning English has been recognized by both students and teachers as evidenced in the recent mushrooming of 'Spoken English' classes or *isspoken kadu panthi* throughout the country. What Kandiah identifies as a heuristic device, the learners consider an indispensable tool of upward mobility. However, for reasons detailed elsewhere in this book, the particular brand of Spoken English learned, by and large, is non-standard Lankan English, which the élites vilify and ridicule. It is a not unimportant irony that the most distinctive marker of Lankan English – pronunciation – is also the very means by which it is policed, through class-marked indices.

Kandiah's most radical formulation of the problematic of (post)-colonial English, or in his preferred nomenclature, New Varieties of English (NVEs), is the springboard for my argument on their theoretical importance *vis-à-vis* language as such. All I can claim for myself is the extension of Kandiah's insight beyond his provisional pause: he uses the contradiction between the systemicness (i.e. that it is rule-governed) of the NVEs and the virtually unlimited acceptance of variation within each variety as pointing to weaknesses in the specific ways of classifying/theorizing the NVEs currently employed by Kachru and others. I say that this is not merely the individual failing of hegemonic theories describing these NVEs, but, more importantly, a fundamental problematizing of received notions (deduced via Standard British/'American' English) on the nature and function of linguistic rules themselves. In other words, it is not that we need a 'better' theory to make these NVEs look more like StE, but that we need to see how StE measures up to the 'bad' theory thrown up by the serious examination of the NVEs. What is at stake in this view is not the validity of the NVEs, but of linguistic theory itself. Here is an example of how the NVEs have helped 'improve' linguistic theory, but as a result of simply trying to stop the cracks, as it were, instead of redoing the foundation, this 'improvement' is inadequate to deal with the challenge of the NVEs. The vexed question of 'native speakers' of the NVEs has led progressive linguists, influenced by this problematic, to enhance their definition. I cite below Tay's new and improved version from the endorsement given to it by Platt *et al.* in *The New Englishes* (p. 166):

(1)    A 'native speaker' of English is not identified only by virtue of his [*sic*] birthright. He need not be from the UK, US, Australia, New Zealand, or one of the traditionally 'native speaking' countries.
(2)    A 'native speaker' of English who is not from one of the countries mentioned above is one who learns English in childhood *and* continues to use it as his dominant language *and* has reached a certain level of fluency. All three conditions are important. ...

So now the 'native speaker' has been salvaged by providing us with a simple hierarchy: some native speakers are born great, and so on! The 'birthright' of some native speakers is not called into question *yet*, but, magnanimously, others are allowed to 'be' native speakers if they satisfy 'all three conditions'. To say any more here would be to labour the point.

Let us go through Kandiah's argument meticulously, however, to see whether this possibility of overhauling existent theory is contained within his own far-reaching critique of the Kachruvian paradigms.

The first shortcoming [of the new paradigms that seek to explain the NVEs] ... is that continua like the cline of bilingualism fail to make the very crucial distinction between English *in* countries like India and Sri Lanka on the one hand and rule-governed *varieties of English* like IE and LE on the other. The study of the former indubitably requires attention to be paid to the full gamut of variation in the English usage of Indians or Lankans, not only the variation arising from regional, ethnic group, personal, social and other such factors, but also the variation arising from the different levels of proficiency attained in the language by users (Kachru: 1983, 70). The special historical, social, educational and other such circumstances that surround the language in these countries make a confrontation with this kind of variation inescapable in a study of language *in* them, and continua like the kind mentioned, can indeed contribute to the study of the language in these terms.

Here is the first level of the problem of classification, then. If a complete description of the gamut of variation within, say, Sri Lankan English usage is essential for understanding the particular nexus of language and society in that context, why is such a description/ analysis not relevant to the variety of English called Lankan English? What has not been articulated in this version of the problem is precisely the *relationship* between Lankan English as a variety and the range/diversity of Lankan usages of English. What is the proper, even indispensable, object of study in the latter case cannot surely be irrelevant to the former.

To recognize this, however, is by no means to accept, too, that *all* of the variation observed, including the variation arising from a lack of proficiency or competence, has a role to play in the characterization of the distinct, synchronic, rule-governed *varieties* that have emerged in these communities. To seek to characterize these varieties and their systems on the basis of the usage not just of those who have acquired control of their distinctive rules but also of those who lack proficiency or competence in them is, to say the very least, an extremely unusual procedure. In countries which use OVEs, students at various levels writing essays, young children learning to speak or read or write and various other members of the speech community, including even very highly educated people, come out at times with forms and expressions that no one has any hesitation in characterizing as 'mistakes', or 'slips' or violations of the operative rules or some such, and, in this way, excluding [them] from the characterization of the varieties of English in question. Quite incommensurably with this, however, scholars, whether liberal or not, working on NVEs persist in treating any expression whatever that purports to be English and issues from the mouths and pens of the natives of the countries which use NVEs, as a valid datum for the characterization of those varieties. Indeed, Mehrotra (1982) insists that this is how it *should* be.

I cannot imagine that Kandiah means literally his claim that the *variation* observed in Lankan usage of English has no role to play in classifying the *variety* of Lankan English. To stick with this formulation would be to imply that non-standard (but non-idiosyncratic) forms have no impact on standard forms at all, but we know that in the dynamic of standardization there are continuous negotiations taking place between these two categories of usage. In fact, there is a sense in which we can legitimately say that the NVEs themselves function as 'non-standard' forms of the OVEs and that they have, in this way, not only influenced the OVEs over time, but have also helped to reformulate the theoretical premises on which these OVEs are understood. The issue, moreover, concerns the mechanisms of classification themselves, as we move to question the validity of a variety of English that cannot account for systematic variation within it. To seek to exclude the vast majority of users of a language on the basis of (in)competence is merely to make questionable assumptions as to the nature of linguistic competence/performance itself. It can and has been shown that the so-called incompetent users of English in, say, Sri Lanka employ sets of 'distinct rules' which, however, appear unacceptable to other 'more competent' users since they involve direct translations, 'odd-mixings', extensive borrowings, systematic 'mispronunciations' and so on.

In fact, the irony of the NVEs is precisely that the 'variation resulting from a lack of proficiency or competence' is much more easily systematized and much more readily distinct (from the OVEs, for instance) in its usage than the so-called variety of, say, LE. The precise problematic of LE is that, unlike in the case of the OVEs, there is a great deal of 'hesitation' in characterizing not merely 'mistakes' or 'slips' but also distinctive usage. My thesis is that the possibility of agreement on 'mistakes' within the OVEs is itself predicated on similar exclusions and coercions, which are, however, dissimulated by a panoply of 'neutral' legitimations. The NVEs pre-empt the hoax that takes the form of such 'innocent' lack of hesitation described by Kandiah, by laying bare its agendas and interests. The only versions of language that are clearly 'mistaken' in this sense are those that are private and idiosyncratic – that is, languages/lects that have not been shared in any meaningful way.

Let me examine examples from the variety of Lankan English to establish the validity of my claim that the issue of distinct rules/ endonormativity *versus* variation is symptomatic rather than acci-dental to NVEs. In Chapter 1 of this book, I quoted Antoinette Fernando, an educated user of Lankan English and a linguist, who did not accept Kandiah's examples of distinct Lankan usage. Fernando is not the exception. In fact, the entire debate on Lankan English centred (and still does) around the issue of which 'legiti-mate' uses are 'distinct' and which 'distinct' uses are 'legitimate'. Halverston argues with Passe, for instance, that many of Passe's examples are common to Standard English, whereas Goonetilleke opines that too much is being made of the non-phonological differ-ences between Standard (British) English and Lankan English, which lacks sufficient distinctiveness. On the other hand, the major-ity of clearly distinct forms and structures are classified (and dero-gated, willy nilly) as 'Singlish' or explained away by linguists in the field in terms of 'interference' or a lack of control/competence. Examples of these arguments have been discussed in the body of this text, and the situation is clearly not endemic to Sri Lanka, as an examination of, say, Indian or 'South Asian' English will establish.

For these systems to be 'well-formed [and] rule-governed' as well as endonormative, competent users of NVEs must be able to make judgements about 'defensible standards and good examples' (Kandiah quoting Sledd, p. 39). Yet competent users cannot agree about such standards and examples as we have seen above. In Kandiah's own work this contradiction receives its most powerful articulation, thereby raising it beyond the realm of personal failing or narrow lin-guistic prescriptivism.

In his seminal essay 'Lankan English Schizoglossia', Kandiah pro-vides six examples of 'acceptable' Lankan English usages that we have seen other users may not find 'as acceptable'.[160] Examples 12a,

---

160. See also Chapter 1, p. 34, for another angle on this.

13a, 14a and 15a, however, are ones in which the Lankan usage is 'clearly ungrammatical' according to Kandiah (p. 70). He explains these 'errors' in terms of hypercorrection, by identifying their systemicity and non-randomness, saying that though they contain errors, these are not, 'however simply random or unmotivated'. Example 13a deserves special attention since it is so common a category of utterance:

13a. Upali returned the book, isn't it?

Kachru uses a similar example as typical of Indian English, and hence in no way 'wrong'. Many others, including a Lankan linguist I canvassed, say that 'isn't it' is a blanket tag used often by 'educated' speakers too, and that, therefore, by any criterion used by Kandiah to decide on the acceptability of the acceptable Lankanisms, this should be accepted as well. The usage is widespread, systematic and rule-governed, so why is it 'a good example' to some and not to others? Kandiah himself in explaining the motivation for this misuse writes, 'This is the kind of sentence that is produced by the many people who have come to stigmatize and reject their own distinctive tag-element, "no?"'

In this case, how can Kandiah legitimize as 'their own distinctive tag' one expression, and say that an analogous is not? Is it because 'no' corresponds directly to, say, the Sinhala 'neda'? Why can't 'isn't it' also be seen to correspond to this question marker in colloquial Sinhala? How can we say with certainty what are the precise motivations of the hundreds of diverse users of this form? My sense, here, is that the tag 'no' is easier on the 'very habitual' speaker's ear because he/she has heard it more often, because descriptive linguistic work legitimizing its existence has long predated any analysis of 'isn't it' and because there are parallels with other bilingual situations elsewhere. None of these motivations are sufficient in a rigorous theoretical sense. This, then, is the challenge/risk of the NVEs, and the descriptive power of Kandiah's conclusion.

What all this implies is that, from an internal point of view, there can, in NVEs, be no mistakes, violations of rules and so on; *everything* belongs. But, the only state of affairs in which there can be no mistakes is one in which there *are* no rules governing conduct. So that, what might initially appear to be a very liberal, even perhaps, radical view, accommodating anything and everything in the English usage of Indians, Lankans, and so on, turns out, in fact, to be profoundly subversive of the central claim of the paradigm, the claim that the varieties these users command are, indeed, well-formed rule-governed systems.

In this sense, 'everything' does belong, but this process of 'belonging' becomes the object of critical enquiry too. How and why does linguistic 'possession' (or belonging) take place? The processes, not merely the rules, are 'up for grabs' here. What is at stake, then, is not the absence of rules but their fraught nature and, therefore, their flexibility. We are aware, even within mainstream linguistic literature, of variable rules, but, as legitimate varieties of English, the NVEs push these notions to their limits. NVEs do not accommodate 'anything and everything', (Kandiah is surely being hyperbolic here since 'private' languages are not sharable in any circumstances), and my disappointment is that they are not yet accommodating enough. But they are profoundly subversive of received notions that model *all languages* on the basis of certain 'well-formed rule-governed systems' (such as Standard English, for instance) since they bring each of these categories to crisis.[161]

## LANGUAGE ATTITUDES: A SURVEY AND ITS LIMITATIONS

In early 1988 I conducted a survey of attitudes to English in Sri Lanka. A questionnaire was presented to statistically significant numbers of the following categories: urban high school students, rural high school students, university (English) instructors, rural (English) teachers and junior administrators (Sri Lanka Institute of Development Administration Trainees).

---

161.  See p. 127, n. 125 for an account of the extent and function of rules as they may be said to operate in non-standard Lankan English.

The limitations of such a study are obvious, and yet this effort marks an important development in linguistic research in Sri Lanka since most similar work to date has been of an *ad-hoc* and anecdotal nature. The restrictions on movement at that time and the closure of universities prevented more extensive data collection in other geographic and 'demographic' areas such as undergraduates, and in marking the rural/urban dichotomy in the teacher and administrator categories. I did interview 'native speakers' of English whose responses will be incorporated into the analysis, though the number was insufficient for statistical viability. The questionnaire was long and detailed in order to provide the respondent with as many possible options without pre-empting certain ones, or appearing to privilege others. As a result, responses were quite varied, even divergent. One of the most important 'findings' was the truism that is so often forgotten in work of this kind: that the sociolinguistic reality is much more complex and much less uniform than is comfortable for all concerned!

The complex interrelationship between language attitudes and linguistic competence on the one hand, as well as the correlation between social pressures and language attitudes on the other, has been outlined, both empirically and theoretically, elsewhere in this text. It is important at the outset to recognize that no survey of attitudes can be innocent, nor is the expression of such attitudes readable outside of existing power relations within the society in question. This means that perceptions shared by users (or non-users for that matter) of a dialect/language are always tied to extra-linguistic realities. Linguists cannot, therefore, avoid responsibility for the language status quo through the appeal to current generalized perceptions because these perceptions are always influenced by the very status quo that linguists help keep in place.

Moreover, perceptions themselves are tricky things at the best of times, not even prone to self-consistency, much less 'translatability' across time and space. This is why the respondents need to be identified in the most precise demographic terms possible, and why future studies should be repeated for consistency. What the articulation of these language perceptions tell us, perhaps more than anything else, is that a social space has opened up recently in Sri Lanka where non-élite language users can *directly* intervene in the debates. Kandiah's work on the double-edged Sinhala colloquial term for

English, *kaduva*,[162] meticulously marks the genealogy of its ascendance/currency as a function of the epistemic space available to the Sinhala youth to perceive and comment on discrimination and frustration. Yet, this use of a 'new' lexical item (in the sense that it is put to a use that is far removed from its 'usual' terrain) points to the nature and limits of the ability of the youth to intervene directly. The arena of contention is somewhat displaced here, and this reflects the power relations that obtain which define the possibility of such protest. Perhaps what we are seeing now is a more direct confrontation and the space opening up for a more 'open' anger against hegemony. I would identify this tendency through the persistent refusal to 'correct' certain mistakes, the venturing into the privileged domain of language classification itself, and the non-insistence on the social injustices that an emphasis on English entails. It is as if we are at the moment where the rules of the language can be opened up like the proverbial can of worms by direct confrontation, as opposed to pleas to de-emphasize English which originate from outside. The old battle cry, 'English is the colonial language which must be destroyed because it confers unfair advantages on its users and perpetuates social inequities even today' is now changing in some arenas to something like, 'If it's English you want, we'll give it to you, but you might not like what you get, or what it does both to your language and to your privileges.' At the moment such a scenario retains elements of wish-fulfilment, but it is important to mark a perceptible shift in this collective attitude to English as 'something to be comfortable with' and, therefore, as a means of subverting the

---

162.  This term appears to have influenced some sections of Tamil youth, such as Peradeniya University students, and even in Jaffna an analogous use of *kaduhu* (literally mustard seed, which is clearly a Tamilized version of *kaduwa*) is now current, if less widespread. What requires further analysis, moreover, is an emerging paired use of *Soduhu* for Sinhala, the other oppressive language for Tamil-speakers. In this case, the word is itself a 'nonsense term' that derives its meaning from the association with *kaduhu* or English, as well as the powerful analogy between these two types of linguistic (and extra-linguistic, of course) colonialism.

  Here, as elsewhere in dealing with examples from Tamil, I am grateful to M. Yoganathan and S. Nanthikesan for their explications and insights.

system.[163] I can explain this discursive shift somewhat schematically if I were to identify three broad stages in the de-hegemonization of the once-colonial language, noting in addition that these phases can operate in the same temporal space as well as being chronologival steps. First, is the time when active intervention is near-impossible within the language in question due to the systemic lack of access to facilities for basic learning and so on; the next phase is characterized by intervention in the form of creating different lexical items, borrowing extensively from the 'native' languages and using 'new' and antagonistic descriptors of the language context that receive wide currency (such as the use of *kaduva*); and the third stage marks the direct intervention by non-élite users who confront the hegemonic meanings and norms of standard dialects through alternate meanings and anti-norms for the 'same' practices. This third type of resistance is much less easy for the élites to deal with since it cannot be simply dismissed through avoidance: for instance, élites can 'ignore' the criticisms implied in the term *kaduva* by simply not using this word, whereas they cannot so blithely avoid the connotations of *habichole*, especially if the usage becomes more widespread. It is no accident that examples of such direct confrontation are not yet available, since we are only at the threshold of this third stage.

---

163.   If one were to consider, as an example, the persistence of 'mistakes' such as those characterized by hypercorrection, and if one were not blinkered by received theoretical 'sacred cows', it seems much more plausible to analyse these moves as stubborn, resistant, even subversive, than as disabilities which are then supposedly constitutive of the 'essence' of certain categories of language users. This means, if we cut through the fine-tuned rationalizations and 'empirical evidence' (both types of arguments have been shown to be wrong in the case of Black English in the past), we must either opt for a kind of collective 'pathology' or dyslexia, or look for other sociopolitical reasons for, say, the $p/f$ consonantal substitution in Lankan English usage. The problem is compounded by the fact that we cannot see active agency or, in fact, opposition of any kind unless it conforms to the norms that we have been taught and/or can see ourselves performing. Here, then, is another theoretical minefield that the NVEs can help us negotiate. This process of 'mistakes' leading to standardization is, moreover, the history of language in microcosm, but here too we are more comfortable with understanding this phenomenon through hindsight.

   I am grateful here as elsewhere for the insights of Lilamani de Silva with whom I have discussed many of these arguments, though the errors remain my responsibility alone!

The onus on those in some tenuous relation to linguistic authority (such as teachers, for instance) at such a time is doubly difficult since we need to encourage and nurture such incipient confrontation without pretending that we are its bandwagon. In this connection, I shall merely point to possible areas for further work by examining briefly the genealogy of a charged current term in the Sri Lankan polity, *thuppahi*.[164]

At around the turn of the century a great deal of etymological and archival work was undertaken in Ceylon to uncover the 'real' origins and meaning of the word. We have access to scholarly research of the philological kind by S. G. Perera, Louis Nell, R. C. Temple, A. Mendis Gunasekara and John M. Senaveratna in the pages of the *Orientalist*, the *Ceylon Antiquary* and so on, but no indication why, around 1880–1920, such an interest/controversy arose of this term. This is specially intriguing since none of the extant glossaries and supplements of 'Native, Foreign and Anglicised Words' issued by the colonial administration even includes *thuppahi* among the thousands of words explained.[165] My sense here is that such an exclusion is a directly political choice and, as always in such political choices, one of access, since the term referred, at least in part, in its Lankan

---

164. See, for instance, the furor generated in the Sri Lankan press in 1989–90 over Reggie Siriwardena's attempt to 'resurrect' this word by reading it positively as a critique of all notions of cultural purity and homogeneity. The careful analysis of this debate will provide us with much more than linguistic arguments from etymology and usage, beyond a simplistic critique of cultural and ethnic blindnesses, to the recognition of cultural (and individual) self-representation through 'safe' arguments and 'risky' ones which pre-empt the mutual contamination (used here as a 'positive') of self-contained discourses whether they be from the right or the left, the nationalist or the internationalist, and of the sexist or non-sexist stripes.

165. See, for instance, *Glossary of Native, Foreign, and Anglicised Words* published in 1894, *The Manual of the NCP* (1899), and the older *Ceylon Civil Service Manual* (1865) as well as the *Administrative Report of 1872*, all of which contain extensive word lists and include quite restricted/obscure lexical items. I have not had access, however, to S. A. W, Motha's just-published book *Glossary of Terms used in official correspondence of the Government of Sri Lanka, compiled from research at the National Archives, 1640–1947*, so I cannot make a definitive statement about its exclusion.

use to the realm of protest and derogation. The 'definitive' analysis of the etymology of *thuppahi* is contained in the *Ceylon Antiquary* (vol. VII, part IV, 1921, pp. 210–19) which includes an article in the *Indian Antiquary* with S. G. Perera's refinements. The summary of this long essay is that the word

> is an early Portuguese corruption, through a form *topashi* in Malayalam (the first Indian language the Portuguese learnt), of the Indian [*sic*] *dubashi* (Skr. *dvibhashi*), one with two languages, i.e., a half-breed servant of Europeans; thence a soldier, especially a gunner, and among sailors, a ship's servant, a lavatory or bath-room attendant, and incidentally, on occasion, an interpreter.
> (p. 210)

In the specifically Lankan variations of this usage, however, the 'incidental' and 'occasional' deviant form as 'interpreter' appears to be dominant. In fact, in 1884, *dubash* and *tuppahi* are described in the *Orientalist* as 'dittonyms' in which the latter applies to 'that class of Eurasians who are commonly called "the Mechanics" – the descen-dants of the Portuguese by native women. … [T]he off-spring of the Portuguese by native women spoke *two languages*, the language of the father and that of the mother' (p. 212). Moreover, it would appear that the Sinhala usage did not come directly from the Sanskrit but via Tamil (see, for instance, 'Derivation of "Tuppahi"' by S. G. P[erera] in the *Ceylon Antiquary and Literary Register*, Notes and Queries, vol. 2, part 1 (1916) pp. 62ff), thereby articulating yet another necessary connection in the linguistic contact situation of the country. *Thuppahi* today has strong negative connotations of 'mongrelization', 'dilution', 'corruption' and 'impurity', which has mapped the purely linguistic space onto the broadly cultural arena. Thus, the westernized upper classes are derogated by this term, but so also are those who are of 'mixed' (that is the 'Burghers' or Eurasians, though this latter term is never used in Sri Lanka) descent, irrespective if their class or cultural affiliations.

If, in some sense, 'knowing two languages', both then and now a sign and criterion of upward mobility, social prestige and/or wealth, has become also a 'mongrel' and symbol of cultural 'bas-tardization', surely this points to a productive contradiction within the processes of signification that constitute a language? What we can do with this 'epistemic violence' remains to be seen in empirical terms (such as perhaps Siriwardena's attempt cited above) and it is in these 'new' practices that we can hope to 'norm' a theory that transcends our own particularities. It is in this spirit that I offer, somewhat back-handedly, the following discussion of current language attitudes since the qualitative components of my interviewing requires a much more nuanced treatment than can be undertaken here.

As regards the identification of the varieties of English heard at home, at work/school and in public places (Figure 5.1),[166] it appeared that the rural students were unable to distinguish clearly among the alternatives offered, though there was a dominant recognition of Broken English[167] as spoken, if English were spoken at all, at home. For the young rural English teachers, who are a part of the government's recent drive to 'broadbase' English education, Lankan English was the predominant variety heard at work, at home and in public places. The upwardly mobile administrators felt, however, that they heard one-and-a-half times as much Good English as Lankan English at work, though Mixed English predominated at home and in public places. The most counter-intuitive response was from the English Instructors at the university level who work in an environment where 'educated Lankan English' is explicitly legitimized. This group felt that at work they heard equal amounts of Lankan and Good English, whereas at home and in public places Lankan English predominated. In fact, at home Good English came a close second to Lankan English, while in public places Broken English was heard at greater frequency than Good English, and Lankan English appeared nearly a third of the time. This would seem to indicate that Lankan English contains pejorative connotations for this group, a hypothesis that is borne out by Figure 5.2 in

---

166. I am most grateful to Kithsiri Jayananda who prepared the figures for me and did such a fine job. My friends Anil Rupasinghe, J. G. Jayaratne, Lakshan Fernando, S. P. Senadheera and G. G. Prematilleke helped with the collection and analysis of the data. I acknowledge this assistance with sadness since two of them are not alive to see this work in print.

167. Since the survey considered self-perceptions and attitudes to English, the distinctions among these various types and descriptors of English remain the individual respondent's prerogative. No attempt was made to make the underlying linguistic assumptions uniform, since I wished to establish the nature of the divergence, if any, between specialist and language-user perceptions.

194

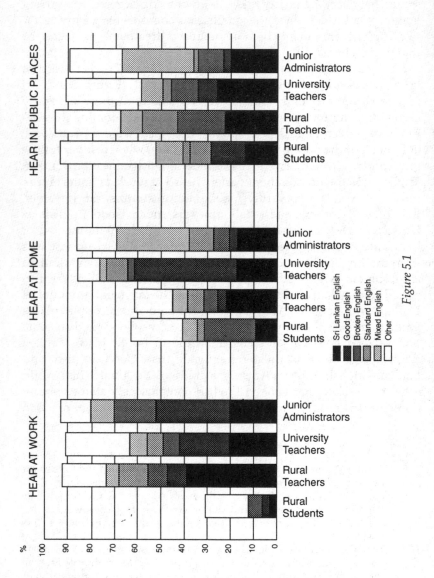

Figure 5.1

which they indicate the desire to speak either Good English or Standard English over Lankan English. Overall, Lankan English came a poor third in the category of wish-fulfilment for the preferred language of speech, declining in all cases. Interestingly enough, however, as regards writing, the university teachers showed a greater interest in Lankan English, which rose three-fold but still lagged behind the Good and Standard forms (Figure 5.3). This no doubt reflects the increasing attention that Lankan English has received in the realm of 'creative writing'.[168] In comparing their speech with 'foreigners' (that is native speakers of British, American, Canadian or Australian English) (Figure 5.4), the majority of university teachers felt that there was no difference while 30 per cent felt that a comparison could not be made. Twice as many of this group felt that they speak better than foreigners, as did those who thought they are worse. Thus, it does seem that members of this group have a positive sense of their English speech even as compared with native speakers of Standard English (RP), a feeling not shared by any other of the categories polled, with the notable exception of the few near-monolingual native speakers of Lankan English who felt that their knowledge of the language exceeded most others internationally! Among this group, there was even a sense of mission to maintain and reinforce old standards in the face of changing usage in England and elsewhere.

As regards the recognition of the 'quality' of English spoken by others (Figure 5.5), the respondents showed clear divergences in identifying crucial judgement criteria. The rural students tended to locate good speech with (proper) grammar (19.0 per cent) and vocabulary equally, whereas for the rural teachers fluency (26 per cent) and pronunciation (21 per cent) were paramount; this was echoed by the administrators who also rated confidence high. For the university teachers fluency was fundamental, with nearly 50 per

---

168.  See, for instance, Kandiah's critical analyses on Lankan poetry and fiction. Most importantly, this phenomenon bears out my oft-repeated contention that linguistic description, however intentioned, influences language-user perceptions normatively.

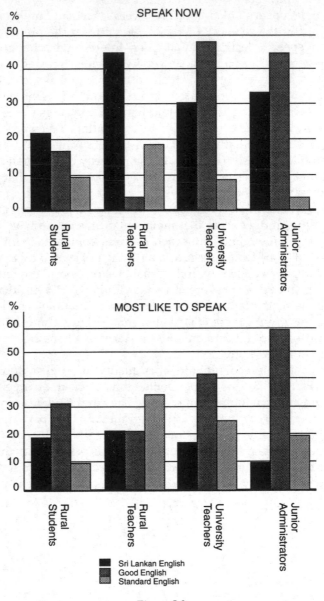

*Figure 5.2*

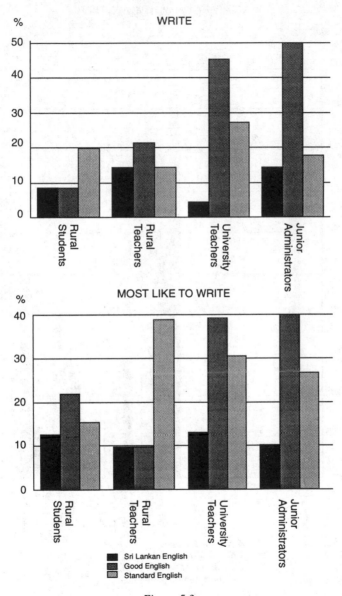

*Figure 5.3*

COMPARISON WITH FOREIGNERS

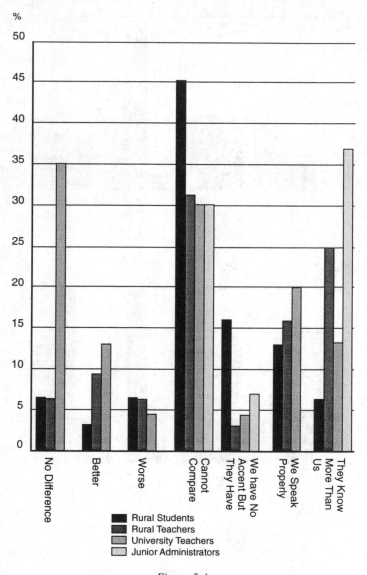

*Figure 5.4*

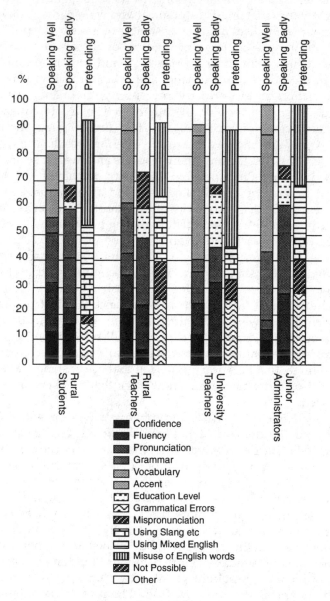

*Figure 5.5*

cent listing it as the main criterion of evaluation. In terms of the negative determinants, however, some of these judgements were vitiated. Only the rural English students (who were perhaps those least 'proficient' in English) made consistent responses by identifying the same phenomena in their evaluation of a person who speaks English badly. Both the rural teachers and junior administrators (next in ascending order of language skills, probably) singled out pronunciation as the primary measure, with fluency coming in second. The instructors, on the other hand, opted for fluency and grammar over pronunciation. The few first-language users pinpointed pronunciation as the key to inferior speech. The disagreement here between the university teachers and the rest seems to be a productive one. Pronunciation has long remained the area of marked agreement among linguists and first-language users of English in Sri Lanka, both in classifying Lankan English as a distinctive variety and in terms of distinguishing between levels of use. It may be that those who are the butt of pronunciation jokes (the 'nɔt pɔt' speakers referred to by C. Fernando) and those who are excluded by élite snobbery are aware of a subtle shift in the class-marker (from mere knowledge of English to 'proper' pronunciation), but those at the margins of acceptance (the instructors) have not been made aware of its sting. In unmasking pretenders, however, a uniform reliance on misuse of English words and grammatical errors was identified across the four categories. It is important to note, though, that the rural groups felt that use of slang was an indication of pretence to greater knowledge than the speaker actually possessed.

Figures 5.6 and 5.7 locate the mixing of English with Sinhala/ Tamil, and the domain of English use in personal relationships, respectively. The data derived from these are important in that they point to the self-perception of more or less 'natural' or 'habitual' mixing and switching as opposed to the self-conscious or artificial 'ragged' variety identified in the literature. In addition, both figures show that there is much more use of English, of whatever stripe, than is generally acknowledged nationally. There is no doubt that questions such as this are loaded, but in this, as in other aspects of the sociology of language, self-perceptions of different categories of users are just as important as 'objective' data and empirical evidence. It appears, moreover, from Figure 5.7 that English has invaded the home of the non-standard speaker as well as the upwardly mobile professional. This feature requires further

USE OF SINHALA/TAMIL AND
ENGLISH WORDS

(Code Mixing)

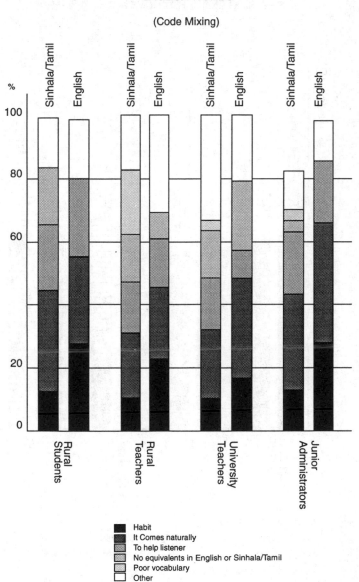

*Figure 5.6*

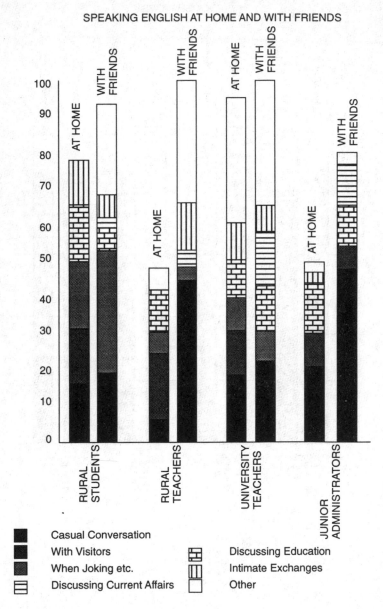

*Figure 5.7*

analysis,[169] since it seems to contradict the contention of Siromi Fernando that the domain of English (particularly for L1 users) is shrinking. My sense is, however, that this is only a seeming contradiction: while on the one hand the near-monolingual English speaker in Sri Lanka is being forced into becoming more and more bilingual, the near-monolingual Sinhala speaker too is coming across English in the strangest places.

In its hegemonic form as educated standard, the language of colonialism is still the prerogative of the élite, renewing the status quo through new dissimulations and justifications which have taken the place of the old discourse of the civilizing mission. Yet, at the same time, in its 'contaminated', 'non-standard', 'uneducated' form, this language is also fundamentally subversive of the old order.[170]

---

169.  I collected data from a sample of students attending private tutories in Sri Lanka in early 1988. It seems that over 56 per cent of those aged 15–35 in rural and semi-rural areas and 48 per cent of those from around the capital, Colombo, attend fee-levying English tuition classes of one kind or another! Among the 200 or so student responses, the majority said they studied English 'for employment', while 'education', 'international language', and 'necessity' were other popular reasons.

 This sort of preoccupation with English is bound to have repercussions in the domestic and recreational spheres. What is troubling in this regard is the absence of any kind of input or even interest, on the part of linguists and English academics in general, in the 'tuition class phenomenon' (with its emphasis on (is)spoken English) and in its effects on language learning in the country.

170.  Figure 5.8 indicates how misguided the dogmatic anti-English arguments, invariably made in English, from the left are today: of those questioned, only small numbers of the 'alienated' English-speaking élite responded wholly negatively to English, whereas at the 'lower' ends of the cline of bilingualism, the old arguments were adduced with much less frequency than before.

## LANGUAGE PLANNER/TEACHER/LINGUIST[171] AS ACTIVIST

It is not, however, only in the broadest, and therefore least interventionist, areas that the arguments made here have subversive potential. For example, Milroy and Milroy (1985) find that 'Persons in positions of authority are often prepared to be openly critical of a speaker's language when they would not be prepared to reject publicly other aspects of his [*sic*] identity or culture' (p. 98), and this statement receives Joseph's acquiescence. However, the situation that obtains in Sri Lanka today is almost exactly its opposite, particularly as concerns the English language. Here, knowledge of English (primarily pronunciation) is dissimulated in other less politically charged ways, as 'personality', even 'intelligence', for instance, in the case of Goonetilleke cited above. In addition, within academe, even in the United States, certain class-marked and race-marked elements of non-standard writing by students provide tacit license for the criticism of 'extra-linguistic' ideas and arguments contained in these assignments in disciplines as diverse as history and philosophy.[172]

The predicament of the linguist-as-activist is contained in Joseph's formulation of the problematic of language planning, though I am less unequivocal about the potential benefit of standardization, and have serious reservations about the efficacy of planners' results to date:

> The planners have learned from the artificial language movement, which after hundreds of attempts over several centuries failed to establish an 'international' language, ... the futility of trying to impose *ex novo* creations. But they also have historical evidence that direct human intervention is not only possible, but

---

171. I use these terms as nearly synonymous in the Lankan context because the field is sufficiently confined so as to provide considerable overlap in respective roles and responsibilities. Moreover, linguists, planners and educationists comprise a tiny minority. This is not to say that there are not immensely powerful figures at the apex of the various hierarchies who command huge resources, but, rather, to point to the essential similarity of function at the middle level.

172. See, for instance, work in this area conceived by Chris Abbott of the University of Pittsburgh, in her doctoral project proposal. Her empirical analysis of this claim will validate/refute what remains only an assumption based on one or two examples.

essential, in the establishment of a standard language. To their credit, the planners have managed to transcend the Romantic naturalism inherited by structural linguists, and believe that standardization has the potential for great social good (as in the classical view), if properly planned by a trained linguist giving due attention to history. (Joseph, 1987, p. 15)

The linguist must, it seems to me, intervene actively in the process of standardization and in the valorizing of a broader standard. This denies him/her the luxury of pure description (whatever that is) of languages at work on the one hand, but on the other it frees him/her from being the unwitting lackey of the status quo. In the specifically Lankan context, Kandiah, more than any other in the field, has understood that

the quality of life in Sri Lanka is not going to be measured finally along a scale of proficiency in English, as it seems to be presently believed. It is necessary to go further and to realize that the solutions that are being sought today, even by the English teacher, lie finally outside the walls of the English classroom. (1989, p. 152)

It may, however, be equally necessary to understand that one of these solutions that lie outside the classroom is the responsibility, at least in part, of the English teacher(s) since it directly concerns linguistic power relations, which are reproduced as language values. Kandiah is quite right in saying that the best English teaching in the world is not going to change real social inequalities drastically. Yet this does not mean that language teachers are doomed to passivity or to being pawns of the socio-economic system. Such a conclusion would be the ultimate alibi for intellectual and moral apathy.

The force of Kandiah's formulation, if we take it seriously, is the paradox that the English teacher's responsibility cannot be circumscribed by the academic environment alone. In working against the hegemony of élite linguistic usage by giving back to the non-élites a measure of linguistic power, the language teacher is effecting change both inside and outside the classroom at the same time. If, however, (s)he is entirely successful, then, with poetic justice, (s)he would be out of a job!

# Bibliography

Adamson, Walter L., *Hegemony and Revolution: A Study of Antonio Gramsci's Political and Cultural Theory* (Berkeley: University of California Press, 1980).

*Administrative Reports, Ceylon 1872* (Colombo: Government Printer, 1873).

Ashcroft, Bill, Helen Tiffin and Gareth Griffiths, *The Empire Writes Back* (London: Routledge, 1989).

Austin, J. L., *How to do Things with Words* (Cambridge, Mass.: Harvard University Press, 1975).

Baldick, Chris, *The Social Mission of English Criticism, 1848–1932* (Oxford: Oxford University Press, 1983).

Bloor, David, *Wittgenstein: A Social Theory of Knowledge* (New York: Columbia University Press, 1983).

Bourdieu, P., *Distinctions: A Social Critique of the Judgement of Taste*, trans. Richard Nice (Cambridge, Mass.: Harvard University Press, 1984).

Bourdieu, P. and Jean-Claude Passeron, *Reproduction in Education, Society, and Culture*, trans. Richard Nice (London: Sage, 1977).

Bourdieu, P. and M. Boltanski, 'Le Fetichisme de la Langue', extract trans. John B. Thompson in *Studies in the Theory of Ideology* (Berkeley: University of California Press, 1984).

Brakel, C. A., 'Language Structure and Social Structure', *Michigan Academician*, vol. 9, no. 2 (1978) pp. 157–63.

Brown, Cecil H., *Wittgensteinian Linguistics* (The Hague: Mouton, 1974).

*Census of Population and Housing 1981 (Sri Lanka)* (Colombo: Government Publications Bureau, 1983).

*Ceylon Antiquary and Literary Register*, Colombo.

*Ceylon Civil Service Manual, 1865* (Colombo: Government Printer, 1865).

Chatterjee, Partha, *Nationalist Thought and the Colonial World: A Derivative Discourse?* (Tokyo: Zed, 1986).

Colonial Office Records (London): vols CO 54/ and CO 55/ which contain Despatches (and annexures) to/from Ceylon (unpublished materials).

Cooray, Reginald, *A Short & Sweet Way to Spoken English* (in Sinhala: ingriisi kathaawa), 3rd edn (Kalutara, Sri Lanka: 1986).

Cornforth, Maurice, *Marxism and the Linguistic Philosophy* (New York: International Publishers, 1971).

Crowley, Tony, *Standard English and the Politics of Language* (Urbana: University of Illinois Press, 1989).

Crystal, David, *A Dictionary of Linguistics and Phonetics* (London: Blackwell, 1985).

Das Gupta, J. and Gumperz, J. J., 'Language, Communication and Control in North India', in *Language Problems of Developing Nations*, ed. J. A. Fishman, C. A. Ferguson and J. Das Gupta (New York: John Wiley, 1968) pp. 17–26.

de Mel, Neloufer, 'Responses to History: The Rearticulation of Post-Colonial Identity in the Plays of Wole Soyinka and Derek Walcott 1950–1976', Ph.D. thesis, University of Kent at Canterbury (1990).

de Silva, K. M., *Letters on Ceylon 1846–50: The Administration of Lord Torrington and the 'Rebellion' of 1848* (Kandy, 1965).

de Silva, K. M. (ed.) *Sri Lanka – A Survey*.

de Silva, Sugathapala, 'Some Consequences of Diglossia', in Haas (ed.), *Standard Languages, Spoken and Written* (Manchester: Manchester University Press, 1982).

de Souza, 'Tests and Targets', in *Socio Economic and Other Factors Affecting the Teaching of English in Sri Lanka* (Colombo: Sri Lanka Foundation Institute, 1977).

Derrida, Jacques, *Limited Inc. abc...*, in *Glyph 2* (Baltimore, Md.: Johns Hopkins Textual Studies, 1977).

Derrida, Jacques, *Signature Event Context*, in *Glyph 2* (Baltimore Md.: Johns Hopkins Textual Studies, 1977).

Devonish, Hubert, *Language and Rebellion: Creole Language Politics in the Caribbean* (London: Karia Press, 1986).

Dharmadasa, K. N. O., 'Diglossia and Nativism: The Case of Sinhalese', *Ceylon Studies Seminar*, 1975 series, no. 3.

Dillard, J. L., *Black English: Its History and Usage in the United States* (New York: Vintage, 1973).

Edwards, J. R., *Language, Society and Identity* (Oxford: Basil Blackwell, 1985).

Fasold, R., *The Sociolinguistics of Society* (Oxford: Basil Blackwell, 1984).

Fernando, Antoinette, 'Culture and Communicative Confidence: A Study of ESL at the Tertiary Level in Sri Lanka', unpublished Ph.D. thesis (Edinburgh University, 1986).

Fernando, Chitra, 'English and Sinhala Bilingualism in Sri Lanka', *Language in Society*, vol. 6 (1976).

Fernando, Siromi, 'Changes in Sri Lankan English as Reflected in Phonology', *University of Colombo Review*, vol. 5 (December, 1985).

Fishman, Joshua A. (ed.), *Readings in the Sociology of Language* (The Hague: Mouton, 1972).

Fishman, Joshua A., Charles A. Ferguson and Jyotindra Das Gupta (eds), *Language Problems in Developing Nations* (New York: John Wiley, 1968).

Forbes, J., *Recent Disturbances and Military Executions in Ceylon* (London: Blackwood, 1850).

Foucault, Michel, *The Archaeology of Knowledge and the Discourse on Language* trans A. M. Sheridan Smith (London: Tavistock, 1972).

Fromkin, V. and R. Rodman, *An Introduction to Language*, 3rd edn (Holt: New York, 1983).

Garvin, P. L. and M. Mathiot, 'The Urbanization of the Guarani Language: A Problem in Language and Culture', in J. Fishman (ed.), *Readings in the Sociology of Language* (The Hague: Mouton, 1968).

*Glossary of Native, Foreign, and Anglicised Words* (Colombo: Government Printer, 1894).

Gooneratne, Yasmine, 'Treading Delicately', *Navasilu*, vol. 9 (1987).

Goonetilleke, D. C. R. A., *Between Cultures: Essays on Literature, Language and Education* (Delhi: Sri Satguru, 1987).

Gramsci, A., *Selections from the Prison Notebooks*, ed. and trans. Q. Hoare and G. Nowell Smith (London: Lawrence & Wishart, 1971).

Greenbaum, Sidney (ed.), *The English Language Today* (Oxford: Pergamon Press, 1985).

Guha, Ranajit (ed.), *Subaltern Studies: Writings on South Asian History*, vols 1–5 (Delhi: Oxford University Press, 1981–1986).

Guha, R., *Elementary Aspects of Peasant Insurgency in Colonial India* (Delhi: Oxford University Press, 1983).

Guha, R. and Gayatri Spivak (eds), *Selected Subaltern Studies* (New York: Oxford University Press, 1988).

Gumperz, John J., *Discourse Strategies* (Cambridge: Cambridge University Press, 1982).

Guneratna, R., *Sri Lanka: A Lost Revolution?* (Colombo, 1990).

Gunesekera, Manique, 'Discourse Genres in English Newspapers in

Singapore, South India and Sri Lanka', Ph. D. thesis, University of Michigan, Ann Arbor (1989).

Gunawardena, R. A. L. H., 'The People of the Lion: Sinhala Consciousness in History and Historiography', in *Ethnicity and Social Change in Sri Lanka* (Colombo: Nawamaga Printers, 1985).

Halliday, M. A. K., *Language as Social Semiotic: The Social Interpretation of Language and Meaning* (London: Open University, 1978).

Halliday, M. A. K., Angus McIntosh and Peter Strevens, *The Linguistic Sciences and Language Teaching* (London: Longman, 1964).

Halpe, Ashley, 'Creative Writing in English', in *Sri Lanka – A Survey*, ed. K. M. de Silva.

Halverston, John, 'Prolegomena to the Study of Ceylon English', *University of Ceylon Review*, vol. 24 (1966).

Haugen, E., 'Dialect, Language, Nation', *American Anthropologist*, vol. 68 (1966) pp. 922–35.

Henderson, *The History of the Rebellion in Ceylon, During Lord Torrington's Government* (London, 1865).

Honey, John, *Does Accent Matter?* (London: Faber, 1989).

Hymes, D. (ed.), *Pidginization and Creolization of Languages* (London: Cambridge University Press, 1971).

James, C. L. R., *Beyond a Boundary* (New York: Pantheon, 1984).

Jones, Daniel, *English Pronouncing Dictionary* (1917); reprinted as *Everyman's English Pronouncing Dictionary* (London: Dent, 1956).

Joseph, John Earl, *Eloquence and Power: The Rise of Language Standards and Standard Languages* (London: Francis Pinter, 1987).

Kachru, Braj (ed.), *The Other Tongue: English across Cultures* (Urbana: University of Illinois Press, 1982).

Kachru, Braj, *The Indianization of English: The English Language in India* (Delhi: Oxford University Press, 1983).

Kachru, Braj, *The Alchemy of English: The Spread, Functions and Models of Non-native Englishes* (Oxford: Pergamon Press, 1986).

Kandiah, Thiru, 'Lankan English Schizoglossia', *English World-Wide*, vol. 2, no. 1 (1981a).

Kandiah, Thiru, 'Disinherited Englishes: The Case of Lankan English (Part II)', in *Navasilu*, vol. 4 (1981b), pp. 92–113.

Kandiah, Thiru, 'New Varieties of English: The Creation of the Paradigm and its Radicalization', *Navasilu*, vol. 9 (1987).

Kandiah, Thiru, 'On So-called Syntactic Deletion in Lankan English Speech: Learning from a New Variety of English about --', unpublished paper (1989a).

Kandiah, Thiru, '"Kaduwa": Power and the English Language Weapon in Sri Lanka', in *A Festschrift for E. F. C. Ludowyk* (Colombo, 1989b).

Kaplan, Robert B., *The Anatomy of Rhetoric: Prolegomena to a Functional Theory of Rhetoric* (1972).

Kaplan, Robert B., 'Cultural Thought Patterns in Inter Cultural Education', *Language Learning*, vol. 16, pp. 1–20.

Krapp, George P., *Modern English: Its Growth and Present Use* (Oxford: Blackwell, 1985).

Kratochvil, *The Chinese Language Today: Features of an Emerging Standard* (London: Hutchinson, 1968).

Labov, William, 'The Notion of "System" in Creole Languages', in D. Hymes (ed.), *Pidginization and Creolization of Languages* (London: Cambridge University Press, 1971).

Labov, William, *The Social Stratification of English in New York City* (Washington, DC: Center for Applied Linguistics, 1966).

Labov, William, *Language in the Inner City: Studies in the Black English Vernacular* (Philadelphia: University of Pennsylvania Press, 1972).
Labov, William, *Sociolinguistic Patterns* (Philadelphia: University of Pennsylvania Press, 1972).
Laclau, E. and Chantal Mouffe, *Hegemony and Socialist Strategy: Towards a Radical Democratic Politics* (London: Verso, 1985).
Leith, Dick, *A Social History of English* (London: Routledge, 1983).
MacCabe, Colin, 'Righting English or Does Spelling Matter?', unpublished paper (1990).
MacCabe, Colin, *Tracking the Signifier* (Minneapolis: University of Minnesota Press, 1985).
MacCabe, Colin, 'Language, Literature, Identity: Reflections on the Cox Report', *Critical Quarterly*, vol. 32, no. 4 (Winter 1990).
Macdonell, Diane, *Theories of Discourse* (Oxford: Blackwell, 1986).
*The Manual of the NCP* (Colombo: Government Printer, 1899).
Marx, Karl, *Capital*, vol. 1 (New York: Vintage, 1977).
Milroy, James and Lesley Milroy, *Authority in Language: Investigating Language Prescription and Standardization* (London: Routledge, 1985).
Milroy, Lesley, *Language and Social Networks* (Baltimore, Md.: University Park Press, 1980).
Moag, Rodney F., 'The Life Cycle of Non-native Englishes: a Case Study', in B. Kachru (ed.), *The Other Tongue: English across Cultures* (Urbana: University of Illinois Press, 1982).
Motha, S. A. W., *Glossary of Terms Used in Official Correspondence of the Government of Sri Lanka, Compiled from Research at the National Archives, 1640–1947* (Colombo, 1990).
Musa, Monsur, *Language Planning in Sri Lanka* (Dacca: Bhuiyan Muhammed Imran, 1981).
*Navasilu (Journal of the English Association of Sri Lanka)*, Colombo, Sri Lanka (irregular).
Negri, Antonio, *The Politics of Subversion: A Manifesto for the Twenty-First Century* (Cambridge: Polity, 1989).
Ngugi wa Thiong'o, *Decolonising the Mind: The Politics of Language in African Literature* (London: James Currey, 1986).
Paikeday, Thomas M., *The Native Speaker is Dead!* (Toronto: Paikeday, 1985).
Parakrama, Arjuna, *Language and Rebellion: Discursive Unities and the Possibility of Protest* (London: Katha, 1990).
Parakrama, Arjuna, 'Ass Backwards: Notes Toward "Empowering" Bad Taste in the Languages of Teaching Culture and in the Cultures of Teaching Language', unpublished paper (December 1990).
Passe, H. A., 'The English Language in Ceylon', Ph.D. thesis, University of London (1948).
Pecheux, Michel, *Language, Semantics, Ideology* (New York: St Martin's Press, 1982).
[S. G. Perera] 'Derivation of "Tuppahi"', in *Ceylon Antiquary and Literary Register, Notes and Queries*, vol. 2, part 1 (1916) pp. 62ff.
Pieris, Ralph, 'Bilingualism and Cultural Marginality', *British Journal of Sociology*, vol. 2 (1951) pp. 328–39.
Platt, John, Heidi Weber and Ho Mian Lian, *The New Englishes* (London: Routledge, 1984).
Prator, Clifford, 'The British Heresy in TESL' in Joshua A. Fishman, Charles A. Ferguson and Jyotindra Das Gupta (eds), *Language Problems in Developing Countries* (New York: John Wiley, 1968).

210                          *Bibliography*

Quirk, Randolf, *Essays on the English Language* (Bloomington: Indiana University Press, 1968).
Rao, Venkat, 'Self Formations: Speculations on the Question of Postcolonial-ity', *Wasafiri*, no. 13 (Spring 1991) pp. 7–10.
*Redpower* (English journal of the Janatha Vimukthi Peramuma), Special Edition (May 1988).
Renfrew, Colin, *Archaeology and Language* (New York: Cambridge University Press, 1988).
Rossi-Landi, F., *Language as Work and Trade: A Semiotic Homology for Linguistics and Economics* (1983).
Ryan, Michael, *Marxism and Deconstruction* (Baltimore, Md.: Johns Hopkins University Press, 1982).
Samaranayake, W. H., *Practical English* (Colombo: Lake House, 1982).
Scott, J. C., *Weapons of the Weak: Everyday Forms of Peasant Resistance* (New Haven, Conn.: Yale University Press, 1985).
Schuhardt, Hugo, *Pidgin and Creole Languages: Selected Essays by Hugo Schuhardt*, ed. and trans. Glenn Gilbert (London: Cambridge University Press, 1980).
Shapiro, Michael C. and Harold Schiffman, *Language and Society in South Asia* (The Netherlands: Foris, 1983).
Smith, Larry E. (ed.), *English for Cross-Cultural Communication* (New York: St Martin's Press, 1981).
Smith, Larry E. (ed.), *Readings in English as an International Language* (Oxford: Pergamon Press, 1983).
Smith, Larry E. (ed.), *Discourse Across Cultures* (New York: Prentice Hall, 1987).
Special Committee on Education Report, Ceylon Sessional Paper XXIV of 1943.
Spivak, Gayatri, 'Revolutions That as Yet Have No Model: Derrida's *Limited Inc*', *Diacritics*, 10 (Winter 1980).
Spivak, Gayatri, *In Other Worlds: Essays in Cultural Politics* (New York: Methven Press, 1987).
Spivak, Gayatri, 'Can the Subaltern Speak?', in *Marxist Interpretations of Culture*, ed. L. Grossberg and Cary Nelson (Urbana: University of Illinois Press, 1987).
Spriano, Paolo, *Antonio Gramsci and the Party: The Prison Years*, trans. John Fraser (London: Lawrence and Wishart, 1979).
[Tennent, Emerson] 'Statement [Submitted to a Committee of the House of Commons] of the Rebellions of Ceylon 1817–1848' in the Colonial Office Confidential Print CO 882/1.
Terdiman, Richard, *Discourse/Counter-Discourse* (Ithaca, NY: Cornell University Press, 1985).
Thambiah, S. J., 'The Politics of Language in India and Ceylon', *Modern Asian Studies*, vol. I (1967) pp. 215–40.
Thompson, John B., *Studies in the Theory of Ideology* (Berkeley: University of California Press, 1984).
Trudgill, Peter, *Accent, Dialect and the School* (London: Edward Arnold, 1975).
'Tutoring Non-Native Speakers of English', undated, anonymous mimeo (16pp), produced for the Writing Workshop of the Department of English, University of Pittsburgh.
Valdman, Albert (ed.), *Pidgin and Creole Linguistics* (Bloomington: Indiana University Press, 1977).
Venkatachalam, M. S., *Genocide in Sri Lanka* (Delhi: Gian, 1987).

Viswanathan, Gauri, *Masks of Conquest: Literary Study and British Rule in India* (New York: Columbia University Press, 1989).

Vittachi, Tarzie, *Trials of Transition in the Island in the Sun* (Colombo: Lake House, n.d.).

Volosinov, V. N. and Baxtin, M. M., *Marxism and the Philosophy of Language*, trans. L. Matejka, and I. R. Titunik (Cambridge, Mass.: Harvard University Press, 1986).

Weinrich, U., *Languages in Contact: Findings and Problems* (The Hague: Mouton, 1953).

Wickramasuriya, Sarathchandra, 'English Literature in Nineteenth-century Sri Lankan Schools: A Survey of Courses of Study, Prescribed Texts, and Methods of Teaching', *Modern Sri Lanka Studies*, vol. 1, no. 2, (1986).

Wittgenstein, Ludwig, *Culture and Value*, trans. Peter Winch (Oxford: Blackwell, 1980).

Wittgenstein, Ludwig, *The Blue and Brown Books* (New York: Harper, 1960).

Wittgenstein, Ludwig, *Philosophical Investigations*, 3rd edn, trans. G. E. M. Anscombe (New York: Macmillan, 1968).

Yule, H. and A. C. Burnell, *Hobson Jobson: A Glossary of Colloquial Anglo-Indian Words and Phrases* (London, 1886, reprinted 1986).

# Index

*I am grateful to Priya Abeywickrema, Kaushalya Fernando, Dharshini Seneviratne, Minoli Sirimanne, Lakshan Fernando and T. Kumarendran who helped to compile this index. The index would not have been possible without the assistance I received from Dr Lilamani de Silva and Udaya Sirivardhana who have contributed so much to the preparation of this book.